Andreas Hemming, Gentiana Kera,
Enriketa Pandelejmoni (Eds.)

Albania

Studies on South East Europe

edited by

Prof. Dr. Karl Kaser
(Graz)

vol. 9

LIT

ALBANIA

Family, Society and Culture in the 20th Century

edited by

Andreas Hemming
Gentiana Kera
Enriketa Pandelejmoni

LIT

∞

Gedruckt auf alterungsbeständigem Werkdruckpapier entsprechend
ANSI Z3948 DIN ISO 9706

Bibliographic information published by the Deutsche Nationalbibliothek
The Deutsche Nationalbibliothek lists this publication in the Deutsche Nationalbibliografie; detailed bibliographic data are available in the Internet at http://dnb.d-nb.de.

ISBN 978-3-643-50144-8

A catalogue record for this book is available from the British Library

Klosbachstr. 107
CH-8032 Zürich
Tel. +41 (0) 44-251 75 05
Fax +41 (0) 44-251 75 06
e-Mail: zuerich@lit-verlag.ch
http://www.lit-verlag.ch

LIT VERLAG Dr. W. Hopf
Berlin 2012
Fresnostr. 2
D-48159 Münster
Tel. +49 (0) 2 51-620 320
Fax +49 (0) 2 51-23 19 72
e-Mail: lit@lit-verlag.de
http://www.lit-verlag.de

Distribution:
In Germany: LIT Verlag Fresnostr. 2, D-48159 Münster
Tel. +49 (0) 2 51-620 32 22, Fax +49 (0) 2 51-922 60 99, e-mail: vertrieb@lit-verlag.de

In Austria: Medienlogistik Pichler-ÖBZ, e-mail: mlo@medien-logistik.at

In Switzerland: B + M Buch- und Medienvertrieb, e-mail: order@buch-medien.ch

In the UK: Global Book Marketing, e-mail: mo@centralbooks.com

Contents

Introduction: Albanian Family, Society and Culture in the 20th Century

Enriketa Papa-Pandelejmoni, Gentiana Kera and Andreas Hemming

The idea for this book emerged in discussions several years ago on ways in which Albanian studies as practised both by Albanian and foreign scholars of the subject could be promoted. The publication of an edited volume that would collect under one roof examples of the work of Albanian and foreign scholars of anthropology and history was deemed to be one possibility. The idea was then discussed with Karl Kaser who generously offered to include the publication in the series Studies on South East Europe.

The idiosyncratic nature of Albania on the margins, as much Mediterranean as it is Balkan, not really part of the Occident but not quite Orient either, neither Christian nor Muslim but a bit of both, with its own language, a late-comer to nationalism (Skendi 1967; Zavalani 1969) with a socialism all its own (Tönnes 1980) – not to speak of its postsocialist history – make make it both a fascinating (counter-)example and difficult to locate in traditional academic structures. Where Albania is not the explicit focus it is often relegated the margins as exotic case study (i.e. Bartl 2000; Hemming 2006). This work can thus be seen in the tradition of a number of edited volumes (Zhelyazkova 2000; Kressing and Kaser 2002) or special journal issues (i.e. Österreichische Osthefte Vol. 45 2003; Anthropological Notebooks Vol. 14(1) 2008) in which the work of various scholars are presented that under different circumstances may have suffered similar fates.

The steady growth in scholarly interest in Albania – a much welcomed trend – has much to do with the work done in centres such as the Centre of Southeast European History and Anthropology at the Karl Franzens University Graz or within the framework of the Nash Fellowship at the SSEES at University College London. Of equal importance is the work of several Albanian colleagues at the Instituti i Antropologjisë Kulturore dhe Studimeve të Artit (Institute of Cultural Anthropology and Art Studies), at the Centre for the Albanian Studies (QSA-Qendra e Studimeve Albanologjike), and at the Department of History of the Faculty of History and Philology of the University of Tirana, who have acquaint themselves with the international disciplines. The emergence of ever new universities and university departments in Albania is also a much welcomed development. The chance for young scholars of history and anthropology to find employment in their disciplines is thus greatly improved. It can only be hoped that this development continues, expanding the basis for future research in these disciplines.

Looking at the themes that have found the interest of scholarship in and on Albania in the last two decades, the country has often – tragically, in a sense – been a ready case study for many contemporary social phenomena. Most prominent of these is probably the issue of migration (cf. for example Kaser et al. 2002; King et al. 2005; King and Mai 2008 or the bibliographic essay by Vullnetari 2007; see also the numerous special issues of various journals: Journal of Ethnic and Migration Studies Vol. 29(6) 2003, Journal of Southern Europe and the Balkans Vol. 7(2) 2005; Southeast European and Black Sea Studies Vol. 9(4) 2009).

Questions of the creation of new identities also rank among those issues that find ready material here (i.e. Saltmarsche 2001; Schwandner-Sievers and Fischer 2002; Schubert 2005) Often in combination with these two issues, gender and the role of women (i.e. Whitaker 1981; Sugarman 1997; Lazaridis 2000; Young 2001, 2002) has also found much interest, as have issues of religion Morozzo della Rocca 1990; Clayer 2002; Pettifer and Nazarko 2007) and border regimes (i.e. Hensell 2005; de Rapper 2010). The particular situation of the Albania transition after the collapse of the socialist regime, interpreted at the time as model development (Vickers and Pettifer 1997) followed by a deep fall into chaos and international intervention in 1997 has also provided scholars with opportunities to observe self-organisation in what is euphemistically known as a weak state (Voell 2003, 2004).

There remains an important facet in the study of Albania and Albanians that remains closed to the greatest part of the international scholarly community - for the simple reason that it is a discourse taking place in the Albanian language. Although much of the anthropological and historical discourse in Albania itself remains marked by the socialist scholarly tradition and its focus on various aspects of 'folklore', 'popular culture' and materialist ethnography (Hysa 2010; Voell 2011), the influx of new ideas, the return of young scholars to the country to take up teaching positions and the gradual internationalisation of the local discourse is slowly making its mark. Much of this work remains in the Albanian language with only a few select studies being translated into more internationally accessible languages. Progress is nevertheless being made.

In 2005 we decided to focus our attention in this volume on contemporary research on the Albanian family, society and culture. In doing so, we consciously excluded specific issues such as those of religion and migration. This difficult decision was made in the knowledge that we would be leaving significant aspects of Albanian studies such as religion or migration unrepresented. At the same time it took place in the knowledge that just these issues have received significant attention elsewhere. In our selection of articles, we have sought to cover a broad range of topics and forms of analysis central to historical anthropology.

In planning the volume it was also important that it cover the whole of Albania, including some areas, such as the northern Has region, that have rarely made an appearance in international scholarship. It was also important for us to include recent research on urban Albania. This complex sphere has in younger research often been ignored at the cost, for example, of traditionalist revivalism or self-organisation in rural and semi-rural areas. Although a trend among ethnographers, anthropologists and historians to look increasingly at contemporary urban issues can be perceived, there is still a lot of research to be done. With chapters dealing with Shkodra, Tirana, Elbasan and Gjirokastra, we hope to take a step forward in urban research on Albania. But issues of self-organisation or local identity processes should not be ignored either; thus we have tried to do justice to them as well. A third core issue for us is the continued analysis of new and revealing demographic sources for the analyses of the Albanian family.

The volume is organised into three parts, each corresponding to one of our subheadings. The study of family and family structures is our first point of focus. This approach has a long tradition both in anthropology (Lévi-Strauss 1969) and in history (Wall et al. 1983; Mitterauer 1990). Well-developed classification systems have emerged as a result. One of the biggest problems in studying kinship and family structures in Albania today is that Albanian scholars have in the past and often continue to consequently ignore this terminology. Albanian scholars still use variations of the terms *familje e vogël/familje e madhe* (small family/large family) (i.e. Muka 2001; Elezi 2002; Xhemaj 2005) and each of them tend to define them in their own way, making any form of comparative study all but impossible. And it gets even more confusing when terms like the democratic family or the contemporary family appear in such classifications.

During the communist era, Albanian historians and ethnologists used terms like peasant family and urban family to describe various types of household forms. Classifications of family based on class were also used, thus the emergence of terms such as *familje fshtare* (peasant family) *familje punëtore* (worker family) and *familje borgjeze* (bourgeois family) in publications of that period (i.e. Elezi 1967; Zojzi 1969). The differentiation of socialist and capitalist family forms was also attempted (Mejdiaj 1976). In Kosova other issues such as nationality also found their way into the study of the family (Krasniqi 1979).

Of course the study of the Albanian family does have its own complexities, one of the most interesting of these being that the term household cannot easily be translated into the Albanian language. Most often, household is simply translated as *shtëpi* (house), but *familje* (family), *oborr* (court), *oxhak* (fireplace/chimney) or *zjarr* (fire) can also be used depending on the context (Luarsi 2001). The various uses of these terms and the reasons behind their specific uses have unfortunately not ever been examined in detail. On the contrary, they are used interchangeably, which can also lead to confusion (for an attempt to differentiate between the immanent meanings of *shtëpi* and *familje* see Voell 2004: 167-176)

Another major obstacle in the historical study of the family and family structures in Albania for the period before 1944 is characterised by a lack of grounded data on family and household structures. The greatest part of writing on the issue to date has been based on the writings of early travellers primarily to northern Albania (i.e. Durham 1909; Nopçsa 1907, 1910, 1912) Various attempts have been made to come to terms with the phenomenon (Mosley 1976; Kaser 1996) but there has always remained an aftertaste of conjecture. In the last decade however, detailed data from the Albanian Population Census of 1918 (Seiner 1922) has been made available for detailed demographic study and has resulted in some cases in the verification, in others in the relativisation of given theories (Gruber and Pichler 2002; Kera and Papa 2002; Kera 2003; Papa 2003; Kera and Pandelejmoni 2008). Here, three members of the project group involved in this landmark project present their analyses of various aspects of this data.

The chapters by **Gentiana Kera** and **Enriketa Papa-Pandelejmoni** focus on marriage patterns and family in two cities and demonstrate the different patterns that existed in urban Albania regarding marriage and household. Enriketa Papa-Pandelejmoni analyses marriage patterns in Shkodra, revealing deviances from marriage and households structures in the rest of the country. She asks why this city differs as it does and finds the answer for the local variation of the general pattern in culturally, socially and economically structured behavioural patterns. Gentiana Kera on the other hand looks at the age at marriage in Tirana in the interwar period. She argues that marriage behaviour changed slowly in this time, traditional values of marriage and family continuing to persist, as in the rest of the country, despite the implementation of new legislation and the rapid modernisation that the city experienced in this time. On the whole, this analysis shows that marriage and the factors influencing nuptiality among the urban population were characterised by a marriage pattern different from that common in rural areas. Village exogamy in rural areas, which, for example, broadened the marriage field for rural men and women and resulted in a low age at marriage for both, stood in contrast to urban endogamy combined with religious endogamy. The existence of dowry and the uneven sex ratio narrowed the marriage field, thus increasing the age at marriage for women. The diversity of economic and cultural activities outside the home and higher education in urban areas affected the way people looked at marriage and the family as well.

Siegfried Gruber also analyses household and family patterns on the basis of the data of the population census of 1918. Here he looks to fit the Albanian household within the theoretical patterns of family and household for Southeastern Europe and the Balkans. The data of the Albanian population census of 1918 shows that even if more simple family households existed than to date has been assumed, more people lived in multiple family households than in simple family households. Albania must thus be placed within the region of joint household systems. The data also reveals considerable differences within the territory in which the census was taken – Austro-Hungarian occupied northern Albania – especially between rural and urban residents and people of different religious and ethnic affiliations.

Two further chapters augment this section with its focus on demography-based approaches to the issue of family and household structures. **Nebi Bardhoshi** discusses norms and practices associated with landed family property as they are delineated in Albanian customary law (*kanun*) in a case study from the northeastern region of Has. Bardhoshi approaches his research historically, looking at the period from the turn of the 20th century to collectivisation in the late 1960s, and at attempts to reinstate this status quo in the transition period. Whilst before collectivisation (1946-1967), families in the Has region lived in multiple family households, they were forced to split with collectivisation. After 1991 the collectivised land was returned to its former owners. But the process of de-collectivisation met with series of problems, the solutions to which were often sought in the *Kanun*, which brings the author to the conclusion that is plausible to speak for a revival of *Kanun* in Albania in the 1990s, especially in the sphere of property relations.

Gilles de Rapper on the other hand gives an account of kinship and social organisation in the district of Devoll (southern Albania). Based on his long-term fieldwork in this region, he shows how local conceptions of kinship and social organisation are embedded in wider representations of society in Albania. The Devolli share for the most part the frame of 'Balkan patriarchy', but in regard to family organisation, they claim to be different from northern Albania's *fis* (lineages) ideal. These claims are based in fact and differences do exist in regard to kinship and social organisation from the northern Albanian case. De Rapper goes one to identify these differences in lineage generation depth, segmentary organisation, to the role of the lineage as political and military organisation and to patrilineality.

The second group of chapters analyse various aspects of Albanian society in the course of the 20th century. Two historical chapters by **Andreas Hemming** and **Nathalie Clayer** focus on the interwar period. Clayer deals with the question of the development of education structures and national integration in the province of Gjirokastër, examining the conflict between state authorities on the one hand and local actors on the other. She demonstrates the role of education as a crucial aspect for the building of the state and the nation but concludes that the implementation of a succinct state policy was hindered by financial shortcomings, by conflicting policies between central and local actors on the implementation of education reforms and by difficulties inherent in building one system out of many heterogeneous pieces. Andreas Hemming, in turn, looks at how the newly independent state of Albania was received in Western media, more specifically in German-language travel writing. Based on close readings of three very different travel reports written and reporting on the situation in Albania in the interwar period, he looks at the motifs that run across the various approaches and that remain present even in travel writing on Albanian today.

This link to the present day is mirrored in the next three chapters. **Gerda Dalipaj** shifts the focus to the Roma, one of Albania's many minority populations. In her introductory examination of the Roma community in Elbasan she develops encompassing lines of development from the early 20th century to the present day. Having settled in three in three periods in three well distinguishable quarters in the centre, periphery and extreme periphery of Elbasan, the Roma community is highly differentiated. They have survived as a distinct community only because they have actively promoted their distinctiveness. The vital Roma values of freedom and space, which have been frequently translated as defiance or animosity vis-à-vis greater society and the ideals of a modern state society, are not symptoms of isolationism. The periphery remains a motif in **Stéphane Voell's** chapter on the persistence of discourse based in the Albanian customary law *kanun* among postsocialist migrant communities in new, peripheral suburbs of Tirana. He discusses how patriarchal, segmentary and specific traditional economic structures and ideologies continue to be important for these communities. But while they have served a clear purpose in structuring local, postsocialist suburban society to a certain degree, they are at their core hopelessly antiquated and thus a very present source of conflict. The actors in these communities find themselves negotiating between estimable traditional values and the realities of modern society. The 'sworn virgins' described in the next chapter by **Jenna Rice and Antonia Young** might at first also be described as trapped in hopelessly antiquated patriarchal Albanian social structures. But this is not necessarily the case. The authors show how this very traditional way to meet the demands of a society that is very ridged in the distribution of gender roles is being occupied in new or modified ways, opening spaces for the negotiation of gender roles and traditions. Today's 'sworn virgins' draw on the letter of the *kanun* to undermine the rigidity of gender roles and access new freedoms. Like many other aspects of traditional patriarchal society, it is difficult to predict the course this intermediary gender role will take; this example nevertheless shows that reference to such structures can very well be a step forward.

The third group of chapters is dedicated to various aspects of Albanian culture. In her chapter, **Armanda Hysa** continues her extended project to tell the history the Balkan bazaar, this time focusing on the old bazaar in Tirana. The growth of bazaar was, like many others, spontaneous; only later did 'urban planning' begin to play a role in its organisation and structure. In the 19th century a shift from the sale of agricultural goods and livestock from the outlying countryside to a focus on trade production could be noted, resulting in the emergence of the trade guilds as the organising authority. But with Tirana's rapid modernisation in the 1920s and 1930s the old bazaar lost continually in importance until, finally, the bazaar was demolished, making way for a new, socialist city centre.

The memories of this socialist system form the core of **Smoki Musaraj's** paper. Based on a series of individual and group interviews with Albanian emigrants in New York, Musaraj addresses the question of how day-to-day life in socialist Albania is reflected upon. Looking at two sets of daily practices that were marginal to the official discourse of historical progress, namely, the milk queue [*rradha e qumshtit*] and consumption of Italian and Yugoslavian television programming, she concludes that the memory of both embody the lived experience of the regime. Existing today as unconscious 'structures of feeling' of the official regimes, both practices produced at their core a subtle but enduring tension with the official discourse. People experienced queues as a physical burden, a painful memory of the planned economy. In contrast to the queues, the consumption of foreign television, a practice perhaps more specific to Albania than much of the rest of Eastern Europe, represented an alternative use of the time and space of imagination. This practice created another form of sociality and public intimacy that capitalised on pleasure rather than deprivation; it reclaimed that sense of the private that would come alive in exhilarating informal conversations about the fetishised foreign.

Eckehard Pistrick, finally, examines cultural change on the basis traditional folk music practice, especially since the collapse of the old regime. The effects of migration, demographic shifts, urbanisation, economic collapse and a deeply-rooted identity crisis since 1991 have lead not only to dramatic social ruptures but to a redefinition of the role of traditional folk music forms. Pistrick's case study on the, of the epic historic song repertoire (*këngë epike historike*) in the Saranda region of southern Albania shows how singing has shifted from being a participatory, community activity strengthening social bonds to one that has, especially in urban contexts, been professionalised, acquiring the character of a performative genre reserved for a few cultural associations.

ACKNOWLEDGEMENTS

This book has been a long time in coming. We would like to thank all our contributors for their cooperation and their unending patience as well as Richard Kisling from the LIT Verlag for his continued support. We would also like to say a special thanks to Karl Kaser, for offering us the opportunity to publish this collection in his Studies on South East Europe and for his continued support despite long distances. The book was printed with the support of the Austrian

Federal Ministry for Science and Research in Vienna. Siegfried Gruber assisted in preparing some of the graphs and data analysis with SPSS. Last but not least, we would like to thank our families for their patience and their not always opportune – but always welcome – distraction.

BIBLIOGRAPHY

Bartl, Peter 2000 Zum Geschichtsmythos der Albaner In: Dittmar Dahlmann and Wilfried Potthoff (eds.) Mythen Symbole und Rituale. Die Geschichtsmächtigkeit der „Zeichen" in Südosteuropa im 19. und 20. Jahrhundert. Frankfurt a.M.: Peter Lang.

Clayer, Nathalie 2002 Religion et Nation chez les Albanais XIXe-XXe siècles. Istanbul: Les Éditions Isis.

De Rapper, Gilles 2010 Religion on the Border: sanctuaries and festivals in post-communist Albania. In: Galia Valtchinova (ed.) Religion and Boundaries: Studies from the Balkans, Eastern Europe and Turkey. Istanbul ISIS Press pp. 247-265.

Durham, M. Edith 1909 High Albania. London: Edward Arnold.

Elezi, Ismet 1967 The Vendetta in Albania. In: Albanian Notes Vol 8. pp 1-5.

Elezi, Ismet 2002 E drejta zakonore e Labërisë. Tiranë: Toena.

Gruber, Siegfried and Robert Pichler 2002 Household structures in Albania in the Early 20th Century. The History of the Family, Vol. 7 pp 351-74.

Hemming, Andreas 2006 Die Rolle Skanderbegs im albanischen politischen Selbstverständnis. Zur politischen Mythologie in Albanien. In: Heidi Hein-Kircher and Hans-Henning Hahn (eds.) Politisch Mythen im 19. und 20. Jahrhundert. Marburg: Herder Institut pp 349-466.

Hensell, Stephan 2005 Die Grenzen der Gesetzeshüter: zur bürokratischen Praxis in der albanischen Polizei. Hamburg: Institut für Friedensforschung und Sicherheitspolitik.

Hysa, Armanda 2010 Ethnography in Communist Albania: Nationalist Discourse and Relations with History. In: Katarina Keber and Luka Vidmar (eds.) Historicni seminar 8. Ljubljana ZRC SAZU pp 103-125.

Kaser, Karl 1996 Familie und Verwandtschaft auf dem Balkan. Analyse einer untergehenden Kultur. Vienna: Böhlau Verlag.

Kaser, Karl, Robert Pichler and Stephanie Schwandner Sievers (eds.) 2002 Die Weite Welt und das Dorf. Albanische Emigration am Ende des 20. Jahrhunderts. Vienna: Böhlau Verlag.

Kera, Gentiana 2003 (MS) The Albanian Population Census of 1918: Basic Statistics and Analyses. Diploma thesis submitted to the Faculty of Arts, Karl Franzens University Graz.

Kera, Gentiana and Enriketa Pandelejmoni 2008 Marriage in Urban Albania (during the first half of the twentieth century. History of the family vol 13 pp 126-137.

Kera, Gentiana and Enriketa Papa 2002 Karakteristikat e familjes shqiptare sipas rregjistrimit të popullsisë në vitin 1918. Politika dhe Shoqëria Vol. 1 pp 83-96.

King, Russell, Nicola Mai and Stephanie Schwandner-Sievers (eds.) 2005 The New Albanian Migration. Brighton and Portland: Sussex Academic Press.

King, Russell and Nicola Mai 2008 Out of Albania: From crisis migration to social inclusion in Italy. New York: Berghahn Books.

Krasniqi, Mark 1979 Gjurmë e gjurmime. Prishtinë: Instituti Albanologjik i Prishtinës.

Kressing, Frank and Karl Kaser (eds.) 2002 Albania - A Country in Transition. Aspects of changing identities in a South-East European country. Baden-Baden: Nomos.

Lazaridis, G. 2000 Filipino and Albanian Women: Multiple Layers of Oppression. In: F. Anthias and G. Lazaridis (eds.) Migration and Exclusion in Southern Europe. Aldershot: Ashgate pp 49-79.

Lévi-Strauss Claude 1969 The Elementary Structures of Kinship London: Eyre & Spottiswoode.
Luarasi, Aleks 2001 Marrëdhëniet familjare. Studime për të drejtën zakonore shqiptare. Tiranë.
Mitterauer, Michael 1990 Europäische Familienformen im interkulturellen Vergleich. Historisch-Anthropologische Forschungen: Fragestellungen und Zugangweisen. Vienna: Böhlau.
Mejdiaj, Bajram 1976 Disa aspekte të martesës para Çlirimit In: Etnografia shqiptare Vol. 8 pp 33-108.
Mosely, Philip E. 1976 The Peasant Family: The Zadruga, or Communal Joint-Family in the Balkans, and its Recent Evolution In: Robert F. Byrnes (ed.) Communal Families in the Balkans: The Zadruga. Essays by Philip E. Mosely and Essays in his Honour. London: Notre Dame.
Muka, Ali 2001 Banesa fshatare dhe familja e madhe. Tiranë: Akademia e Shkencave, Instituti i Kulturës Popullore.
Morozzo della Rocca, Roberto 1990 Nazione e religione in Albania (1920–1944). Bologna: Il Mulino.
Nopçsa, Franz Baron 1907. Das katholische Nordalbanien: Eine Skizze. Vienna: Gerold und Co.
Nopçsa, Franz Baron 1910. Aus Sala und Klementi. Albanische Wanderungen (Zur Kunde der Balkanhalbinsel: Reisen und Beobachtungen, 11). Sarajevo: Kajon.
Nopçsa, Franz Baron 1912. Haus und Hausrat im katholischen Nordalbanien (Zur Kunde der Balkanhalbinsel. Reisen und Beobachtungen, 16). Sarajevo: Institut für Balkanforschung.
Papa, Enriketa 2003 (MS) The Albanian Population Census of 1918: Household and Family. Diploma thesis submitted to the Faculty of Arts, Karl Franzens University Graz.
Pettifer, James and Mentor Nazarko (eds.) Strengthening Religious Tolerance for a Secure Civil Society in Albania and the Southern balkans. Amsterdam: IOS Press.
Saltmarsche, Douglas 2001 Identity in a post-communist Balkan state: an Albanian village study. Aldershot: Ashgate.
Schubert, Peter 2005 Albanische Identitätssuche im Spannungsfeld zwischen nationaler Eigenstaatlichkeit und europäischer Integration. Frankfurt a.M. Peter Lang.
Schwandner-Sievers, Stephanie and Bernd Fischer (eds.) 2002 Albanian identities: Myth and History. Bloomington: Indiana University Press.
Seiner, Franz 1922 Ergebnisse der Volkszählung in Albanien in dem von österreichisch-ungarischen Truppen 1916-18 besetzten Gebiete. Vienna: Hölder-Pichler-Tempsky.
Skendi, Stavro 1967 The Albanian National Awakening 1878–1912. Princeton, NJ: Princeton University Press.
Sugarman, Jane 1997 Engendering Song. Singing and Subjectivity at Prespa Albanian Weddings. Chicago: University of Chicago Press.
Tönnes, Bernhard 1980 Sonderfall Albanien. Enver Hoxhas "eigener Weg" und die historischen Ursprünge seiner Ideologie. Munich: R. Oldenbourg Verlag.
Vickers, Miranda and James Pettifer 1997 Albania: From Anarchy to a Balkan Identity. New York: New York University Press.
Voell, Stéphane 2003 The Kanun in the City. Albanian Customary Law as a Habitus and Its Persistence in the Suburb of Tirana, Bathore. In: Anthropos Vol. 98 pp 85-101.
Voell, Stéphane 2004 Das Albanische Gewohnheitsrecht und seine mündliche Dimension. Marburg: Curupira.
Voell, Stéphane 2011 The Kanun in Ethnographic Self-Description. Research into Albanian Traditional Law during Socialism. In: Ulf Brunnbauer et al. (eds.) Sociology and Ethnography in East-Central and South-East Europe: Scientific self-description in state socialist countries. Munich: Oldenbourg pp 227-294.
Vullnetari, Julie 2007 Albanian Migration and Development: state the Art review Working Paper No. 18. IMISCOE.
Wall, Richard, Robin Jean and Peter Laslett (eds.) 1983 Family forms in historic Europe Cambridge: Cambridge University Press.

Whitaker, Ian 1981. "A sack for carrying things": The traditional Role of Women in Northern Albanian Society. In: Anthropological Quarterly Vol. 54 pp 146-56.
Xhemaj, Ukë 2005 Shtresime kulturore. Prishtinë: Instituti Albanologjik i Prishtinës.
Young, Antonia 2001 Women Who Become Men: Albanian Sworn Virgins. Oxford and New York: Berg.
Young, Antonia 2002 Women's Lack of Identity and the Myth of their Security under Albanian Patriarchy in Albania In: Frank Kressing and Karl Kaser (eds.) Albania - A Country in Transition. Aspects of changing identities in a South-East European country, Baden-Baden: Nomos Verlagsgesellschaft pp 93-104.
Zavalani, T. 1969 Albanian Nationalism In: Peter F. Sugar and I.J. Lederer (eds.) Nationalism in Eastern Europe. Seattle and London: University of Washington Press pp 55-92.
Zhelyazkova, Antonia (ed.) 2000 Albania and the Albanian Identities. Sofia: International Center for Minority Studies and Intercultural Relations.
Zojzi, Rrok 1969 Mbeturina të familjes patriarkale që bëhen pengesë emancipimit të gruas In: Studime Historike Vol. 23 pp 33-37.Zojzi, Rrok 1969 Mbeturina të familjes patriarkale që bëhen pengesë emancipimit të gruas In: Studime Historike Vol. 23 pp 33-37.

1. Household and Family in Albania at the Beginning of the 20th Century

Siegfried Gruber

Little is really known about household and family structures in Albania at the beginning of the 20th century. Clear evidence of this fact is the general absence of Albania in publications about household and the family in Europe; Albania is not mentioned in the 4th volume of the French History of the Family (Burguière et al. 1986) or the 3rd volume of The History of the European Family (Kertzer and Barbagli 2003), both dealing with the 20th century. It is also not mentioned in any German history of the family in the chapters dealing with the 20th century (Gestrich et al. 2003) or in the division of Eastern Europe proposed by Plakans and Wetherell (2005: 120). Goody mentions Albania only once in his book about the European family (Goody 2000: 111).

Eastern and Southeastern Europe are generally under-represented in histories of the family in the European context - and Albania even more so. This is not simply negligence or prejudice on the part of scholars from the western half of Europe, who generally write these volumes based on the small number of publications in Western languages. The field of family history in general is much more elaborated in the western half of the continent and publications in the respective languages of Eastern Europe are much more limited in number. One of the main reasons for this, besides the lack of scientific knowledge in this field in Eastern European countries, is the lack of available data. And in the absence of adequate statistical data, incidental, often extraordinary cases have the potential to be interpreted as the norm or at least as the ideal type of family. This is for example the case with Karadžić, who cited a multiple family household with 62 members and 13 married couples in his dictionary under the term zadruga, the term he used for this type of household (Karadžić 1818).

Albania around 1900

Albania was incorporated into the Ottoman Empire in the 15th century; for a number of reasons, Albanians became the nation with the highest percentage of Muslims within the European part of the Ottoman Empire, which played a role in significant number of people of Albanian descent who were successful in making a career within the military and civil administration of the Ottoman Empire. In the 18th and 19th centuries, regional holders of office established themselves as semi-independent rulers in Albanian territories; an irredentist movement began only at the end of the 19th century with successive Ottoman withdrawal out of Europe. Albanian independence occurred only in 1912 with the de facto collapse of Ottoman rule in Europe (with the exception of the region around Constantinople) against the will of its neighbours, who would rather have partitioned the Albanian territories between them. But the new Albanian state was nevertheless smaller than the region settled by ethnic Albanians; and even then, to speak of a national identity realised in an ethnic state would be too much. The northern Albanian mountain regions had never really been incorporated into the Ottoman Empire and the people of this region continued to bet on their independence from an outside ruler when this was an Albanian state.

The urban centre of this region, Shkodra, grew in the first half of the 19th century to 40,000 inhabitants (Shkodra 1988: 22); in the second half of the century the importance of the city decreased and the city suffered heavily from an earthquake in 1905 and the retreat of the Ottoman Empire with the creation of new borders. Shkodra was a regional commercial centre and thus attracted the interest of neighbouring Montenegro, which tried to incorporate it. In the Balkan Wars and Word War I, Montenegrin and Serbian armies repeatedly invaded northern Albania with the goal to shift the borders. During the period of Austrian occupation in World War I, Shkodra was the administrative centre and by far the largest city in the Albanian territory then occupied by the Austrian forces, with 23,099 inhabitants (Seiner 1922: 7).

By that time, this area has attracted many scholars because of its alleged 'otherness' as compared to Western and Central Europe. Berit Backer explains that the "existence of a traditional social structure based on kinship in northern Albania has caught the attention of many Western scholars. This together with the blood feud and the traditional legal code has aroused the enthusiasm of ethnographers. A fully fledged tribal society in the middle of Europe had been found (Backer 2003: 59).[1]" Ethnographers and travellers were long both irritated by and at the same time attracted to the practice of blood feuding and swearing virginity (cf. Young 2000 and Boehm 1984 for studies of these practices). But this lead, for example, to Mary Edith Durham to "devoted more attention to the exotic Albanian 'Virgins', the women who dressed as men and vowed never to marry, than to any of the hard-working wives and mothers she met (Goldsworthy 1998:200)."

The image of Albanian society was shaped in the period of colonialism, mostly by men coming from the West and writing for a Western audience. This kind of colonialism has been called "internal colonialism" (Verdery 1979) or "frontier orientalism" with "the Turk" as the bad and "the Bosnian" as the good Muslim (Gingrich 1998: 117). Austrian ethnography (*Volkskunde*) was especially interested in the Balkan countries, this region being politically interesting with occupation (1878) and annexation (1908) of Bosnia-Herzegovina. WWI and the occupation of Serbia, Montenegro and Albania provided the opportunity to study in territories, which had not been easily accessible before. Scientific expeditions were conducted in close co-operation with the occupying army and were intended to facilitate local administration (Häußer 2005).

---

1 Berit Backer's work is based on her PhD-thesis (Backer 1979). Backer still uses the term 'tribe', the term used by ethnographers to describe the society in northern Albania a century ago. When the term 'tribe' is used in the following, I am referring to cited literature. Otherwise the Albanian term *fis* will be used.

THEORY OF THE BALKAN FAMILY

John Hajnal distinguished two different marriage patterns in Europe divided by a line from Leningrad/St. Petersburg to Trieste: a "(Western) European Marriage Pattern" characterised by a high age at marriage, especially for women and a high proportion of never-married persons and a "Eastern European Marriage Pattern" characterised by a low age at marriage and almost universal marriage (Hajnal 1965: 101f.). He did not deal with Albania as a unit in his study since it was not an independent state at the beginning of the 20th century and statistical data was not readily available. While there is still not enough material available from Eastern Europe to allow a complete picture (Plakans and Wetherell 2005: 109); Plakans and Wetherell propose a division of Eastern Europe into three subregions or subzones, namely a northern, central and southern zone (Plakans and Wetherell 2005: 120). What also needs to be considered in these categorisations are differences not only between regions and states, but also between urban and rural areas, between different ecotypes and the influence of religion, status and class.

Almost two decades after proposing his model, Hajnal added household formation patterns to marriage patterns. The formation rules common to the northwestern European simple household system were

> late marriage for both sexes (mean ages at first marriage are, say, over 26 for men and over 23 for women). After marriage a couple are in charge of their own household (the husband is head of household). Young people before marriage often circulate between households as servants (Hajnal 1983: 69).[2]

In contrast, the formation rules common to joint household systems were "earlier marriage for men and rather early marriage for women (mean ages at first marriage are under about 26 for men and under 21 for women). A young married couple often start life together in a household of which an older couple are in charge (usually the household of which the young husband has been a member). Households with several married couples may split to form two or more households, each containing one or more couples (Hajnal 1983: 69)." In joint household systems it is not necessary that the majority of households were joint households, but that "the majority of people were members of a joint household at some stage in their lives (Hajnal 1983: 69)." In the same volume, Laslett designed a set of tendencies in domestic group organisation in traditional Europe, which yielded in four regional trends (West, West/Central or Middle, Mediterranean and East). The criteria were occasion and method of domestic group formation, procreation and demographic criteria, criteria of kin composition of groups and criteria of organisation of work and welfare (Laslett 1983: 526f.). Overall, the "Hajnal line remains a good on-the-ground predictor for the Balkan Peninsula, where strong tendencies toward household complexity and low mar-

---

[2] This article was first published in 1982 (Hajnal 1982), but the version from 1983 has become more popular.

riage ages continued to exist well into the twentieth century. But as Maria Todorova and others have noted, these tendencies cannot be attributed to the entire Balkan region, especially if that region includes Romania and Bulgaria (Plakans and Wetherell 2005: 112)."

But as Plakens and Wetherell indicate, there have been tendencies to challenge the difference in household formation systems between Western Europe and Southeastern Europe on the basis of quantitative studies, which have to date been rare for this region. But the generalised argument that "in view of basic characteristics – size, structure and function, the Serbian family of the mid-19th century did not differ much from that in other European countries" (Vuletić 2002: 201) does not convince either since it is based largely on urban population figures (Todorova 1993) or a completely new household typology (Vuletić 2002). Rather, the multiple family household, in Serbia as elsewhere, must "be considered primarily a patrilocal unit existing within a society which places stress on patrilineal descent and where the formal authority patterns are patriarchal (Halpern and Kerewsky-Halpern 1972: 17);" i.e. the family must be seen in its social context. Karl Kaser argues that the family played a very complex role, in a Balkan family household the property is owned jointly, religious practises exist for strengthening the bonds within the lineage and blood feuds were a possible means of conflict management between lineages (Kaser 1995: 266).

Kaser divides Southeastern Europe in four different regions according to the patterns of household formation. Albania belongs to the fourth region, characterised by partible equal male inheritance, patrilocality and complexity in the household cycle. "The transmission of property was not related to death or marriage and took place when the household divided into several different groups after generations (Kaser 1996: 383)." This pattern was predominant in Hungary proper, Croatia and Slovakia, most parts of Serbia, western Bulgaria, Macedonia, Bosnia-Hercegovina, Montenegro, Albania and northern Greece with variants in the Maina region of the Peloponnesus and on larger islands like Crete, Corfu and Cyprus. This pattern has a northern and a southern variant, of which the latter was prevalent in Albania (Kaser 1996: 383). This division is based on reports from travellers in the 1st half of the 20th century (i.e. Hasluck 1954; Frashëri 1930: 2002) and the results of the Albanian census of 1918 (Seiner 1922; cf. Kaser 1995: 270). The social and cultural background was described as 'Balkan patriarchy', which includes strong blood ties, ancestor worship, patrilineality, patrilocality, bride-price, blood feuds and a patrilineal kinship structure (Kaser 1992). Since Kaser published this data, the author has shown that household divisions were seldom postponed over generations in Serbia in the second half of the 19th century and that it is questionable whether such a postponement prevailed in the other countries of this pattern (Gruber 2004: 303).

NEW DATA ON THE ALBANIAN FAMILY

An important resource for research on family structures is the population census conducted by the Austro-Hungarian army in 1918 in Albania (see Nicholson

1999). The Austro-Hungarian army occupied a major part of the territory of what was by then the newly created independent Albanian state and established a new administration in 1916. One of this administration‘s first acts was to organise a census. The collection of the census data was done by officers of the Austro-Hungarian army with the assistance of Albanian officers (Seiner 1922: 3). The census personnel were male and the person responsible for declaring the members of the household was the (overwhelmingly male) household head. In the knowledge that this could lead to data falsification, the census personnel were instructed to be sure that no person was left out, i.e. female children (Seiner 1922: 4). These efforts were successful, since the census counted almost the same number of women as men; in contemporary censuses in other countries in the region a clear male majority was always counted (for Serbia cf. Sundhaussen 1989: 80). This census is the first, whose original data is still available on the level of the persons recorded and it is of high quality considering the circumstances under which it was taken (Gruber 2007: 257); most of the census material was preserved (Seiner 1922: 5). The number of Orthodox believers is quite small in the data used for this article, because a third of the missing data was on Orthodox Christians and constituted about two thirds of all Orthodox Christians within the territory of the census (Seiner 1922: 7f.). This census data is also still widely unknown; for example, a recently published demographic atlas of Albania uses data from 1926 as the earliest population data (Bërxholi 2003). Likewise, Gjonça only mentions the preliminary census of 1916, describing the 1923 census as the first general census conducted in Albania (Gjonça 2001: 38f.).

The research project The 1918 Albanian Population Census: Data Entry and Basic Analyses funded by the Austrian Science Fund (2000-2003) aimed at bringing the data into machine-readable form.[3] The project timetable did not allow for the digitalisation of all the data; thus the data was divided into two groups of settlements, the first group being split into 20 five percent samples to be digitalised as time allowed, while the second group was digitalised completely. This second group of settlements included all settlements with a considerable share of minorities, Orthodox Christians, non-agricultural occupations, an uneven sex-ratio, more than 2000 inhabitants (including all the cities), and an extremely low or high household size.

The following analysis is based only on the population present at the time of the census; the population of Sample 1 is weighted with the factor 18.81 for representing the whole population.[4] The data is still available on the level of the individual, which allows for a much more detailed analysis than aggregate data on the village level. The researcher is able to aggregate data in a variety of ways and is not bound to given categories (cf. Hall et al. 2000: 9). This also enables the analyst to combine different variables on the individual level for research purposes. The census data of 1918 is thus a rich resource for examining a variety of questions related to population structure and behaviour.

---

[3] http://www-gewi.kfunigraz.ac.at/suedost/seiner/index.html

[4] Sample 1 is larger than the average sample since sampling was done on the village level.

Table 1: Database of the Albanian population census of 1918

	Settlements	Population
Twenty 5% samples	1093	333,413
Not included in 5% samples	200	102,423
Total	1293	435,836
Data no longer available	501	88,381
Total for the census	1794	524,217
Not included in 5% samples	200	106,414
Sample 1	54	17,719
Total	254	124,133
Present at the time of the census		117,730
Weighted population		424,009

HOUSEHOLD SIZE

Gopčević claims an average household size of about ten persons in the parishes of the diocese of Alessio/Lezha (Gopčević 1880: 406) and about seven persons for the tribe of Klementi (Gopčević 1880: 411). Nopcsa reported that households with 20 adult men were not rare in Albania around 1906 and he mentioned a household in Thethi that had almost 50 men before its dissolution in 1906 (Baxhaku and Kaser 1996: 284). He estimated the average household size to be seven persons in Mirdita and Malcija e madhe and six persons in Malcija e vogël and Dukagjin (Baxhaku and Kaser 1996: 285). But these large households represent extremes and may thus have attracted so much attention. Analysis of the population census of 1918 reveals that out of seven prefectures, only one had an average household size of more than six persons (Puka with 6.7 persons per household). The available data shows that the average household size in Catholic *fis* was 6.8 persons and in Muslim *fis* 6.1 persons. Large households did exist, five examples with at least 40 members were recorded, but the average household was smaller, 5.2 persons in rural areas and 4.3 in the cities. The data therefore appears to confirm Gopčević's and Nopcsa's estimates, which on the surface might look rather conservative when compared to the largest households, and in light of the fact that a majority of the population was living in multiple family households.

Table 2: Household size in Albania in 1918

Catholic *fis*	6.8
Muslim *fis*	6.1
'Tribal area' overall	6.2
Muslim villages	5.1
Orthodox villages	5.0
Catholic villages	6.4
Villages outside the 'tribal area' overall	5.2
Rural areas overall	5.6
Cities	4.3
Muslims	5.3
Catholics	6.2
Orthodox	4.6
Albanians	5.5
Slavs	3.6
Roma	4.0
Overall	5.4

Forty-five percent of all family households had less than four members and only eight percent had more than ten members. Nevertheless large households did exist; 20 percent of the population were living in households with more than ten members. Some of the differences within the country are to be expected, like the prevalence of the largest households in northern Albania and the generally small household in the cities. Catholics had larger households in the 'tribal areas' and also outside this region. The much smaller average households among Slavs and Roma are unexpected, but can be explained for Roma by the fact that more than half of them were living in cities. Almost half of the Orthodox population was also living in cities (a result of the fact that the missing data includes much of the rural Orthodox population); their average households were smaller than those of Catholics and Muslims.

HOUSEHOLD TYPOLOGY

Hahn reported seeing large households in northern Albania with joint property and a tradition of keeping the household together. He found the largest households with 70 to 80 members in the area of the Mirdita federation (Hahn 1854: Vol. I: 180f.). Gopčević even mentions households of 50, 100 and 200 persons because brothers did not divide the household after the death of their father (Gopčević 1880: 408). Frashëri wrote in the 1930s, that a "Mirditë household may have 10, 20, 30 and sometimes 40 people (Frashëri 2002:9)." But Seiner published the results of the population census of 1918 and mentioned that because of the low average household size, the "Slavic zadruga" did not prevail in northern Albania, but the existence of many households with 20 or more members was evidence of the considerable spread of the "Slavic zadruga" (Seiner 1922: 8).

In a first publication based on data from the Albanian population census of 1918, four zones of analysis were developed (Gruber and Pichler 2002: 355). Zone 1 represented the northern Albanian highlands; in the four villages in this zone between 37.0 percent and 75.2 percent of the people lived in multiple family households. Zone 2 was made up of villages in the plain and the foothills; between 12.2 percent and 61.0 percent of the people there lived in multiple family households. Zone 3 represented three urban quarters; two of them revealed that 15 percent of their residents lived in multiple family households while in the third 65 percent did so. Zone 4 was a single village with a high proportion of male labour migration and 21 percent of the population living in multiple family households. In the meantime, more data has been made available, which allows a much more detailed analysis.

The available data shows a very complex picture of household structure in Albania. Overall, a relative majority of the households were simple family households, but almost half of the population was living in multiple family households. This seeming contradiction is the effect of the different sizes of simple and multiple family households: simple family households contained on average only 3.8 persons whereas multiple family households were made up of 9.1 persons on average. The type of household that was the most prominent among all types was that of the married couple with children (24.5 percent of the households with 20.6 percent of the population).

Simple family households were dominant in the cities, among the Roma and Orthodox populations, both highly urbanised, and among the Slavic minority. Half of the households in Orthodox villages were simple family households and the percentage of people living in multiple family households was only slightly higher than those living in simple family households. Multiple family households were dominant in the 'tribal area', even more so among the Catholic than among the Muslim population. There a relative majority of the households were multiple ones, while in the cities only one in eight households had a multiple structure. The villages outside the 'tribal area' were in between the 'tribal area' and the cities with a majority of simple family households but a majority of the population living in multiple family households. Also in these villages, Catholics tended more towards multiple family households than Muslim and Orthodox believers. Extended family households were about a fifth of all households and contained also about a fifth of the population. They were rather evenly distributed across the country. Solitaries and no families were quite seldom, with higher shares among the urban population.

Table 3: Household typology in Albania in 1918

	Solitaries		No family		Simple family household		Extended family household		Multiple family household	
	HH	P	HH	P	HH	P	HH	P	HH	P
Catholic *fis*	1.2	0.2	2.1	0.9	30.4	20.1	23.0	18.1	43.3	60.8
Muslim *fis*	3.0	0.5	2.6	1.4	34.7	21.4	24.1	21.0	35.6	55.7
'Tribal area' overall	2.7	0.4	2.6	1.3	33.9	21.2	23.9	20.4	37.0	56.7
Muslim villages	3.4	0.6	3.5	2.0	44.7	34.1	22.9	21.2	25.5	42.1
Orthodox villages	3.9	0.7	3.3	1.6	48.4	37.8	18.1	18.7	26.3	41.1
Catholic villages	2.3	0.4	2.8	1.8	34.5	22.2	20.4	17.2	40.1	58.5
Villages outside the 'tribal area' overall	3.3	0.6	3.4	2.0	44.1	33.2	22.5	20.7	26.6	43.5
Rural areas overall	3.0	0.5	3.0	1.6	39.7	27.6	23.1	20.6	31.1	49.6
Cities	6.2	1.4	4.1	2.7	56.2	48.4	20.7	22.9	12.8	24.6
Muslims	3.6	0.6	3.2	1.8	42.8	30.8	23.1	21.3	27.3	45.5
Catholics	3.0	0.5	3.0	1.6	36.7	25.1	21.4	18.4	35.9	54.4
Orthodox	4.5	0.9	3.7	2.0	52.9	42.1	19.6	21.5	19.3	33.4
Albanians	3.4	0.6	3.2	1.8	42.0	29.9	23.0	21.0	28.4	46.8
Slavs	7.5	1.3	2.9	1.6	49.4	41.3	18.1	19.1	22.0	36.7
Roma	5.3	1.2	5.6	4.5	57.7	50.7	15.5	17.0	15.9	26.6
Overall	3.5	0.6	3.2	1.8	42.4	30.4	22.7	20.9	28.1	46.3

Another important factor that needs to be considered is change in the composition of the household over the life-course. Many people experienced different household types throughout their lives, but some also lived all or almost all their life in the same household type. About half of the population was born into multiple family households. This percentage decreases with increasing age until ca. ten years-of-age, when the trend is reversed. The share of people living in multiple family household increases then up to an age of 25 years before it begins to decrease again. After age 35, the share of women living in multifamily households remains constant; for men, it increases again after age 50. Alternatively, the share of simple family households was highest at age ten and between 40 and 45 years-of-age for women and 40 and 50 years-of-age for men. The share of extended family households remained rather constant for men until they reach 50 years-of-age at which time it begins to decrease. For women, by contrast, a rapid increase in extended family households rates could be found after an age 45 to reach half the population by the time they are 80. These changes can be attributed to household divisions when sons leave the household, the death of the elder generation when children are still young and household divisions of middle-aged brothers. The increase in multiple family households can be attributed to the marriages of brothers living in the same household and the marriage of sons later in life. The high share of extended family households among older women is a sign that widows lived with one of their sons. At no age did share of multiple family households drop below 40 percent and it was more than 60 percent only for the oldest men. The share of simple family households was between 20 percent between 20 and 25 years-of-age for women and 25 and 35 years-of-age for men. This rate reached 40 percent at an age of 45 years-of-age for women and 50 years-of-age for men. Among the oldest people, the share fell below 20 percent for men and even below ten percent for women. The share of extended family households was rather constant at about 20 percent with the exception of the oldest age-groups.

Chart 1: Household typology over the male life-course

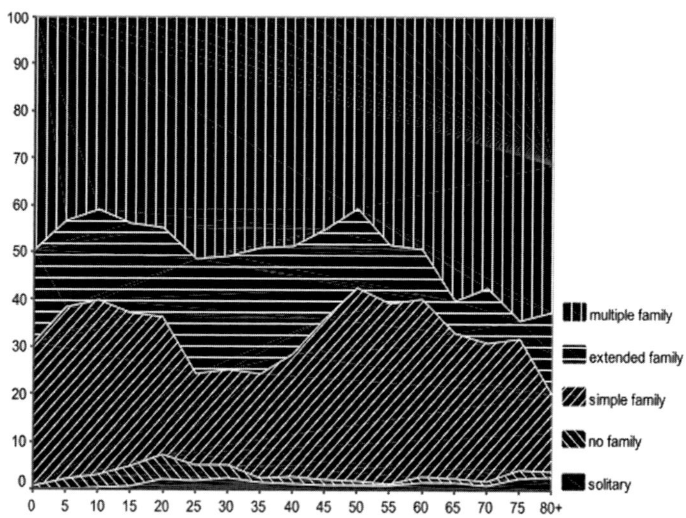

This data shows that Albania falls within the region of joint family households, since at least half of the population was living in a multiple family household at some point in their lives. But this is only valid for the rural population; in the cities the share of multiple family households reached a share of only a third for the women at age 20 and a third for the oldest men. On the other hand the share fell below 20 percent for men at age 20 and for women at age 50. Simple family households reached shares of 60 percent during childhood and for middle-aged people.

HOUSEHOLD HEADS

Households were generally headed by men; only 5.4 percent of the households had a female household head. Although household heads were often referred to as 'elders' (Kaser 1995: 344) their average age was 44 years for male household heads and 47 years for female household heads. More than 20 percent of male household heads were only 30 years old or even younger. Three-fourths of them were married, while more than 90% of female household heads were widowed. Women as household heads lived in much smaller households than those headed by men, they contained only 3.05 persons on average. These households were also different in their structure; more than half of them were simple family households, almost a fifth of these women were living alone, one in seven was living in an extended household and only 5.5 percent were living in multiple family households. In the larger cities (Shkodra, Tirana, Elbasan, Durrës) more than ten percent of the households were headed by women and among the Roma population more than 15 percent had a female head. In contrast only one percent of the multiple family households were headed by a woman and only 1.8 percent of Catholic households in the 'tribal areas'. In most of these households there were no men over 20 years-of-age; only in 14.4 percent of them did such men exist and only in eleven percent was at least one of them present at the time of the census.

When did people become household heads, at which stage in their life-course and as a result of which event? This question is much easier to answer for women: they became household heads after the death of their husband and between the age of 45 to 70; five percent of them were heading a household provisionally until a son or other male member of the household could assume the position. A continuous rise in headship rates for men up to an age of 50 was to be discerned when 80 percent of them were heading a household. Thereafter the rate remains constant, followed by a peak at age 65, when 90% are household heads. Thereafter the rate begins to fall. Therefore there was no definite age at which a man becomes a household head, although most men became household heads at younger ages. The number of men stepping down voluntarily from this position was very low; thus only the death of the father allowed his son to inherit his position. Leaving the parental household was another possibility for becoming household head. This happened most often after the death of the father, since the average number of sons declined only after age 75. Household heads lived with a widowed mother to the same extent that men were not household heads. After the death of the father a constant process of dividing households may be observed; at age 20 the percentage of men living with a brother in the same household began to decrease rapidly. At that age, 69 percent of them had a least one brother in the same household and this rate dropped below 40 percent by age 45. Household heads had higher rates of being married and having children than men who were not household heads and of the same age.

Men were marrying over a longer time period. At age 30, only three-fourths of men were already married. Therefore, marrying may be connected with becoming a household head. The data from the census does not allow the direct analysis of the sequence of marriage and becoming household head, but some indirect conclusions can be drawn. During youth and young adulthood marriage and household head status were clearly not connected, both events occurred independently. Afterwards both sequences were possible, although it seems that men married before becoming household heads more often than afterwards. Between 45 and 50 years-of-age almost only married men became household heads. The birth of a son could also be a decisive event for establishing a new household, because it would be the guarantee of a continuation of the patriline, a very important element of Balkan patriarchy (Kaser 1992: 285). Up to an age of 25 years men became household heads almost exclusively without having a son. At least half of the men had a son before becoming household head in the age category 25 to 35 years. It seems that most of the men became the father of a son only after already being a household head and that they therefore did not see having a son as a prerequisite for becoming household head.

LIVING TOGETHER IN A HOUSEHOLD

The core of the households were the household head, his wife, parents, siblings and children and encompassed three fourths of all members of the households. More distant relatives made up for another 22.3 percent. These were mostly spouses and children of siblings, children-in-law and grandchildren, and cousins. Therefore only 2.5 percent of the members of the households were not related to the head of the household by blood or marriage, being mostly servants.[5] About a tenth of the population experienced such an unrelated individual in their household with almost no change during their life-time.

There was a constant change of the composition of the households over the life-course. At an age of 15 years only half of the population still had a father, but more than two thirds still had a mother. We see here clearly the effects of the high mortality at that time and of the different age at marriage for men and women. Women moved generally into the household of their husbands upon marriage and therefore they stopped living together with their blood relatives around the age of 20 years. Most men also lost their parents during their youth or young adulthood and at an age of 25 years only a third of the men still had a living father and only 60 percent had a living mother. Grandparents were alive only at the beginning of life: at birth about a third of the children had a grandmother living in the same household. This percentage fell to a mere ten percent for grandmothers and two percent for grandfathers at an age of 15 years. By far not all of the boys and girls at that time had siblings, or better surviving siblings: the highest shares were 70 percent for brothers and 60 percent for sisters during childhood. Sisters left the household normally at marriage and brothers died or also left the common household after some time and at an age of 45 years less than 40 percent of the men

[5] These 2.5 percent include also those persons with unclear or missing information about their relation to the head of the household.

still had a brother in the same household. But there were also people moving into these households, beginning with a wife after the marriage and followed by children after some time for most of the people. The late age at marriage for men and an obviously high child and infant mortality are the reasons why at an age of 40 years only half of the men had a son, while women reached this margin already at an age of 30 years. Only about three-fourths of all older people were successful in having a surviving son, while the rate for daughters only exceeded half of the population due to their leaving of the household upon marriage. People could also see their grandchildren in case they lived long enough: half of the women of age 65 and half of the men of more than 80 years had grandchildren in the same household. The high mortality and age gap between spouses in combination with a higher remarriage rate for men caused a high percentage of widows, since at an age of 50 years only half of the women were still married. Other relatives were of importance for a smaller part of the male population. Almost half of them had an uncle in the same household at birth, but this rate continuously decreased throughout life. In contrast nephews became more widespread and reached a rate of about 30 percent at higher ages. About a fourth of all boys had a cousin in the same household and this share remained almost constant during childhood and young adulthood and then slowly diminished.

Chart 2: Living with relatives over the male life-course

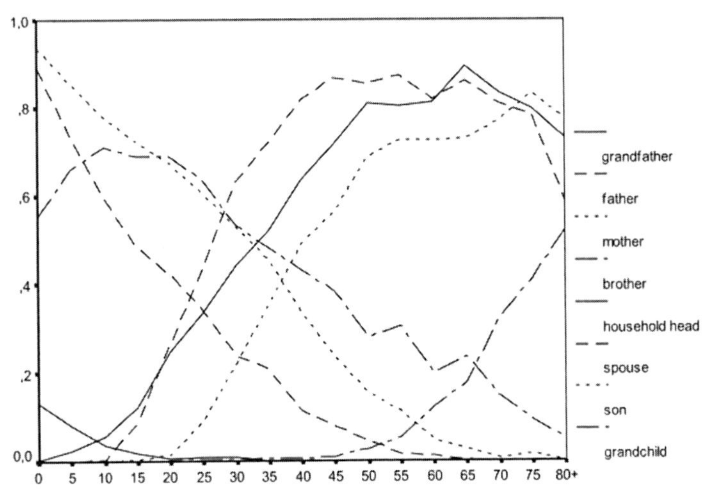

CONCLUSIONS

The Albanian population census of 1918 permits the investigation of Albanian households and families at the beginning of the 20th century. The data confirms average household sizes published already more than a century ago. There were more simple family households than multiple family households but more people were living in multiple family households than in simple family households. A majority of the population was living at some point in their life-course in a multiple family household and therefore Albania can be placed within the region of joint household systems. The data also reveals that there were considerable differences within the Albanian territory occupied by the Austro-Hungarian Army during WWI, especially between rural and urban residents and people of different religious and ethnic affiliations. These differences can also be observed for the life-course of the people: there is no 'standard life-course', even if men and women are separated. About half of the people live in multiple family households at almost any age, but the other half is living in different familial constellations. These constellations could be the same throughout life for a minority of the population, but changed several times for a majority of the population. Most of the men became eventually the head of a household, after the death of their father of after dividing the household with their brother or brothers. Only a small minority of men stayed within the household of an older brother throughout their whole life.

BIBLIOGRAPHY

Backer, Berit 1979 Behind the Stone Walls: Changing household organization among the Albanians in Yugoslavia. Master's thesis; University of Oslo.

Backer, Berit 2003 Behind Stone Walls: Changing Household Organization among the Albanians of Kosova. Peja.

Baxhaku, Fatos and Karl Kaser 1996 Die Stammesgesellschaften Nordalbaniens. Berichte und Forschungen österreichischer Konsuln und Gelehrter (1861-1917). Vienna, Cologne and Weimar.

Bërxholi, Arqile ed. 2003 Atlasi gjeografik i popullsisë së Shqipërisë: Atlasi i Shqipërisë = Demographic Atlas of Albania. Tiranë.

Boehm, Christopher 1984 Blood Revenge. The Anthropology of Feuding in Montenegro and Other Tribal Societies. Lawrence.

Burguière, André, Christiane Klapisch-Zuber, Martine Segalen, and Françoise Zonabend, (ed.) 1986 Histoire de la famille. Paris.

Durham, Mary Edith 1909 High Albania. London.

Filipović, Milenko S. 1976 Zadruga (Kućna Zadruga). In: Robert F. Byrnes (ed.) Communal Families in the Balkans: The Zadruga. Essays by Philip E. Mosely and Essays in His Honor (International Studies of the Committee on International Relations). Notre Dame and London pp. 268-279.

Fischer, Bernd J. 1999 Albanian Highland Tribal Society and Family Structure in the Process of Twentieth Century Transformation. In: East European Quarterly, Vol. 33(3) pp. 281-301.

Frashëri, Stavre Th. 1930 Përmes Mirditës në Dimër. Korçë.

Frashëri, Stavre Th. 2002 Through Mirdite in Winter (East European Monographs). New York.

Gestrich, Andreas, Jens-Uwe Krause and Michael Mitterauer 2003 Geschichte der Familie (Europäische Kulturgeschichte, vol. 1). Stuttgart.

Gingrich, Andre (1998) Frontier Myth of Orientalism: The Muslim World in Public and Popular Cultures of Central Europe. In: Bojan Baskar and Borut Brumen (eds.):

Mediterranean Ethnological Summer School, Vol. II, Piran/Pirano Slovenia 1996. Ljubljana pp. 99-127.
Gjonça, Arjan 2001 Communism, Health and Lifestyle: The Paradox of Mortality Transition in Albania, 1950-1990 (Studies in Population and Urban Demography, No. 8). Westport and London.
Goldsworthy, Vesna 1998 Inventing Ruritania: the Imperialism of the Imagination. New Haven and London.
Goody, Jack 2000 The European Family: An Historico-Anthropological Essay (The Making of Europe). Oxford.
Gopčević, Spiridon 1880 Ethnographische Studien in Ober-Albanien. In: Dr. A. Petermann's Mitteilungen, Vol. 26 pp. 405-420.
Gruber, Siegfried and Robert Pichler 2002 Household structures in Albania in the early 20th century. In: The History of the Family, Vol. 7 pp. 351-374.
Gruber, Siegfried 2004 Lebensläufe und Haushaltsformen auf dem Balkan: das serbische Jasenica im 19. Jahrhundert. PhD-thesis; Karl-Franzens-Universität Graz.
Gruber, Siegfried 2007 Die albanische Volkszählung von 1918 und ihre Bedeutung für die Wissenschaft. In: Helga Kostka (ed.) SeinerZeit Redakteur Franz Seiner und seine Zeit (1874 bis 1929). Graz pp. 253-265.
Hahn, Johann Georg von 1854 Albanesische Studien. Jena.
Hajnal, John 1965 European Marriage Patterns in Perspective. In: David Victor Glass, David Edward Charles Eversley, eds., Population in History: Essays in Historical Demography. London pp. 101-143.
Hajnal, John 1982 Two Kinds of Preindustrial Household Formation System. In: Population and Development Review 8 (3) pp. 449-494.
Hajnal, John 1983 Two kinds of pre-industrial household formation systems. In: Richard Wall (ed.) Family forms in historic Europe. Cambridge pp. 65-104.
Hall, Patricia Kelly, Robert McCaa and Gunnar Thorvaldsen, (eds.) 2000 Handbook of International Historical Microdata for Population Research. Minneapolis.
Halpern, Joel M. and Barbara Kerewsky-Halpern 1972 A Serbian Village in Historical Perspective. New York.
Häußer, Christian 2005 "Balkan-Expeditionen" und Österreichische Volkskunde. Zur Erkundung des "Fremden" und zur "Erfindung" einer Wissenschaft in Österreich-Ungarn. In: Kakanien Revisited (http: www.kakanien.ac.at/beitr/materialien/MHaeusser1.pdf).
Hasluck Margaret 1954 The Unwritten Law in Albania by the late Margaret Hasluck. Cambridge.
Karadžić, Vuk Stefanović 1818 Lexicon serbico-germanico-latinum. Vienna.
Kaser, Karl 1992 Hirten, Kämpfer, Stammeshelden. Ursprünge und Gegenwart des balkanischen Patriarchats. Vienna, Cologne and Weimar.
Kaser, Karl 1995 Familie und Verwandtschaft auf dem Balkan. Analyse einer untergehenden Kultur. Vienna, Cologne and Weimar.
Kaser, Karl 1996 Introduction. In: Karl Kaser (ed.) Household and Family Contexts in the Balkans (The History of the Family, Vol. 1(4)) pp. 375-386.
Kertzer, David I. and Marzio Barbagli (eds.) 2003 Family Life in the Twentieth Century (The History of the European Family: Vol. 3). New Haven and London.
Laslett, Peter 1983 Family and household as work group and kin group: areas of traditional Europe compared. In: Richard Wall (ed.) Family forms in historic Europe. Cambridge pp. 513-563.
Liebert, Erich 1909 Aus dem Nordalbanischen Hochgebirge (Zur Kunde der Balkanhalbinsel. Reisen und Beobachtungen, Vol. 10). Sarajevo.
Louis, Herbert 1927 Albanien. Eine Landeskunde vornehmlich auf Grund eigener Reisen. Stuttgart.
Mosely, Philip E. 1940 The Peasant Family: The Zadruga, or Communal Joint-Family in the Balkans, and Its Recent Evolution. In: Caroline F. Ware (ed.) The Cultural Approach to History. New York pp. 95-108

Nicholson Beryl 1999 The census of the Austro-Hungarian occupied districts of Albania in spring 1918. A preliminary note on the manuscript (Centre for Scandinavian Studies Papers No. 5).
Plakans, Andrejs and Charles Wetherell 2005 The Hajnal line and Eastern Europe. In: Theo Engelen and Arthur P. Wolf, eds., Marriage and the family in Eurasia: Perspectives on the Hajnal hypothesis (Life at the Extremes, vol. 1). Amsterdam pp. 105-126.
Seiner, Franz 1922 Ergebnisse der Volkszählung in Albanien in dem von den österr.-ungar. Truppen 1916-1918 besetzten Gebiete (Schriften der Balkankommission, Linguistische Abteilung, vol. XIII). Vienna and Leipzig.
Shkodra, Zija 1988 La ville albanaise au cours de la renaissance nationale (1831-1912). Tirana.
Sundhaussen Holm 1989 Historische Statistik Serbiens 1834-1914. Mit europäischen Vergleichsdaten (Südosteuropäische Arbeiten 87). Munich.
Todorova, Maria 1993 Balkan Family Structure and the European Pattern. Demographic Developments in Ottoman Bulgaria. Washington.
Todorova, Maria 1997 Imagining the Balkans. New York and Oxford.
Verdery, Katherine 1979 Internal Colonialism in Austria-Hungary. In: Ethnic and Racial Studies Vol. 2(3) pp. 378-199.
Vuletić, Aleksandra 2002 Porodica u Srbiji sredinom 19. veka (Istorijski Institut, posebna izdanja, vol. 35). Belgrade.
Young, Antonia 2000 Women Who Become Men: Albanian Sworn Virgins (Dress, Body, Culture). Oxford and New York.

2. AGE AT MARRIAGE IN INTERWAR TIRANA

GENTIANA KERA

Research on the Albanian family in the first half of the 20th century has been concerned primarily with the rural family, in particular, the complex patriarchal households in Northern Albania (see Coon 1950; Stahl 1986; Kaser 1997; Fischer 1999). Both Albanian and foreign scholars have taken an interest in this type of household, drawing on ethnographic observations made by foreign travellers who visited Albania from the nineteenth century onward (i.e. Nopcsa 1907; Siebert 1910; Cozzi 1912; Durham 1928; Cordignano 1931). Hitherto there has been a scarcity of research that has used demographic data due in large measure to the paucity of statistical data and the poor quality of much of that which exists. Ethnographic studies of marriage in the interwar period deal almost exclusively with issues such as marriage customs and ceremonies, dowry, and differences between religious groups and in different cities.

The urban family, by contrast, has received less attention. This paper analyses the marriage pattern in Tirana, comparing demographic data of the population censuses of 1918 and 1930.[1] In the decades following 1912, when Albania gained its independence from the Ottoman Empire, and especially after 1920, there were important political, social and administrative changes in Albania. The new state took over administrative and civil issues that had been previously handled by religious institutions and the Civil Code of 1929 legally regulated marriages and divorces. By analysing age at marriage on the basis of demographic data, I intend to identify changes in marriage behaviour in Tirana during the interwar period. I argue that marriage behaviour changed slowly in the course of the two decades and that traditional values of marriage and family continued to persist in Tirana, as in the rest of the country, despite the implementation of new legislation and modernisation trends. Nonetheless, age at marriage increases during the interwar period, although universal marriage continued to be the case. Age at marriage is analysed for different religious and ethnic communities living in Tirana in the interwar period.

During the socialist period, studies of the interwar family by Albanian scholars usually took the form of negative descriptions of marital practices before World War II, primarily with the goal to emphasise the positive effects of policies implemented by the socialist government to reform marriage and family life (i.e.

[1] The research project "The 1918 Albanian Population Census: Data Entry and Basic Analyses" funded by the Austrian Science Fund (Fonds zur Förderung der Wissenschaftlichen Forschung) aimed to bring the data into a machine-readable format. The project team at the University of Graz consisted of Helmut Eberhart, Karl Kaser, Siegfried Gruber, Gentiana Kera and Enriketa Papa. The data entry of the population census of 1930 for Tirana was made in the course of the project, Tirana and Shkodra: Demographic and historical-anthropological trends in two Albanian cities (1928-1938) at the University of Graz funded by the Austrian Science Fund (Fonds zur Förderung der Wissenschaftlichen Forschung).

Nova 1969; Mejdijaj 1970; Tirta 1970; Dojaka 1972; Zojzi 1972; Sinani 1986). The traditional patriarchal family was considered an obstacle to the emancipation of women (Zojzi 1969), whereas the new socialist family should become the preferred model of family (Uçi 1968: 51-54). Ethnographic studies on marriage in Albania aimed to identify traditional elements of marriage behaviour before World War II, which continue to exist and hinder the "complete triumph of the new marriage" (Mejdijaj 1976: 33).

Efforts made in the interwar period to improve the position of women within the family and in society, and the outlawing of practices such as polygamy, bride price, child betrothal, and under-age marriage, were either ignored or dismissed as insufficient and superficial.

In a joint article published in 1989, it was argued that the National Liberation War "is to be considered as involving the first step taken towards the emancipation of Albanian women." The active participation of women in the war was a sign of revolt against conservative and oppressive forces in the very vein of the society (Danermark et al. 1989: 22). The authors argue that during the socialist period, the Albanian family had, for the first time, features of an ordered and legal institution consisting of the fact that only the civilian marriage was recognised to be legal. The creation of families was arranged in accordance to civil codes, and not in accordance to canonistic or religious laws as it was previously the case (Danermark et al. 1989: 22). The Civil Code of 1929 was indeed the first attempt made by the Albanian state to regulate marriage and family.

DEMOGRAPHY IN ALBANIAN TOWNS

In 1923, only 15.9 percent of the Albanian population was living in towns (Breu 1968: 310). An indicator for the slow urbanisation in the interwar period was a light increase in the absolute numbers of the urban population, while the percentage of urban population was even lower in 1938 (15.4 percent) (Breu 1968: 310). The reasons need to be sought in the slow industrialisation of the country and higher fertility rates in villages which influenced a higher increase of rural population during the interwar period.

Table 1 shows the population of the main Albanian towns in 1923 and 1938. With the exception of Korça, other cities experienced a population increase, which was at highest in Tirana. A plausible explanation for this rapid population increase in Tirana in comparison to other towns is migration. Better employment opportunities in Tirana because of intense construction activities and the establishment of new administrative and governmental structures attracted persons from all over the country.

Although Tirana experienced rapid urban development after becoming the capital, other urban centres with a larger population, more solid urban structure, more historical tradition or other cultural and economic advantages experienced an economic and demographic decline, primary among them Shkodra (Castiglioni 1941: 11).

Korça, the largest town in 1923, witnessed the strongest population decrease among Albanian towns in the interwar period because of emigration, especially to United States; Gjirokastra and Kruja had a slight population decrease. Despite the considerable population increase in Tirana, in 1938, Shkodra was the largest town in Albania. Population in Durrës and Vlora, two important port towns, also increased in the interwar period.

Table 1: Population of Albanian towns between 1923 and 1938

Town	1923	1927	1938
Tirana	10,845	16,513	25,079
Durrës	4785	5175	10,506
Vlora	5942	6210	9948
Shkodra	21,580	23784	25,293
Korça	25,598	25598	21,221
Elbasan	10,408	10,399	12,718
Berat	8000	8505	9584
Kavaja	6307	6307	7272
Gjirokastra	8906	9578	8820
Kruja	3783	4027	3708

Source: Breu, Josef (1968). Das Wachstum der Städte Albaniens 1923-1965, Geographische Informationen, 2/3, p. 307; Selenica, Teki (1928). Shqipëria më 1927, p. CXXII.

The occupational structure of towns reflected the slow industrialisation of the country. In 1918, the most significant group of occupations in towns were those relating to production and transport. In Durrës, this group reached 40 percent, whereas in Elbasan and Tirana their share was only half of this. Second place was occupied by sales workers, comprising between 22.7 percent in Durrës and 16.2 percent in Elbasan. Service workers accounted for five to twelve percent of the male workforce, whereas agriculture was still of importance in Tirana, Elbasan and Kruja. White-collar jobs were rare and the highest percentage was to be found in Shkodra (Gruber 2008: 142-143).

Even in 1930, 80 percent of the population in Albania were still dependent on agriculture. Taking into account the number of people engaged in state administration, armed forces, transportation, and communications, there were few engaged in industry (Skëndi 1958: 58-59). At the beginning of the 1930s, the ratio of males gainfully occupied in mining and industry to males gainfully occupied in agriculture was 8.33:100 (Skëndi 1958: 59). Agricultural products comprised the majority of exported products from Albania, whereas imported goods were mostly manufactured goods, cars, machines (Selenica 1928: 185). In the 1920s, several fabrics were opened in the main towns, mainly fabrics for the production of cigarettes, alcohol, soap, rice, oil or printing houses (Selenica 1928: 188).

TIRANA

Contemporary observers described Tirana in the first half of the twentieth century as a town with agricultural-commercial character. An Italian traveller who visited Tirana in 1916 noted that "Tirana is an interesting town, rich of tree shadows and waters which retains all the magic of a pure oriental town with its low buildings circumcised by gardens, with its rich market and its coffee houses and above all with its elegant mosques with high minarets" (Marteli 1917: 83). Tirana was an important centre of agriculture and manufacturing, and is especially well known for the production of arms, ornaments, wool, and silk (Marteli 1917: 83).

After the proclamation as capital of Albania, Tirana changed rapidly acquiring new urban forms and characteristics deriving from its political function as capital, and at the same time, preserving her agricultural-commercial character (Mauro 1940: 247-248). The proclamation of Tirana as capital was considered frequently by contemporary observers as the starting of the new history of Tirana as a real city and of its urban transformation (Mauro 1940: 256; Castiglioni 1941: 16). Di Mauro considered the combination of natural and political aspects as the reason for the interesting and strong contrasts in Tirana, where traditional and modern elements coexisted (Mauro 1940: 247).

Nevertheless, the urbanisation and industrialisation of Tirana in the interwar period, as in the rest of the country, were relatively slow. The population of the town increased as a result of in-migration of people searching for job opportunities, but many of these migrants were seasonal workers. Industrialisation, which would have stimulated the urbanisation of Tirana, was slow and insufficient.[2] Table 2 shows the occupational structure of adult males in Tirana in 1918.

Table 2: Occupational structure of adult males in Tirana in 1918

Occupation	Percentage
Professional, technical and related workers, administrative and managerial workers, clerical and related workers	6.2
Sales workers	19.8
Service workers	10.4
Agricultural, animal husbandry and forestry workers, fisherman and hunters	20.1
Production and related workers, transport equipment operators and labourers	23.2
Domestic work, co-working relatives, not working	4.3
Data missing	16.0

Source: (Gruber 2008:143)

[2] A ka urbanizëm 1936: 2.

The development of industry was low, also because of the world economic depression, which also affected Albania. Only a few factories had opened for the processing of agricultural products, some oil and soap plants, some tobacco mills, carpenters workshops and brick kilns. After 1934, industrialisation proceeded more quickly (Frashëri 2003: 167-168). In 1927, Tirana was home to factories for metal processing, clothing and foodstuffs; various trades continued to prevail in the city (Frashëri 2003: 167).

The proclamation of Tirana as the capital of Albania in 1920 played a decisive role in the further development of the city and the population increased rapidly from 10,416 in 1918 to 30,806 inhabitants (including provisional inhabitants) in 1930. 91.7 percent of the population of Tirana in 1918 were Moslem, 7.9 percent Orthodox, 0.3 percent Catholic, and 0.1 percent Jewish. The data of 1930 show an increase in the percentage of Catholics living in Tirana (4.1 percent) and a slight decrease in the number of Orthodox (7.4 percent). 87.7 percent of the population were Moslem in 1930. The increase of the number of Catholic inhabitants should be related to in-migration from other regions.

The majority of the population in 1918 was ethnically Albanian (92.1 percent), 7.5 percent Roma, 0.2 percent Slavs, and 0.2 percent other. Illiteracy rates were very high and in 1918 only 8.3 percent of the population was literate, whereas in 1930 this percentage rose to 19.1 percent. Both censuses show an evident increase in the literacy of both males and females. In 1918, only 1.5 percent of females were literate in comparison to 15.0 percent of literate males. In 1930, the percentages of literacy arose to 8.6 percent for females and 29.1 percent for males.

Regarding age structure, in 1918, 38.4 percent of the population of Tirana were younger than 15 years of age, and only 8.7 percent of the population were 60 years old or older. We have almost the same figures for 1930, when 36.3 percent were younger than 15 years of age, and 6.7 percent were 60 years or older. In 1918, there were 101.8 men for every 100 women in the population, and by 1930, this ratio had risen to 105.6. The reason for the higher male majority in 1930 was that men were involved in migratory processes to a higher degree than women.

MARRIAGE BEHAVIOUR IN INTERWAR ALBANIA

In the course of the preparation of the Civil Code of 1929, despite the orientation toward Italian and Swiss civil codes, traditional values related to marriage were taken into account. Just to mention one example, the custom of engagement preceding the marriage was included into the Civil Code of 1929. Engagement was legally considered as a promise for a future marriage between the engaged persons, although no person could be forced to get married. In case one of the engaged persons wished to end the engagement, the respective families had to find an agreement. If this was not the case, a court would have to make a decision (Kodi Civil 1998: 46-48).

The law did not define any minimum age of engagement, which permitted the engagement of persons at very young ages in the whole country, but especially in rural areas. Engagement preceded marriage and ethnographic records show that girls were usually engaged at the age of twelve to 14 and boys a few years later, at the age of 16 to 18 (Dojaka 1980: 9). Engagement was usually made by a matchmaker, and its social importance was comparable to that of the actual marriage (Luarasi 2001: 73-75).

The importance given to engagement and the social problems that could be caused by the dissolution of such an engagement between the families led to the passing of a special law to regulate engagements, which prohibited the engagement of girls younger than 14 and boys younger than 16 years-of-age.[3] The legal age for a girl to get engaged was lower than a previous decision of the Council of Ministers in 1926 in which any engagement of girls younger than 17 years-of-age was prohoibited because of the problems that accompanied the engagement of very young girls.[4] This is an indication that the tendency to engage girls at younger ages continued to persist in Albanian society.

The reasons for the young engagement age were varied. A letter sent to the Ministry of the Interior by the Prefect of Elbasan in 1934 stated that the payment made by the groom-to-be to the family of his fiancé continued to exist and constituted a financial burden for the family. Reasons for the persistence of this tradition were a lack of women at marriage age in comparison to men (about 17 percent less women than men) and also the function of women as a working force in agriculture. As a result of the hard work, mortality was very high among the female population, which on the other hand influenced the low number of births. A solution to limit abuse in the amount of payment was found in defining a minimum and a maximum amount that could be paid to the family of a future bride.[5]

A young engagement age is also an indicator of a young age at marriage because engagement usually lasted one year. At the beginning of the 20th century, marriage was, as a rule, arranged by the parents of the young women and men. Marriage was considered to be an agreement between two families with the principal aim to strengthen the family's social status, power and wealth, and the decision was made on the basis of family interests, although sometimes the opinions of the potential candidates for marriage were heard. The absolute power of the parents regarding the marriage decision originated as a result of the concentration of the whole family wealth being in the hands of the household head. Young men usually worked on the family property or ran the family business, therefore lacking the necessary financial independence to make their own decision on marriage (Dojaka 1980: 4-5).

Marriage behaviour was strongly influenced by several important obstacles to marriage such as the exogamy of the kinship group, which prohibited marriage between persons related by kinship ties, and the existence of spiritual connections between the couple or different religious affiliations (Mejdiaj 1976: 49; see also Luarasi 2001: 79-82). There were also some other obstacles such as the health of the bride and groom and their family members, and the wealth and social status of the family. In the inter-war period, in particular, marriage usually took place between people of the same social class (Mejdiaj 1976: 63-64). These obstacles

[3] Ministria e Punëve të Brendshme (152) 1934, file 286, AQSH, p 15.
[4] Komuniteti Mysliman (482) 1926, file 28, AQSH, p 1.
[5] Ministria e Punëve të Brendshme (152) 1934, file 286, AQSH, p 12.

could strongly influence the age at marriage, especially in relatively small and closed communities.

Aleks Luarasi mentions among the main functions of the family its economic function, meaning that the family was an economic unit, with common property over the means of production, the reproduction and child-rearing function, and the defence function against possible threats from the outside (Luarasi 2001: 28-29). Marriage was an economic institution where women were welcomed as labour power and child rearers (Danermark 1989: 21).

The marriage rules in Albania were exogamic with respect to the kinship group, and often of the locality (especially in villages), whereas endogamy was the rule in relation to religious affiliation, social class, and locality (cities) (Kera and Pandelejmoni 2008: 31). In cities such as Korça, Tirana, Vlora, and Gjirokastra, marriage was endogamous in the locality and urban families could get brides from the villages but did not marry their daughters into the villages. The reasons for this were related to the different religious affiliations, the differences in economic conditions between rural and urban areas, the difficulties of village life, and the differences in family wealth (Mejdiaj 1976: 66-67).

DATA

The main statistical data sources for this paper are the data of the population censuses of 1918 and 1930 for the city of Tirana. The Austro-Hungarian Military Administration in the occupied territories of Albania, which included Tirana, conducted a population census on 1 March 1918, whereas the population census of 1930 was carried out by the Albanian government on 25 May 1930.

The 1930 census served as basis for the population registers of the Civil Office of the Municipality of Tirana. These registers contain information on all births, deaths, marriages, and divorces in registered households from 1930 to 1945. For creating the database of the census of 1930, only data on persons registered on the census day were entered, excluding all those who joined or left households thereafter. These registers include only permanent residents of Tirana, omitting temporary residents who must have been recorded in census enumeration lists on census day. According to archival data, Tirana had, in 1930, a total of 30,806 inhabitants,[6] but only 19,801 inhabitants are included in our database. This explains the discrepancy between the number of inhabitants according to the published census statistics, and those included in our database. The above mentioned figure on Tirana's population in 1938 (25,079) strengthens the argument, as it is highly improbable that a population decrease occurred in Tirana in the 1930s. Official statistics on the population of Tirana give a number of 24,603 residents in 1937, without including temporary inhabitants.[7]

---

[6] Selenica, Teki (441), file 590, AQSH (Albanian Central State Archive, Tirana).
[7] Bashkia Tiranë (380) 1938 file 35, AQSH, p 2.

A special commission established in 1932 for checking the data of the population census of 1930 with the data of the population census of 1923 concluded that there were no cases of unregistered persons and very few cases of incorrectly registered persons.[8]

Both censuses contain information on first name, family name, relation to household head, sex, age, religious affiliation, birthplace, literacy and profession. The census of 1918 also includes data on ethnic affiliation, whereas in the census of 1930, this information is missing, except for a few cases of registered Roma.

AGE AT MARRIAGE IN TIRANA

An analysis of marriage in Albanian cities on the basis of the population census of 1918 showed that the marriage pattern in Albanian cities was closer to the Mediterranean set described by Laslett, because Albanian cities showed characteristics typical for the Mediterranean set, such as the low age at marriage for females, high age at marriage for males, high proportions marrying, the wide gap between spouses at first marriage, and low numbers of wives older than their husbands (Kera and Pandelejmoni 2008: 136-137). The city endogamy combined with religious endogamy, the existence of dowry and the uneven sex ratio narrowed the marriage field, thus increasing the age at marriage for women. In addition, the diversity of economic and cultural activities outside the home, and the higher levels of education in urban areas affected the way that people looked at marriage and the family (Kera and Pandelejmoni 2008: 137).

In a joint article, Gruber and Pichler investigated household structures in Albania in the early 20th century based on the data of twelve villages or parts of cities on the basis of the Albanian census of 1918 and found a mean age at marriage of about 20 years for women, with women in cities marrying later and an age at marriage for men that ranged from 20 to more than 30 years (Gruber and Pichler 2002).

The information on both marital status and age that both censuses provide enables the calculation of Singulate Mean Age at Marriage (SMAM, cf. Schurer 1989). The census of 1918 shows a SMAM of 18.3 years for Albanian women. There was a difference of about two years between the age at marriage of women in urban and in rural areas, with women in cities marrying at the age of 19.8 years, and those in villages at the age of 18.1 years. For men, the mean age at marriage was 27.0 years and men living in cities married about three years later than those living in villages. The age at marriage was 30.2 and 26.6 years, respectively.

Age at marriage for women in Tirana in 1918 was slightly higher than the country average (18.6 years). In 1930, women married at the age of 19.9 years. According to data of 1918, 81.2 percent of the females in Tirana were already married at the age of 20, whereas in 1930 the percentage of married women at the age of 20 had declined to 70.5 percent. In 1918, only 1.8 percent of women in the

[8] Prefektura Tiranë 1932 file 34, AQSH.

age group 45-49 were never married while in 1930 this percentage was even lower (1.3 percent).

For men in Tirana, the mean age at marriage in 1918 was 28.0 years. It was surprising to see that age at marriage of men in 1930 was 27.2 years, which means a decline in age at marriage for men in comparison to 1918. One plausible explanation for the decrease in age at marriage for men was sought in the in-migration from other areas of Albania, including persons from rural areas, who used to marry earlier. Taking this fact into consideration, we assumed that persons coming from other parts of the country would show a lower age at marriage. An analysis of birthplaces of married and widowed persons in Tirana in 1918 and 1930 indeed showed that the percentage of persons born in the place of residence (Tirana) was much lower in 1930 for both men and women (see Table 3).

Table 3: Birthplace of married and widowed men and women in Tirana in 1918 and 1930 (in percent)

Place of birth	1918		1930	
	Women	Men	Women	Men
In place of residence	90.1	94.0	57.9	61.1
In district of residence	2.9	1.1	4.5	3.6
In prefecture of residence	2.7	1.1	7.0	3.4
Rest of the country	4.3	3.8	30.6	31.9
Total	100.0	100.0	100.0	100.0

Source: Albanian Population Censuses of 1918 and 1930 (calculated by author).

A detailed analysis of age at marriage of persons according to their place of birth showed that in 1918 the age at marriage of women born in Tirana was 18.6 years, while of women born outside of Tirana was 17.1 years, confirming our thesis that persons coming from other parts of the country lowered age at marriage of women. In 1930, women married at the same age whether they were born in Tirana or not. We have a different picture regarding age at marriage of men. In 1918, men born in Tirana married at the age of 27.7 years, whereas those born outside of Tirana married at the age of 28.7 years. The difference was striking in 1930, with men born in Tirana getting married at the age of 24.7 years, whereas those born outside of Tirana married at a much higher age (30.1 years). In-migration influenced the age at marriage of men on the opposite direction of what I initially supposed it had. Migratory processes influenced age at marriage of men in Tirana, increasing the age at marriage of men in Tirana, which otherwise would have been much lower, especially in 1930. The higher age at marriage of men in Tirana in 1918 may have been influenced by the effects of World War I, which possibly delayed marriage. This implies that age at marriage of men in Tirana was normally lower than the data of the population census of 1918 showed.

In 1918, only 23.9 percent of men at the age of 24 were married, a very low percentage in comparison to women that were married at the same age (76.3 percent). In 1930, the percentage of married men at this age was higher (40.4 percent). Seven percent of men in 1918 and eight percent in 1930 never married throughout their lives. Although the tendency to universal marriage continues to persist, the age at marriage for women increased in the interwar period, while age at marriage of men decreased. Taking into consideration the fact that the legally defined age at marriage for both men and women was even lower than actual age at marriage, the new legal framework did not directly influence the increase in age at marriage. The Civil Code of 1929 defined as the lowest age at marriage as 16 for women and 18 for men, although girls aged 14 and men aged 15 could be married in special cases. Men and women under 20 years-of-age could not get married without the permission of their parents, or, in case their parents had died, of their grandparents (Kodi Civil 1998: 48-50).

The tendency toward an increase in age at marriage, especially for women, might be related to a better position of women in the society, as a result of the efforts for the modernisation of Albanian society. One important element was the increase in the number of girls who attended schools, which were opened all over the country. Nevertheless, the number of girls attending schools was still much lower than the number of boys. In 1927, there were 25,828 boys attending schools, whereas the number of girls was only 5734 (Skëndo 1928: 281). In 1938, there were 17,000 female students attending elementary schools in Albania, 10,000 in towns. The number of girls attending a higher education institution was small. There were 723 girls who finished secondary school and 20 who completed a higher education degree in the towns. There were 358 female teachers, 283 of which taught in a town (Schwanke 1968: 62).

Literacy was an important factor that delayed marriage because educated men and women married at higher ages in 1918. Literate women in cities married about five years later than illiterate ones and in villages about six years later. The difference at age at marriage of men was about four years (see Table 4).

Table 4: SMAM and literacy (1918)

	SMAM cities		SMAM villages		SMAM total	
	Women	Men	Women	Men	Women	Men
Illiterate	19.1	28.8	17.9	25.8	18.3	26.7
Literate	24.6	32.3	24.2	29.8	21.5	31.9

Source: Albanian Population Census of 1918 (calculated by author).

The same phenomenon was observed for Tirana in 1930. The percentage of literate women in 1918 was too low for analysis purposes, but in 1930, literate women married about five years later that illiterate ones. Literate men married also later in 1930, although the difference was smaller than for women.

Table 5: SMAM according to literacy in Tirana

	1918		1930	
	Women	Men	Women	Men
Illiterate	-	27.9	19.3	26.5
Literate	-	27.8	24.5	28.4

Source: Albanian Population Censuses of 1918 and 1930 (calculated by author).

The difference in mean age at marriage between men and women in Tirana resulted in a high age difference between partners, the mean age difference being 10.2 years in 1918. In only 1.4 percent of the marriages were the partners the same age and in only 6.5 percent of them was the wife older than her husband. There was, in addition, a difference in age difference between spouses in rural areas of the prefecture of Tirana and in the city itself. In rural areas, women were eight years younger than their husbands, whereas in the city of Tirana women were ten years younger. The reason for this difference is the younger age at marriage in rural areas than in the city, especially for men. There was no difference in the age gap between spouses, taking into consideration the literacy of the partners. In 1930, women were about 9.5 years younger than their husbands.

AGE AT MARRIAGE, RELIGION AND ETHNICITY

The marriage rules in Albania in the first half of the 20th century were exogamic with respect to the kinship group, and often to the locality (especially in villages), whereas endogamy was the rule in relation to religious affiliation, social class, and locality (cities). The influence of religion in age at marriage is difficult to measure but there are obvious differences in age at marriage among religious communities in Albania during the interwar period. The Albanian ethnographer Bajram Mejdiaj wrote that in the Muslim regions in central and southern Albania, age at marriage was lower for Muslims than for Catholics (Mejdiaj 1976: 85-86, cf. Kera and Pandelejmoni 2008). Muslim families having only one son, in particular, showed a tendency to marry him at a young age because of the parents' desire to experience the marriage of their only son (Mejdiaj 1976: 86).

In Tirana, the SMAM in 1918 was 20.3 for Orthodox women and 18.4 for Moslem women. As a result of the small number of Catholics in Tirana, it was not possible to calculate the SMAM for this category. Orthodox men married at the age of 27.9 years and Muslim men at the age of 27.8. The Orthodox population had a higher age at marriage for women. The analyses of sex ratios showed a female majority for the Orthodox community (97.4) and a male majority for the Muslim community of Tirana (102.1). The combination of a female majority and urban endogamy influenced the higher age at marriage of Orthodox women in Tirana.

Ethnographic records indicate that for the Orthodox population, dowry played an important role in marriage. Orthodox girls and boys in Tirana were engaged when they turned 16 usually with the help of a matchmaker, but also directly by their parents, most commonly, the parents of the future groom taking the initiative. As a rule, the engagement did not last long and the delay of the marriage for any reason, for example if the engaged men was studying abroad, resulted in its annulment (Beduli et al. 2007: 43). Age at marriage was usually more than 18 years-of-age. Depending on its financial situation, the family of the engaged girls gave her a dowry when she got married (Beduli et al. 2007: 44-45).

An article in 1937 also mentioned dowry as a very problematic tradition especially because of an uneven sex ratio between persons at marriage age (30 women to 10 men). This resulted in the nfamilies of Orthodox girls making high payments to potential marriage candidates (Meksi 1937: 3). The cited sex ratio was much overestimated, but it draws attention to effects that an uneven sex ratio can have on age at marriage, especially for smaller religious communities.

The picture changed in 1930 when the higher percentage of Catholics in Tirana enabled the calculation of SMAM for this religious community. Catholics married at latest, whereby men married at the age of 33.4 years and women at the age of 24.8 years. In particular, the age at marriage of Catholic women is distinctly higher than Orthodox (20.5) and Muslim women (19.5). For men, age at marriage was 26.6 years for Muslim men and 29.9 years for Orthodox men.

Table 6: SMAM in Tirana according to religious affiliation

Religion	Women		Men	
	1918	1930	1918	1930
Catholic	-	24.8	-	33.4
Muslim	18.4	19.5	27.7	26.6
Orthodox	20.3	20.5	27.9	29.9

Source: Albanian Population Censuses of 1918 and 1930 (calculated by author).

The uneven sex ratio in 1930 influenced especially the age at marriage of women as urban endogamy narrowed their marriage field. City inhabitants did not prefer to marry their daughters in villages because of worse living conditions in rural areas in comparison to the city. In Tirana, as in other cities, such as Korça, Vlora or Gjirokastra, urban families did not marry their daughters into villages, although they could get daughters-in-law from rural areas (Mejdiaj 1976: 66). Therefore, the decision of men to marry was less conditioned by sex ratio. When comparing age at marriage of Muslim women we see an increase of about one year in 1930 in comparison to 1918.

The analysis of age at marriage in the six quarters of Tirana showed interesting distinctions. In 1918, the quarters with the highest age at marriage for women (Ali Bej and Sulejman Pasha) were the quarters with the highest percentage of Orthodox and Catholic populations (27.3 percent and 11.8 percent). It is highly probable that an uneven sex ratio for the Orthodox community (97.4) was the cause.

Table 7: SMAM in the quarters of Tirana

Quarter	1918		1930	
	Women	Men	Women	Men
Abdulla Bej	17.8	26.6	19.8	25.6
Ali Bej	19.4	27.9	19.3	27.3
Ismail Efendi	17.9	29.3	20.1	28.8
Mahalla e Re	18.1	26.3	19.8	27.2
Sulejman Pasha	19.4	29.1	19.7	28.5
Xhami Sherif	17.7	26.4	20.5	26.0

Source: Albanian Population Census of 1918 and1930 (calculated by author).

In 1930, only 1.3 percent of the women and eight percent of the men living in Tirana had never been married. There were no unmarried Catholic or Orthodox women between the ages of 45 and 49, and only 1.5 percent of Muslim women in this age group were unmarried. Of Catholic men, only 23.1 percent were unmarried in this age group, and 7.8 percent of Muslim men were not married. The high percentage of unmarried Catholic men may have to do with the limited number of cases in this age group.

One important issue regarding marriage behaviour, especially for the Muslim population, was polygamy. Although not frequent, cases of polygamy in Tirana an be found in both censuses. Of all married men in Tirana in 1918, 3.6 percent were married to a second wife. Second wives were usually younger than the first ones and the mean age difference rose to 19.9 years for the second wives in 1918. In 1930, only 1.9 percent of married men lived with a second wife. The age difference to second wives was about 18.5 years.

The reasons for the decision to marry a second wife differed. In her article on polygyny in southern Albania at the beginning of the twentieth century, Nicholson mentions as possible reasons for polygyny the absence of children (or male children), the fear that children might not live to adulthood because of high mortality, the need to increase the family's labour reserves or even the desire of some household heads to obtain young wives for themselves (Nicholson 2006: 52-54).

The permission to marry a second wife was granted in cases when the first wife was suffering from any incurable disease, had not given birth to children, was handicapped or mentally ill with the condition that the husband was financially capable of maintaining both wives.[9] In 1926 a resident of Tirana living in the Abdulla Bej quarter asked for the permission to marry a second wife because he did not have any children from his first marriage.[10]

Polygamy was legally prohibited in 1929 and a second marriage could not be celebrated before the divorce of the previous marriage (Kodi Civil 1998: 48-50). The law on marriage was also strictly exogamous, prohibiting marriage between persons related by kinship (Kodi Civil 1998: 53).

It can be supposed that men already living in a polygamous marriage continued to cohabit with both their wives even after the prohibition of polygamy in 1929. This assumption was confirmed during an interview with a person who was born in Tirana in 1930. He stated that his mother was his father's second wife and that they had lived together all in the same house. He considered himself as having been "brought up by two mothers" and remembered relations between his mother and stepmother as very good. He mentioned as the main reason for the marriage of his father to the second wife the fact that all six sons born to his stepmother had died and the desire to have a son, who would inherit the family fortune; so his father married a second wife with the approval of the first. The interview showed that although new trends were spreading among the inhabitants of the capital, traditional values continued to persist.

---

[9] Komuniteti Mysliman (482) 1926, file 28, AQSH, p 132.
[10] Komuniteti Mysliman (482) 1926, file 28, AQSH, p 131.

The traditional trend to marriage within the same religious or ethnic community continued to be prevalent in Tirana. The database for Tirana in 1918 contains no cases of inter-confessional marriages. In Albania as a whole, only 0.1 percent of women were married to a man belonging to another religious community. In 1930, 7.2 percent of Catholic women were married to Orthodox or Muslim men. Only 0.8 percent of Orthodox women were married to Catholic or Muslim men, while the percentage of Muslim women married to men of other religious affiliation was only 0.1 percent.

Despite the increase in the number of inter-confessional marriages, such marriages continued to be exceptional in the interwar period. The marriage of a Muslim woman to a Catholic man in Tirana in 1930 is cited in the local press as an exceptional case and a step to modernity:

> The most radical tool for the uprooting of a tradition which more or less hinders the pure harmony of feelings among different religious communities. This tradition was the prohibition of marriage of Muslim women to Catholic men. The first step in this direction was taken: The daughter of Maliq Bej Frashëri [Muslim] is married to Joan Basho [Catholic].[11]

The analyses of age at marriage of persons with different ethnic affiliations are possible only for the population census of 1918, as the population census of 1930 does not provide information on ethnic affiliation. In order to facilitate the calculations of the mean age at marriage, persons having another ethnic affiliation than Albanian are categorised into three groups: Roma, Slavs, and Others. The category others include all the persons who are not included in the other categories, and they are grouped together because they were very small in number.

For the whole Albania, the mean age at marriage for Albanian women was 18.2 years and of the Albanian men 27.0 years. Roma women married at the age of 19.2 years and men at 23.0 years. Among the Slav population, the mean age at marriage was 19.8 years for women and 27.5 years for men. Albanian women in Tirana married at the age of 18.6 years, and Albanian men at the age of 28.1. Roma women married at the age of 18.0 years and men at the age of 23.2 years. The low age at marriage of Roma men lowered the age of marriage of men overall. The neighbourhoods with the lowest age at marriage for both women and men (Abdulla Bej, Mahalla e re and Xhami Sherif) were those with the highest percentage of Roma population.

When analysing the marriages between persons with different ethnic affiliation, results show that again a low percentage of women were married to a man with a different ethnic affiliation (only 0.1 percent). The most frequent cases were those of Albanian women married to a man with another ethnic affiliation. In Tirana, cases of intermarriages between persons of different ethnic affiliations were not found in 1918.

[11] Kundrejt njësisë kombëtare të kulluar. Martesa e njëkrishteri me një vajzë myslimane 1930 Arbënia 25 p 1.

CONCLUSION

The comparison of age at marriage in Tirana in the interwar period showed a trend toward an increase of age at marriage for women, whereas age at marriage of men tended to decrease. One important factor that influenced the higher age at marriage of women in Tirana in 1930 was the extension of female education in the 1920s statistically expressed in the increase of the percentage of literate women. Education opened new perspectives for urban women and possibly affected their view on traditional gender roles in the family and society. The interwar period in Albania was characterised by modernisation trends, which were also expressed in the implementation of new legislation and measures undertaken by Albanian governments that challenged traditional values.

Nevertheless, marriage behaviour in the capital, as in rest of the country, continued to be strongly influenced by traditional values and roles. Ethnographic records show that important elements of marriage behaviour, such as religious or ethnic endogamy, continued to influence the decision to marry. Demographic data from the population censuses of 1918 and 1930 show that inter-confessional and interethnic marriages continued to be an exception.

BIBLIOGRAPHY

Beduli, Dhimitër, Dhora Vlash and Mara Kostandin 2007, Shënime për bashkësinë ortodokse të Tiranës, Tiranë: Neraida.

Breu, Josef 1968 Das Wachstum der Städte Albaniens 1923-1965. In: Geographische Informationen, Vol. 2/3 pp 306-314.

Castiglioni, Bruno 1941 Appunti sulla capitale dell'Albania all'alba den Nuovo Regime. In: Bolletino della R.Societa Geografica italiana, Vol. 6 pp 9-27.

Coon, Carleton S. 1950 The Mountains of Giants: A racial and cultural study of the North Albanian Mountain Ghegs. Cambridge.

Cordignano, F. P. 1931 Nell'Albania di Trent'Anni Fa. La Vita Della Montagna. In: Studi Albanesi, Vol. 1 pp 61-87.

Cozzi, Ernesto 1912 La donna albanese con speciale riguardo al diritto consuetudinario delle Montagne di Scutari. In: Anthropos, Vol. 7 pp 309-335, 617-626.

Danermark, Berth et al. 1989 Women, Marriage and Family. Traditionalism vs Modernity in Albania. In: International Journal of Sociology of the Family, Vol. 19 pp 19-41.

Dojaka, Abaz 1972 Disa ndryshime në lidhjet martesore pas çlirimit. In: Etnografia shqiptare, Vol. 4.

Dojaka, Abaz 1980 Karakteri i lidhjeve martesore para çlirimit (gjysma e dytë e shek.XIX deri në prag të çlirimit) In: Etnografia shqiptare, Vol. 11 pp 3-20.

Durham, Mary Edith 1928 Some tribal Origins, laws and customs of the Balkans. London: George Allen & Unwin.

Fischer, Bernd J. 1999 Albanian Highland Tribal Society and Family Structure in the Process of 20th century Transformation. In East European Quarterly, Vol. 33(3) pp 281-301.

Frashëri, Kristo 2003 Tirana. A brief historic overview. In: Besnik Aliaj, Kejda Lulo and Genc Myftiu (eds.) Tirana: The challenge of urban development. Tirana.

Gruber, Siegfried 2008 Household structures in urban Albania in 1918 In: The History of the Family, Vol. 13 pp 138-151.
Gruber, Siegfried and Robert Pichler 2002 Household structures in Albania in the early 20th century In: The History of the Family, Vol. 7 pp 351-374.
Kaser, Karl 1997 Family and Kinship in the Balkans: A declining Culture? In Ethnologia Balkanica, Vol. 1 pp 150-155.
Kera, Gentiana and Enriketa Pandelejmoni 2008 Marriage in Urban Albania In: The History of the Family, Vol. 13 pp 126-137.
Kodi Civil 1998 Kodi Civil i vitit 1929, Tiranë: Toena.
Luarasi, Aleks 2001 Marrëdhëniet familjare, Tiranë: Luarasi.
Marteli, Alessandro 1917 L'Albania adriatica. In: Pagine Geografiche della nostra Guerra, Roma.
Mauro, Giuseppe Di 1940 Tirana. Note di Poleografia morfologica. Bari.
Meksi, Jorgj 1937 Prika. In: Shtypi, Vol. 54 pp 3.
Mejdiaj, Bajram 1976 Mbi të drejtën e gruas për të kërkuar zgjidhjen e martesës, Studime historike, Vol. 30 pp 80-88.
Mejdijaj, Bajram 1976 Disa tipare të martesë para çlirimit. In: Etnografia shqiptare, Vol. 8 pp 33-108.
Nicholson, Beryl 2006 Women who shared a husband: Polygyny in southern Albania in the early 20th century. In: The History of the Family Vol. 11 pp 45-57.
Nopcsa, Franz Baron 1907 Das Katholische Nordalbanien. Budapest.
Nova, K. 1969 Pozita e gruas sipas së drejtës zakonore të Labërisë In: Studime historike, Vol. 23, pp 101-111.
Schurer Kevin 1989 A note concerning the calculation of the Singulate Mean Age at Marriage. In: Local Population Studies Vol. 43 pp 67-70.
Schwanke, Robert 1968, Frauenemanzipation in Albanien. In: East European Quarterly, Vol 2(1) pp 57-73.
Selenica, Teki 1928 Shqipëria më 1927, Tiranë.
Siebert, Paul 1910 Albanien und die Albanesen. Vienna: Manz.
Sinani, Beqir 1986 Lëvizja për emancipimin dhe arsimimin e gruas në vitet 1920-1924, Studime historike, Vol. 40 pp 69-85.
Skëndo, Lumo 1928 Gruaja In: Mësuesi, Vol. 9/10 pp 279-287.
Skëndi, Stavro 1958 Albania, New York: Praeger.
Stahl, Paul H. 1986 Household, Village and Village Confederation in Southeastern Europe. New York: Columbia University Press.
Tirta, Mark 1970 Mbi martesat pas çlirimit mes personave të besimeve të ndryshme fetare. In: Studime Historike, Vol. 25 pp 107-117.
Uçi, Alfred 1968 Mbi disa aspekte të zhvillimit të familjes në vendin tonë. In: Studime Historike, Vol. 22 pp 49-78.
Zojzi, Rrok 1969 Mbeturina të familjes patriarkale që bëhen pengesë emancipimit të gruas. In: Studime Historike, Vol. 23 pp 33-37.
Zojzi, Rrok 1972 Aspekte të kalimit nga familja patriarkale në familjen e re socialiste. In: Etnografia shqiptare, Vol. 4.

3. Marriage in Shkodra in the first half of the 20th century. Micro-level Data and challenges to Macro Theories

Enriketa Papa-Pandelejmoni

After preliminary analysis (Kera and Pandelejmoni 2008) on the Albanian population Census of 1918, Shkodra appeared a city with some deviances from the rest of the country in terms of marriage and households structures. The intention of the author is to investigate Shkodra's marriage pattern in order to understand why this city differs from the general urban marriage pattern. Was the pattern developed under local factors such as social, cultural, economic and educational developments, or was it something else that influenced this 'new marriage pattern'?

Shkodër is characterised by its mixed Moslem-Catholic population as well as its Slavic minority population (Montenegrins and Serbs). The 20th century found Shkodër with a population of around 30,000-40,000 (Ippen 1907: 38; Mantegazza 1912: 89; Nopcsa 1910: 23). After Albanian independence in 1912 the city numbered 23,000 inhabitants (Duka 1997: 9). Surveys in 1926-27 showed the city not to have experienced any relative growth, a figure of 23,784 inhabitants being given (Selenica 1928: CXXII), which was the same figure as confirmed for the data of the population census of 1918, according to which Shkodër in 1918 had a population of 23,099 (Seiner 1922: 7). In Shkodër the majority – two-thirds – of the population was Muslim and one third was Catholic with a small community of Orthodox faith (Martelli 1917: 74) of Slavic and Vlach origin who immigrated to Shkodër during the 19th century (Simini 1898: 9). The city was divided into 12 mahallas, of which nine were inhabited by the Muslim and three by the Catholic population, and a separate bazaar (Ippen 1907: 38). The Muslims were mostly to be found in the quarters on the west side of the city while the Catholics were living in the quarters on the east side of the city. The Orthodox population mostly lived within the Muslim quarters (Beci 1994: 231; Bushati 1998: 608).

The data used in this paper is drawn from the Albanian Population Census of 1918,[1] and is based on a sample of 117,730 persons resident in Albania and 22,631 persons resident in Shkodër at the time of the census.

---

[1] The Population Census of 1918 was conducted by the Austro-Hungarian military administration in the occupied territories of Albania during World War I. The census, stored in the archive of the Austrian Academy of Sciences, covers almost the whole of the country. The Population Census of 1918 provides the point for departure for a demographic history of Albania in the 20th century. For further details of the Albanian Population Census of 1918 see Gruber in this volume and the webpage of the research project "The 1918 Albanian Population Census: Data Entry and Basic Analyses" at the Centre for Southeast European History of Karl-Franzens-University Graz. The research project was financed by the Austrian Science Fund (Fonds zur Förderung der wissenschaftlichen Forschung).

THEORETICAL NOTES

As a starting point in my investigation and analysis I take the theories developed by two distinguished authors on family and household for Europe, J. Hajnal's and P. Laslett, as both dealt in indirect way with Albania as part of Southeast Europe or Mediterranean. Hajnal's theory on 'European marriage pattern' states a significant increase in the age at first marriage (over 26 for men and over 23 for women) and a high proportion of people who never married at all, around 20 percent (Hajnal 1965: 101-102). Hajnal later added that this transition affected only a part of European populations, those to the West of an imaginary line from Saint Petersburg to Trieste, and that the other part, the countries east of Hajnal's line displayed quite a different marriage pattern from the European one. The Eastern European pattern, was characterised by an earlier marriage for men and rather early marriage for women (mean ages at first marriage are under about 26 for men and under 21 for women) and a very low percentage of persons who never married (less than five percent) (Hajnal 1983: 69). The reasons for early and universal marriage have been related to different factors. Hajnal related the high age at marriage in Western Europe with the necessity or a man to defer marriage until he could establish an independent livelihood adequate to support a family; in other societies the young couple could be incorporated in a larger economic unit, such as the joint family. This does not require such a long postponement of marriage (Hajnal 1965: 133).

Peter Laslett made a finer division in 1983 and developed a set of tendencies in domestic group organisation in traditional Europe with four sets: West, West/Central or Middle, Mediterranean and East. These sets are based on criteria for occasion and method of domestic group formation, procreational and demographic criteria, criteria of kin composition of groups and criteria of organisation of work and welfare (Laslett 1983: 526). According to Laslett, in the Mediterranean set, females had a low age at marriage and male a high one, while in the Eastern set both female and male had low age at marriage.

Using Hajnal's theory as a starting point for examining marriage patterns, and despite the fact that Hajnal only analysed rural data from Eastern Europe among 'closed populations' (Hajnal 1965: 197), several scholars have categorised Albania as part of the 'Eastern European marriage pattern', with a low age at marriage and a virtual lack of celibacy, since it is situated east of Hajnal's infamous Triest - St. Petersburg line. When Hajnal described what he called the European marriage pattern, he said that its two distinctive attributes were, first, a late age at first marriage, and, second, a high proportion of final celibacy. It is important to note that this new pattern concerned women. This was one of the first things that Hajnal remarked, comparing Western European with Eastern European data around 1900 (Devolver 1999: 5). Indeed, Hajnal noted that "the uniqueness of the European pattern lies primarily in the high age at marriage of women (often with a small difference between ages of husband and wife) rather than in a high age at marriage for men (Hajnal 1965: 134)."

Hajnal himself did not deal with Albania as a unit in his study since Albania was not an independent state at the beginning of the 20th century and no statistical data on Albania existed at the time. Because of the lack of reliable statistical data for this period, the analysis of marriage in Albania has thus far been based on the reports of foreign travellers who visited Albania in that time. Thus, several scientific publications mention a low age at marriage for Albania, especially for women. The British ethnographer Mary Edith Durham, who travelled through Albania in the first decade of the 20th century, recorded ages at marriage of 13-14 years for girls and of 15 years for boys (Durham 1928: 192). The American anthropologist Carleton Coon notes that "in northern Albania (Malsia e Gegnisë) girls are married as soon as they come to sexual maturity and begin bearing children as soon as they are biologically able. There is no time of peace (Coon 1950: 27)." The Austrian scholar Karl Kaser, arguing based mostly on the above mentioned records, points to a "relatively low age at marriage for women" between 16 and 20 years and between 20 and 23 years for men in the middle of the 19th century (Kaser 2008: 61). Kaser considers marriage behaviour as related primarily to the rules of household formation in the Balkans, especially to patrilocality, the main justification of which was the common male ownership of property (Kaser 1994: 6). All sons had rights to equal portions of the house and the land when a household divided while their sisters hat no rights to this property. This is why having a male heir was considered to be so important and why men were interested in marrying young girls: the period of fertility was longer and they had better chances of giving birth to a son. Kaser describes the 'Balkan family pattern' as characterised by early and universal marriage before and after the First Demographic Transition. This was the case in the whole area of the Balkan family, which stretches from Croatia in the north to Northern Greece in the south, from Albania in the west to Bulgaria in the east (Kaser 1994: 8). Kaser explains the low age at marriage with the urgent need for children in a milieu of patriarchy with high infant mortality, high rates of blood feud, an urgent need for manpower and the continuation of the patriarchal line (Kaser 1995: 153).

The Albanian ethnographer Bajram Mejdiaj related the young age at marriage to two important factors. First, the newly married couple usually did not establish a new household, but was incorporated into the groom's household, so they did not have to deal with many duties and responsibilities and, second, marriage and procreation were considered a way to increase the number of family members for work or defensive purposes. The early marriage of girls was also influenced by the consideration of women as a "burden" for her family (Mejdiaj 1976: 87). The importance laid upon virginity of women at marriage, partly because of traditional values, partly because of religious influence, made parent anxious to marry their daughters as soon as possible.

One of the first contributions on Albanian household structures based on demographic data was a joint article by Siegfried Gruber and Robert Pichler (2002), who investigated household structures in Albania in a case study of 12 villages and city-quarters based on the data of the Albanian census of 1918. They found that the mean age at marriage for women was for most of the analysed settlements 20 years-of-age or less, with the exception of urban environments where it was slightly higher. Mean age at marriage for men ranged from under 20 years-of-age to more than 30 years-of-age (Gruber and Pichler 2002: 360).

MARRIAGE BEHAVIOUR

In the period before the turn of the 20th century, marriages were the result of arrangements between the heads of the two households concerned, and the bride and the bridegroom rarely met before the wedding day (Hasluck: 1933: 191). Love and courtship were rare and arranged marriage was considered a process in which particular attributes of individuals and their families are matched, and the suitability of the prospective spouses was a central issue. Various criteria were brought to bear on the match, expressed in the notions of soj or rod, (literally kin), a common local expression being *do martohesh me dikë të sojit të mirë* (may you marry someone of good kin). Of the criteria of suitability, the economic and educational levels of the two families were very important as was the place of origin as expressed in the considerations of *derë e mirë* (good door, i.e. a good family) or *derë e kênun* (wealthy door). A key figure in this process was the *shkues* (matchmaker). This was an official position often taken up by relatives, close kin or friends, who, in any case, usually played a part in suggesting suitable partners or in discreetly verifying claims on behalf of the party looking for a partner.

Marriage was thus not only a bond between two people but a union of two families and their fortunes. The individuals actually getting married had little if any input in these negotiations (Dibra 2004: 51). In the end, parents would simply announce to their daughter *të kena feju për filanin* (we have betrothed you to a man) (Bushati 1998: 337).

According to the data of the Albanian Population Census of 1918, 93.5 percent of men born in Shkodër were married to women with urban origins while only 81.0 percent of women born in the city were married to men born in city. Only 17.8 percent of married women not born in Shkodër had spouse born in the city. For men quite the opposite was true, 53.4 percent of men who were not born in the city were married to women born in Shkodër. Thus, for men who were not born in Shkodër, but were living there, it was important to have a *Shkodran* wife in order gain status and be integrated into city life (Pandelejmoni 2007: 3).

Table 1: Marriage and place of origin (1918)

Married	Spouse born in Shkodër
Men born in Shkodër	93.5%
Women born in Shkodër	81.0%
Men not born in Shkodër	53.4%
Women not born in Shkodër	17.8%

Source: Albanian Population Census of 1918 (calculation by author).

The Albanian scholar Gjush Sheldia examined this historical process of finding a partner in Shkodër. He writes that it was important to ask if the girl was diligent, honest, good-looking and if she had dowry. For the boy it was important to ask about his economic situation and if he had contributed to his family's economic status. Further, it was verified if he had any bad habits[2].

CHANGING MARRIAGE TRADITIONS

Hamdi Bushati (1998) examined marriage in the city of Shkodër in the interwar period. According to him, marriage arrangements did change significantly from the beginning of the 20th century and these changes were similar for both Moslems and Christians. In his interpretation, these changes were due to western influence, more specifically from Catholic men educated at Western European universities who upon their return demanded changes in their own marriages. Moslem men embraced these new customs only later (Bushati 1998: 354). In this time it became usual for an engaged couple to walk together on the piazza, the shame interpreted into the bride and groom meeting *–paska dalë të shifte të fejuemen!* (the boy is out looking at his fiancée!) (Bushati 1998: 355) – making way for modernity. After getting engaged, a man would organise a banquet and a reception for his friends and all participants could dance and chat freely with one another. Again it took some time until such traditions gained popularity among the Moslem population (Bushati 1998: 339). For their part, Orthodox girls were traditionally isolated in their houses, having only one week of freedom per year in which they were allowed some freedom. A week before Easter, on the feast of St. Lazarus, unmarried girls enveloped (*mërtisun*) themselves in a lone veil (*çarçaf*) and were allowed to go out of the house to the church. That week, they were free to move around. They were courted appropriately by the young men of the community (Bushati 1998: 389). This also changed in the 1920s and 1930s and potential couples could move around freely in the city without any accompanying kin and even went shopping for the wedding (Bushati 1998: 355).

Financial independence was usually a prerequisite for young men if they were considering getting married. In a commercial town such as Shkodër, this often meant that young men would first have to open their own shop in the bazaar or in the city. After finishing primary school, boys would began to work as apprentices with a master tradesman or a merchant in the bazaar or in one of the city shops with a small salary of 150-200 Turkish piasters. But every year, on 5 May, their salaries would be raised until they earned 1500-2000 Turkish piasters. Then the apprentices would be dismissed by their respective masters (Mihačević 1913: 40). The young man was left with two options: to open his own shop in Shkodër or to leave the city, often to emigrate to Bosnia, Herzegovina, Dalmatia or Italy (Simini 1899: 16-20). If he decided to stay and open a shop of his own, the young man's parents would began searching for a wife for their son among the beautiful and wealthy girls of the city, whose dowry would be invested in the business (Mihačević 1913: 40). The

[2] AE- IKP Dosja 6, nr.i. 197/19, 1961 as cited in Dibra 2002: 101

matchmaker began his or her work and the interested partys would meet and begin negotiations, hoping that the whole affair would bear fruit. If they succeeded in matching the young couple, the young man would begin to renovate his parental home and refurnish, while the young woman's family would start to collect the dowry. When the contract was ratified by the hoxha or by a priest, they were married.

This process was often so expensive that in 1910 several regulations were issued with the aim of reducing them. Marriage expenses continued to increase nevertheless, especially among the urban elite (Dojaka, 1980: 14). A groom and his family bought all his bride's clothing and presents for her family, while the bride bought more clothing for herself and presents for the groom's family. Her father paid for furnishing a kitchen and other furniture that the bride took to her new household, a custom that existed in other cities too, even if to a lesser degree (Dojaka, 1980: 17). Raising the money for such an expensive enterprise required time, which caused the postponement of marriage for men until they could open their own business and for women until they cold provide an appropriate dowry (Kera and Pandelejmoni 2008: 135). In Shkodër, the mean age at marriage for men was the highest in the whole of Albania.

INTER-CONFESSIONAL MARRIAGE

The ethnographic records indicate that as a rule marriage took place within the religious community (Mejdiaj 1976: 68). Inter-confessional marriages were nevertheless not unheard of. In Albania, 0.1 percent of women married a man with another religious affiliation, a figure which was no different in Shkodër. This religious exogamy did nevertheless result in delayed marriages among Orthodox and Catholic women because of an uneven sex ratio within these religious communities. While there was a male majority among the Muslim population in the cities (sex ratio 103.0) there was a female majority in the Catholic and Orthodox Christian populations (sex ratios 97.4 and 97.3 respectively) (Kera and Pandelejmoni 2008: 133).

All five inter-religious marriages in Shkodër as indicated in 1918 census were arranged between the two Christian communities. Three were Catholic men married to Orthodox women while two Orthodox men (one of whom was an ethnic Greek) married Catholic women.

AGE AT MARRIAGE

The analysis of the specific situation in Shkodër proves to be interesting for understanding both Albanian and more general Balkan marriage patterns. When referring to age at marriage, I mean Singulate Mean Age at Marriage (SMAM), which is calculated on the basis of the proportion of single individuals at certain ages.[3] According to the census data, the mean age at marriage for women in Albania was 18.3 years. There was a difference of about two years between the age at marriage of women in urban and in rural areas, with women in cities marrying at an age of 19.8 years while those in villages married at a mean age of 18.1 years. For men, the mean age at marriage was 27.0 years with men living in cities marrying about 3 years later than those living in villages, the age at marriage being 30.2 years and 26.6 years respectively. As mentioned, mean age at marriage in Shkodër was significantly higher than for the rest of Albania. The SMAM for woman in the city of Shkodër was 21.4 years. For men it was 34.2 years.

Table 2: Age at Marriage for Women and Men (1918)

	Albania	Urban Albania	Rural Albania	Shkodër
Women	18.3	19.8	18.1	21.4
Men	27.0	30.2	26.6	34.2

Source: Albanian Population Census of 1918 (calculated by author).

In Shkodër the proportion of unmarried women in the age bracket 45-49 was 7.5 percent and for men the rate was 14.7 percent, which was also much higher than in other cities. One can thus not speak of universal marriage in Shkodër as the proportion of those individual remaining unmarried was higher than 5 percent. But the rate nevertheless remained below 10 percent for women, making an association with Hajnal's European pattern, where the percentage of people who never married was much higher (about 20 percent) than in the case of Shkodër. Shkodër was the only Albanian city with a considerable percentage of women who never married. In other cities, less than 3 percent of women never married (Kera and Pandelejmoni 2008: 132), the national average being 2.1 percent (and 4.7 percent for men). This high proportion of individuals who never married may well be linked to the large Catholic community.

An important role in defining age at marriage has been attributed to religion. In her article on nuptiality in Eastern Europe around 1900, June L. Sklar argued that Protestantism and Roman Catholicism reinforced the late-marriage pattern through doctrines and practises that emphasised the social and economic independence of the nuclear family unit from the extended kin group and weakened the moral authority of such large kin groups. Roman Catholicism supports the nuclear family unit at the expense of the extended kinship system with its position that children, not their parents, have the right to determine whom they will marry. It challenged the moral strength of extended kin bonds by discouraging cross-cousin marriages in

[3] The Singulate Mean Age at Marriage (SMAM) is a synthetic cohort measure obtained from a single census – a cross-section of age-specific percentages (Hajnal 1953). It is the mean number of years lived in the single state as implied by a schedule of age-specific percentages single. In practice, data are most often available for five-year age groups from age ten or 15 onward. Here SMAM is calculated as devised by Kevin Schurer (1989).

most circumstances and by maintaining the right of its members to bequeath property to non-kin and competed directly with kin authority by providing an alternative to marriage for those electing to become priests and nuns (Sklar 1974: 237).

Islam, on the other hand, favoured an early marriage pattern in the Balkans because it tended to reinforce the authority of extended kin ties and encouraged the incorporation of the nuclear family unit into the kinship group (i.e. by means of the ideal model of marriage between cousins, which consolidates family power and prestige, the sanctioning of concubinage and poligyny and the legal subordination of a woman to her nearest male kinsman). Unlike the Roman Catholic Church, Islam has neither a separate nor a celibate clergy, nor does it have a Church organisation to rival the family. The lack of a religious institution capable of rivalling the kinship groups for loyalty is also viewed by Sklar as a feature of Eastern Orthodoxy (Botev 1990: 111). In contrast to the Roman Catholic Church, the Orthodox Church was organisationally weak, being a loose confederation of frequently conflicting independent Churches. And unlike the Roman Catholic clergy, the Orthodox clergy lacked monopolistic power and influence over religious matters, to a large extent sharing management and policy-making functions with an educated class of non-clerics. That being the case it interfered little with the pursuit of local customs, including early marriage behaviour favoured by centuries of Moslem influence (Sklar 1974: 238).

The Albanian Census of 1918, providing information about a population with different religious affiliations, offers a concrete opportunity to study the impact of religion on age at marriage. But it does not confirm Sklar's theses, quite the contrary. In the total population, the mean age at marriage for Muslim women was 18.3 years, for Catholic women it was 17.8 years, and for Orthodox women 20.1 years. The same results appear when analysing the mean age at marriage for men. Again, the Orthodox men married later, at an average of 28.5 years. The age at marriage for Catholic men was 25.4 years and for Muslim men 27.3 years. This clearly contradicts the argument that Roman Catholicism reinforced a late-marriage pattern as compared to Orthodoxy or Islam.

Nevertheless, when analysing this same data and taking urban and rural differences into account, we get a more detailed – and more complicated – picture. The highest age at marriage in the cities for both men and women was among Catholics, who were 34.7 and 22.4 years old respectively. Orthodox men got married at the age of 30.1 years and women the age of 20.2 years. Muslim men and women married the earliest at 29.3 and 19.2 years-of-age respectively. In the villages the order was reversed, the Catholics marrying earlier, men at the age of 23.8 years and women at the age of 17.5. Orthodox men married the latest, at the age of 27.1 years, but without any striking difference to Muslim men (27 years). Orthodox women also married late (20.1 years) while Muslim women married at the age of 18.2. The situation in cities appears to correspond to Sklar's theory. The case of rural Albania nevertheless demands that the theory be revised. It should be questioned whether it was the influence of religion that caused the later marriage among Catholics in the cities or whether economic and socio-cultural factors related to the specific characteristics of life in villages and cities also played a role.

CELIBACY

Analysing the proportions of individuals who were never married in urban and rural areas, the highest percentage was found among Orthodox men (9.0 percent), although this was only slightly different to Muslims (6.2 percent) and Catholics (6.5 percent). For women, the highest percentage was among the Catholic population (5.0 percent), while in the other religions this percentage was very low (1.4 percent for Orthodox and 0.6 percent for Muslim women). In the cities the highest proportion of individuals who were never married for both men and women was found among Catholics (17.6 percent for men and 14.6 percent for women), followed by Muslims (9.7 percent for men and 2.0 percent for women) and Orthodox Christians (8.0 percent for men and 2.0 percent for women). Although it is not always possible to understand from the information given in the census sheets why they never married, in most of the cases the reasons were of a religious nature, the individuals becoming nuns or priests for example. Although Catholicism did not influence later marriage, it undoubtedly influenced the proportions of people who never married, especially among women.

In Shkodër 14.8 percent of Catholic women and 10 percent of Orthodox women never married, while only 3 percent of Muslim women never married. Among men, Catholics again show the highest percentage of individuals who never married (18.3 percent), followed by Orthodox and Muslim men with 13.6 percent and 13.5 percent respectively.

Comparing this data from Albania and Shkodër specifically with the respective data from other countries in the Balkans also proves interesting. Table 3 shows that the Balkans do indeed agree with Hajnal's 'European pattern', most people getting married at least once in their lifetime. But also there is sometimes significant deviance from Hajnal's general celibacy rate of five percent and one could be tempted to think that there is something else that increases this rate in urban centres to over ten percent. Further analysis is needed in order to elaborate the different factors which might have affect these marriage patterns, among them the effects of a developing economy, political and social changes or changes in the demographic structure of the population.

Greece provides a marked exception from the overall Balkan pattern. Although the levels typical of Western Europe were not reached in that country too, marriage occurred significantly later and celibacy was higher than in other countries of the region (Botev 1990: 108).

Table 3: The Balkans around 1900: Percentage of individuals who have never married in the 45-49 age cohort

Country	Year	Men	Women	Urban	
				Men	Women
Albania	1918	4.4	2.1	10.4	3.8
Bosnia		6.0	2.0		
Bulgaria	1900	3.0	1.0	6.0	3.0
Greece	1900	9.0	4.0		
Romania	1899	5.0	3.0		
Serbia	1900	3.0	1.0	7.0	0.0
Istanbul	1885			5.5	2.0
	1907			9.5	2.0
Shkodër	1918			14.7	7.5

Sources: Albanian Population Census of 1918 data analysis, Hajnal 1965: 103; Laslett and Clarke 1972: 397; Sundhaussen 1989: 121; Duben and Behar 1991: 123; Todorova 1993: 43

GENDER REGIMES AND AGE AT MARRIAGE

The census data from 1918 shows a relatively high age at marriage for men. In nearly all societies, men marry at higher ages than women and tend to be at least several years older than their wives. In Shkodër the age-gap between spouses was 12.4 years. Readiness to marry, often traditionally defined for young women by physical development, may be economically defined for men. Where men were expected to demonstrate an ability to support a family, they may have not been considered fit for marriage until their mid to late twenties or even later. One factor in a man's economic independence was his status as being free of having to care for any unmarried siblings. This factor was relevant in Shkodër specifically and caused men to delay marriage until their mid thirties. They often had to wait until their sister(s) had all married. The existence of this urban tradition was confirmed to me both by Father Zef Pllumi OFM and Willy Kamsi.[4] To verify this assumption, the data on the number unmarried men living in the same household with their unmarried sisters was examined.

[4] Interviews on 9 August 2006 with Father Zef Pllumi, a Franciscan friar in Arra Madhe Franciscan Monastery in Shkodër and on 24 April 2007 with the Albanian scholar and resident of Shkodër Willy Kamsi.

Table 4: Unmarried siblings living in a single household (1918)

Age cohort	% of unmarried men living with unmarried sister(s)	% of unmarried women living with brother(s)
18-22 years		66.2
23-27 years	43.3	52.8
28-32 years	39.7	54.0
33-37 years	31.6	

Source: Albanian Population Census of 1918 (calculated by author).

In 1918, according to the age cohort analysis, 43.3 percent of unmarried men between 23 and 27 years-of-age lived in the same household with at least one unmarried sister. In the age cohort 28 to 32, 39.7 percent of unmarried men lived with unmarried sister(s) and in the age cohort 33 to 37, 31.6 percent of unmarried men were in this situation. As for the women, in the age cohort from 18 to 22 years-of age, 66.2 percent of unmarried women lived in the same household with their brother(s). In the age cohort from 23 to 27 years-of-age this figure was 52.8 percent and for the 28 to 32 year olds there was even a slight increase to 54.0 percent.

The analysis shows that the number of unmarried women living in the same household with their own brother(s) is quite high, which tends to confirm the hypothesis that the tradition of not getting married for brother(s) until their sisters have done so could have an impact on the relatively high age at marriage for men.

MARRIAGE AND EDUCATION

Education played a significant role in marriage as well. The census data shows that the impact of male education on age at marriage is positive, even if only 33.9 percent of men and only 11.58 percent of women were literate. The level of literacy among married men was 29.3 percent and that of married women was 6.3 percent. The Orthodox population proved to have the highest literacy rates both for men and women. But the number of Orthodox people in city was quite low and does not allow for meaningful comparisons between the three religious communities in this respect. Comparing this specific data based on ethnicity on level of education, Albanians tended to be better educated, both married men and women, than their Slavic counterparts. But again, the number of Slavic people in Shkodër was quite low, which again makes any comparisons questionable.

The SMAMs for women and men were higher for those who were literate. In the city the literate women showed a SMAM of 23.2 years, while illiterate women married on average at 20.8 years. For men, those who were literate had a higher SMAM, 34.6 years as compared to 33.2 years for those who could not read and write (Papa 2004: 10).

Table 5: Literacy of married person born in Shkodër (1918)

Sex	Literacy among married persons born in Shkodër in %									
	Ethnicity Albanian		Religion						Ethnicity Slavic	
	No	Yes	Catholic		Orthodox		Moslems		No	Yes
			No	Yes	No	Yes	No	Yes		
Men	75.8	24.2	75.8	24.2	42.2	57.8	79.2	20.8	84.0	16.0
Women	93.7	6.3	93.7	6.3	59.5	40.5	98.6	1.4	95.2	4.8

Source: Albanian Population Census of 1918 (calculated by author).

NEOLOCALITY

Neolocality has an impact on marriage patterns as well. Neolocality was much more common in the cities and generally delayed marriage until the conditions were fulfilled for getting married and forming a new household. The ethnographic record nevertheless suggest that after marriage, the couple would live for a period of time in the husband family before founding their own household (Bushati 1998, Dibra 2002) a joint family emerging if other married brothers lived there too. It is difficult to trace changes in residence patterns based on a single census. One possibility for tracing neolocality is to see how many men live with their parents in the same household. Graph 1 shows that married men at around 33 years-of-age tend to no longer live with their fathers. Quite similar result emerges in Graph 2 for men living with their mothers in the same household.

Taken together, the graphs show that almost one third of married men while two thirds of unmarried men live with their mothers, which tends to support the neocality thesis for married men. But one should be beware of sweeping conclusions. One reason for no longer living with one‘s father could simply be the fact that one‘s father had already died, a phenomenon which is likely typical for urban Shkodër where men marry and procreate quite late. Married men thus only appear to reside in new households (apparent neolocality). Marriage might well take place in reaction to a father’s death, in order to meet the demands of being head of the household. The large number of nuclear households in a city does not automatically mean neolocality. The data is to date insufficient to say conclusively why married men were living alone in a household without their father.

Graph 1. Shkodër 1918: Man living with father

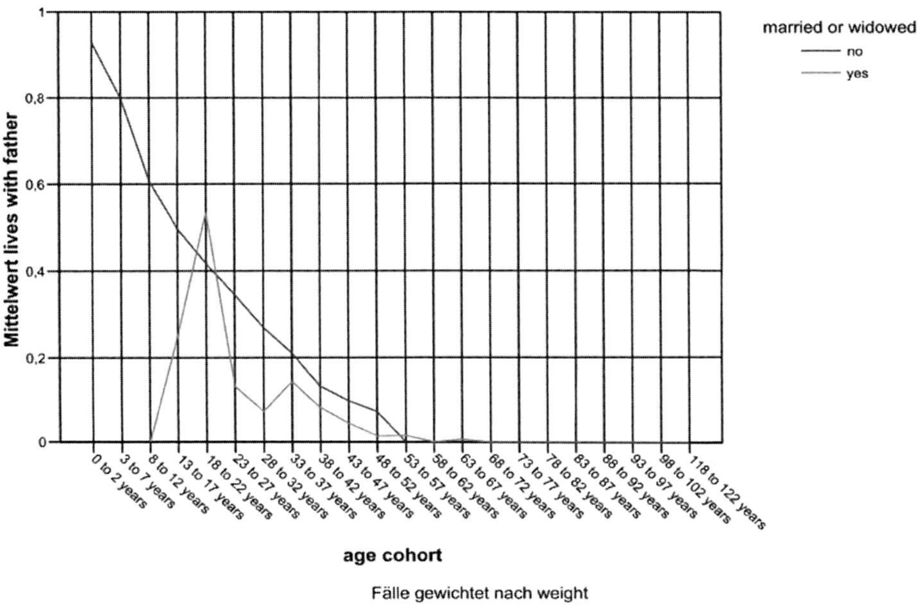

Source: Albanian Population Census of 1918 (calculated by author).

Graph 2. Shkodër 1918: Man living with mother

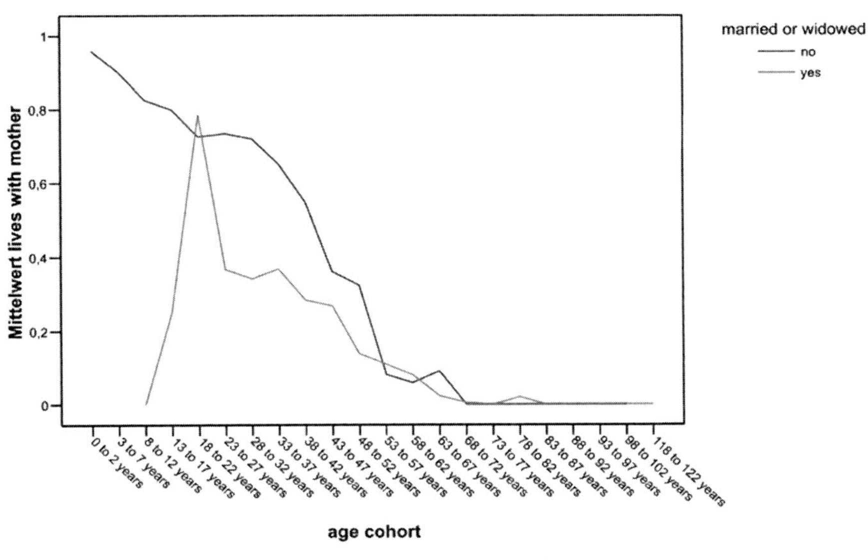

Source: Albanian Population Census of 1918 (calculated by author).

CONCLUSION

Is the Shkodra marriage pattern a unique phenomenon in Albania? This cannot be confirmed exclusively on the basis of the Albania Population Census of 1918 considering that it does not provide data for all of Albania.[5] This is especially unfortunate because Korça, which one could argue to be the southern counterpart to Shkodër in the north, is missing. For the region that was included in the survey (including Durrës and Elbasan) Shkodër proved to have had the highest age at first marriage for both men and women and the city had the highest SMAM for all other categories analysed in this paper. One can raise the question why this is so and if this should be understood as a deviation from Hajnal's Eastern European marriage system model. From what has been analysed in this paper, similarities appear to Laslett's Mediterranean tendencies in domestic group organisation (Laslett 1983: 526). This is true for the low female SMAM of ca. 22 years and the high SMAM for men at ca. 33 years. This high age for marriage for men could be explained with the economic changes that affected marriage and changing education in the urban area as well as the way people looked at marriage. The emerging tradition that men only married after their sister(s) should not be underestimated. In Shkodër the marriage gap was the highest in the country, reaching 12.4 years. The celibacy rate in Shkodër was also the highest for both sexes and far removed from universal marriage.

But it is nevertheless inadvisable to speak of deviance from Hajnal's Eastern European Pattern. Rather, I merely see a form of local differentiation within Albania, the political, social and economic situation in turn of the century Shkodër being what it was. It is an accepted fact that Hajnal's Eastern European and or European Patterns were not uniform for all of Europe but had variations (Plakans and Wetherell 2005: 120, Ehmer 2002: 305, Lynch 1991: 92).

Older customs in the marriage field did prevail in Shkodër in the first decades of the 20th century but these were being challenged by "modern" outside influences. New traditions and tendencies appeared such as for engaged and married couples to stroll in the city streets or in the city park together. Marriage shifted from being a family to being an individual matter. Marriage behaviour was characterised by the persistence of old traditions and by diverse attempts to adapt these traditions to the new circumstances. Demographic data are essential for making such marriage patterns visible but they are less adequate for explaining them. Thus, the local variation of the general pattern may only be explained as part of culturally, socially and economically structured behavioural patterns. These differences warrant more intensive and longer investigation than can be provided here. A close analysis of other Albanian censuses such as those of 1923 and 1930 would shed light on the country's marriage pattern and on its urban variation.

[5] Many southern Albanian cities, including Vlora, Korça, Gjirokastra, Fieri, Lushnja, Saranda and Përmeti among others were not included in the census.

BIBLIOGRAPHY

Beci, Bahri 1994 Dukuri sociolinguistike në qytetin e Shkodrës. In: Seminari i parë Ndërkombëtar "Shkodra në shekuj". pp 229-233.

Botev, Nikolai 1990 'Nuptiality in the Course of the Demographic Transition: The Experience of the Balkan Countries' Population Studies, Vol. 44(1) pp 107-126.

Bushati, Hamdi 1998 Shkodra dhe Motet. Vol. I. Shkodër.

Coon, Carleton 1950 The Mountains of Giants. A Racial and Cultural Study of the North Albanian Mountain of Ghegs. Cambridge.

Devolver, Daniel 1999 Hajnal's European marriage pattern and the evolution of agrarian structures in Western Europe from the fifteenth to the eighteenth centuries. Social Science History Association. Annual Meeting. November 11-14, Forth Worth Texas. Family/Demography Network.

Dibra, Miaser 2002 Vështrim psikologjik i karaktereve në ceremonialin e dasmës shkodrane. Studime Historike, Vol. 56 pp 80-111.

Dibra, Miaser 2004 Ceremoniali i dasmës në qytetin e Shkodrës. Tiranë.

Dojaka, Abaz 1980 Karakteri i lidhjeve martesore para çlirimit (gjysma e dytë e shek. XIX deri në prag të çlirimit). In: Etnografia shqiptare Vol. 11 pp 3-20.

Duben, Alan and Cem Behar 1991 Istanbul household. Marriage, family and fertility, 1880-1940. (Cambridge studies in population, economy and society in past Time Vol. 15.) Cambridge.

Duka, Valentina 1997 Qytetet e Shqipërisë në vitet 1912-1924. Tiranë.

Durham, Mary Edith 1928 Some tribal origins, laws and customs of the Balkans. London

Durham, Mary Edith 2001 Albania and the Albanians. Selected Articles and Letters 1903-1944. London.

Ehmer, Josef 2002 Marriage. In: David I. Kertzer and Marzio Barbagli (eds.) Family Life in the Long Nineteenth Century 1789-1913. Vol. 2. New Haven and London. pp 282-321.

Gruber, Siegfried and Robert Pichler 2002 Household structures in Albania in the early 20th century. In: History of the Family. Vol. 7(3) pp 351-374.

Gruber, Siegfried 2007 The Quarters of Shkodra in 1918: Differences and Similarities. In: Klaus Roth and Ulf Brunnbauer (eds.) Urban Life and Culture in Southeastern Europe: Anthropological and Historical Perspectives (Ethnologia Balkanica 10). Berlin pp 141-158.

Hajnal, John 1983 Two kinds of pre-industrial household formation systems. In: Richard Wall, Jean Robin and Peter Laslett (eds.) Family forms in historic Europe. Cambridge. pp 65-104.

Hajnal, John 1965 European marriage pattern in perspective. In: D. V. Glass and D. E. Eversley (eds). Population in history. Chicago pp 101-143.

Hajnal, John 1953 Age at marriage and proportions marrying. In: Population Studies Vol. 7(2) pp 111-136.

Hasluck, Margaret 1933 Bride-Price in Albania. A Homeric Parallel. In: Man, Vol. 33 pp 191-195.

Ippen, Theodor Anton 1907 Scutari und die nordalbanische Küstenebene. Sarajevo.

Kaser, Karl 2008 Patriarchy after Patriarchy. Gender Relations in Turkey and in the Balkans, 1500-2000. In: Studies on South East Europe Vol (7). Lit Verlag. Vienna and Münster.

Kaser, Karl 1995 Familie und Verwandtschaft auf dem Balkan. Analyse einer untergehenden Kultur. Vienna, Cologne and Weimar.

Kaser, Karl 1994 The Balkan Family Pattern. Conference Paper. Conference of the Cambridge Group for the history of population and social structure: "Where Europe ends?" April 6-9. Budapest.

Kera, Gentiana and Enriketa Pandelejmoni 2008 Marriage in urban Albania (during the first half of the twentieth century). In: History of the Family 13, pp 126-137.

Kera, Gentiana and Enriketa Papa 2003 Familja, feja dhe e drejta zakonore në Shqipëri deri në gjysmën e parë të shekullit XX. In: Politika & Shoqëria Vol. 6(1) pp 31-44.

Laslett, Peter 1983 Family and household as work group and kin group: areas of traditional Europe compared. In: Richard Wall, Jean Robin and Peter Laslett (eds.) Family forms in historic Europe. Cambridge. pp 513-563.

Laslett, Peter and Marilyn Clarke 1972 Houseful and household in an eighteenth century Balkan city. A tabular analysis of the listing of the Serbian sector of Belgrade in 1733-4. In: Peter Laslett and Richard Wall (eds.) Household and Family in Past Time. Cambridge. pp 375-400.

Luarasi, Aleks 2001 Marrëdhëniet familjare. Studime për të drejtën zakonore shqiptare. Tiranë.

Lynch, Katherine A. 1991 The European Marriage Pattern in the Cities. In: Journal of Family History 16(1) pp 79-96.

Mantegazza, Vico 1912 L'Albania. Gli Albanesi. L'appello all'Europa. Montenego e Albania. Scutari e il suo lago. Roma

Martelli, Alessandro 1917 Albania adriatica. In: Pagine geografiche della nostra guerra. Roma

Mejdiaj, Bajram 1976. Disa aspekte të martesës para Çlirimit. In: Etnografia shqiptare, Vol. 8 pp. 33-108.

Mihačević, Fra Lovro 1913 Durch Albanien. Reise Eindrücke. Prague.

Mosely, Philip E. 1976 "The Peasant Family: The Zadruga, or Communal Joint-Family in the Balkans, and its Recent Evolution. In: Robert F. Byrnes (ed.) Communal Families in the Balkans: The Zadruga. Essays by Philip E. Mosely and Essays in his Honour Notre Dame and London.

Nopcsa, Franz Baron 1910 Aus Šala und Klementi. Albanische Wanderungen. Sarajevo.

Pandelejmoni, Enriketa 2007 Family and marriage in urban Albania during the pre-communist era. Micro-level versus macro-level data: The Case of Shkodër quarters. Paper presented at the history of the European family Conference. Limerick.

Papa, Enriketa 2004 Marriage patterns of the Albanian city of Shkodra at the beginning of the 20th century. Paper presented at the European Social Science History Conference. Panel "Changes in urban marital and reproduction behaviour". Berlin.

Plakans, Andrejs and Charles Wetherell 2005 The Hajnal line and Eastern Europe. In: Theo Engelen and Arthur P. Wolf (eds.) Marriage and the family in Eurasia: Perspectives on the Hajnal hypothesis (Life at the Extremes, vol. 1). Amsterdam pp 105-126.

Schurer, Kevin 1989 A note concerning the calculation of the Singulate Mean Age at Marriage. In: Population Studies Vol. 43 pp 67-70.

Seiner, Franz 1922 Ergebnisse der Volkszählung in Albanien in dem von den österr.-ungar. Truppen 1916-1918 besetzten Gebiete (= Schriften der Balkankommission, Linguistische Abteilung, Vol. XIII). Vienna and Leipzig.

Selenica, Teki 1928 Shqiperia me 1927. Tiranë.

Simini, Giacinto 1899 Genni sui costumi di Scutari d'Albania. Proverbi e favole. Lecce.

Sklar, June L. 1974 The Role of Marriage Behaviour in the Demographic Transition: The case of eastern Europe Around 1900 In: Population Studies Vol. 28(2) pp 231-247.

Sundhaussen, Holm 1989 Historische Statistik Serbiens 1834-1914. Mit europäischen Vergleichsdaten. Südosteuropäische Arbeiten 87.

Todorova, Maria 1993 Balkan Family Structure and the European Pattern. Demographic Developments in Ottoman Bulgaria. Washington.

4. FAMILY PROPERTY IN ALBANIAN CUSTOMARY LAW

NEBI BARDHOSHI

In this paper I will discuss the norms and practices associated with landed family property as they are delineated in Albanian customary law or *kanun*. In the first section I will approach the issue historically, from the beginning of the 20th century until collectivisation (1953-1967). In the second section I will deal with the issue the postsocialist period from a more anthropological perspective. Did practices related to property relations ever completely abandon the dictates of customary law? And under what socio-political conditions did the *kanun* 'reappear' in the 1990s?

The division of property in the family is of great importance because this is a matter affecting not only family goods but also persons. This issue has also consequences for the state and nature of neighbourhood relations, economic structures, political relations, justice and so on (Davis 1976: 176-179).

Drawing an exact map of the historical distribution of the kanun is almost impossible, especially for the period after the collapse of the socialist regime. The practice of the kanun was generally more prominent in rural mountainous areas but this was not the same in all regions. And in each regional version had its on name: in the northern Albanian Alps it was known as the *Kanuni i Maleve* (Code of the Mountains), while in the central regions of northern Albania and in Kosova it was mostly known as the *Kanuni i Lekë Dukagjinit* (Code of Lekë Dukagjini) (Gjeçovi 1972; Fox 1989; Meçi 1995, 2002). More to the south it is known as the *Kanuni i Skënderbeut* (Code of Skanderbeg) (Ilia 1993). In Gjirokastra people speak of '*me ba kuvend sipas kanunit të Pirrit*' (to assemble according to the code of Pirri) (Tirta 2003:373). In various regions of Labëria one speaks of the Shartet (conditions), the *Kanuni i Idriz Sulit* (Code of Idriz Suli) or *Kanuni i Labërisë* (Code of Laberia) (Zojzi 1956). Elsewhere on can find references to the *Kanuni i Dibrës*, the *Kanuni i Lumës* or the *Kanuni i Bendës*. These regional associations may be more accurate denominations for the *kanun*; while names like Skendërbeu, Pirro or Lekë Dukagjini are used to identify these various codes and have been conserved in the memory of the population as founders of these laws, the maximum extent of their role in defining these codes was at most a slight reforming of their content (cf. Pupovci 1967).

Research for this paper was done in the region of Has, where the *kanun* is known as the *Kanuni i Lekë Dukagjinit*, the memory of which is still very vivid. The version of the *kanun* applied in this area has not yet been the focus of intensive scholarly interest. No collection of the passages of the *kanun* has yet been undertaken. Fieldwork was carried out in 2002 (May-June), 2003 (October) and 2005 (June-July).[1]

THE BORDER REGION OF HAS

Has is a small region situated in northeastern Albania on the border to Kosova. Much of the historical region (40 villages) is today situated within the borders of Kosova. The part of historical Has situated in Albania (29 villages) is also partially known as *Hasi i Brijës* (Hillside Has) and partially as *Has i Thatë* (Dry Hasi) but I will continue to use the simple denomination Has here.

In 1927, Has had a population of about 5876 persons living in 680 families (Selenica 1928: 346); in 1993 the population numbered 25,265 inhabitants in 5452 families living in 29 villages. In 2003 the population had decreased by 2631 persons to 22,634, which can be attributed to migration movements. Based on new administrative divisions of 1992, Has has three *komuna* (districts) – Gjinaj, Fajza and Golaj and the municipality of Kruma (Law No, 8653, 31.7.2000).

Villages in Has are made up of families belonging to brotherhoods of different clan origins; the village represents a territorial entity where blood relations are of special importance. Brotherhoods are exogamous, as are clans, be they fictive of real. Marriage in the maternal line is also forbidden as long as memory extends, although memory of the maternal line is generally shorter because it does not have as many functions as the paternal line, which is important for property matters, for assembly rights and on the subject of to collective responsibility. Despite the fact that the whole population of Has is Muslim the tradition of parallel cousin marriage was not applied. The thesis authored by Coon that Has as a whole – as a northern Albanian 'tribe' – was exogamous (Coon 1950: 7), although it has found followers among younger scholars (cf. Resta: 1996, 43) is an exaggeration. My research in the region has shown that exogamy as a marriage principle does not extend in the region level. Though the inhabitants of each and every village are aware of one another's different lineage and brotherhood descent, the village still apply exogamic marriage rules. Often on such issues they emphasised the belief that such a rule was imposed by their ancestors to prevent eventual conflicts between families of the village; as a result the locals state that the ancestors lived in peace and considered themselves as brothers. They, also, believe that in this way the honour of the girls is safeguarded within the village realm.

The village families have, beside their rights to family property, rights to common property such as forests, pastures and mountains as well. All families have equal rights over this common property, indifferent from the number of members, the social status or the duration of residence in the village. Brotherhoods also have

[1] The data collected during fieldwork has been archived in the Institute of Folk Culture, Tiranë; cf. Materiale të mbledhura në terren mbi të drejtën dokesore në krahinën e Hasit, Nebi Bardhoshi, 2002, 2003, 2005. The Institute of Folk Culture financed the fieldwork within the framework of the project "Property in Albanian customary law".

common property, which was considered the part divided from the village's common property according to a system *për vllazni* (per brotherhood), each brotherhood having rights to an equal part of the land in question. In small villages this common property was divided *për tym* (per family) In Has, the clan or *bajrak* were not relevant categories when it came to property rights.

DIVISION OF LANDED PROPERTY IN THE FAMILY ACCORDING TO THE KANUN

Based on a tradition that existed well into the period after World War II, family and household in Has are organised, as elsewhere in Albania, on the basis of patriarchal relations. Although simple family households did exist, the majority of the population lived in joint family households of two, three or more brothers living together with their wives and children or extended families of parents living with their married sons. Households of ten persons were common, although cases of 40 to 60 family members in a household were not unheard of, for example the family of Isen Qarrit in the village of Qarri, which counted more than 40 members, or the family of Haxhi Xhafes in the village of Nikoliq.

The big households either joint or extended families, known as *shtëpia e madhe* (big house) were traditionally very useful for the welfare of its members. The old saying *damja e fik derën* (division destroys the door) is a reference to the weakened economic basis of households that had divided. A family division was conceived almost as a day of mourning, especially by parents who saw their sons leave the common household. Visitors to such families consoled them, saying *mos u mërzit! Zoti ju shtiftë lezet ndër veti*! (Do not worry! May God bring joy among you!) and the like. The reasons for a family to divide were of various natures, such as the large number of members, quarrels and disagreements within the family. There was no definite rule to regulate household fission. This option was the only applied if no other solution to a given problem could be found. The case that was most common and to a degree normal was household fission after all sons were married. All family goods were then divided equally; the rights to the use and enjoyment of the fruits of the common brotherhood or village property was recognised for every new household emerging from separation. This new distribution of rights was one reason why the division of a household constituted an event of special importance for the whole community.

The head of the household could decide that the household separate, but each son was free to request a separation as well, under the condition that he explain himself. The *zot shtëpie* (household head) made the final decision and a facilitated the division of property. But the division of a household was often a very delicate moment and the village *pleqtë* (elders) often mediated. This mediation process could take several forms. One option was to name two *pleqtë e dès* (elders of separation) that because of their individual qualities, friendship or kinship with the family in question enjoyed the confidence of all affected persons. It was assumed that they would be *pa hile* (impartial) and arrange the separation in the most equitable way. One of these elders would arrange the separation and the other would assist and help him not to fall into error. This form of mediation by two elders is also described in the written versions of the *kanun* (Gjeçovi 1972: 25). Another option was that each *vëlla* (brother) nominate an elder to represent him. In such cases the number of mediating elders was a factor of the number of *pjesëtar* (parties) involved in the separation. The elders nominated to second the family appointed one of their number – usually the most experienced – as speaker and decide how the property was to be divided. Each *plak* was interested not only in protecting in the best way possible the interests of the family member he represented, he was also interested in doing so based on the respective customary norms. This model can also be found in the written versions of the *kanun* all across Albania (Meçi 1996: 123, 2002: 186; Zojzi 1956: 50). A third option was to nominate a single mediator, a relative who did not represent anyone in particular but simply adjudicated the process from the beginning to the end. In a way he played the role of the household head, as it was the case also in the above mentioned variants as well. This latter mediation model was most practical and is thought to have been more common than the first two variants. It is also to be found in the written versions of the *kanun* (Meçi 1996:124; Prifti 1987: 128).

Relevant *pjesëtar* in the division of landed property were considered to be the brothers of the first generation that had not gone through a separation process earlier. Thus, in a family of more than three generations the *pjesëtar* were either the brothers or sons of the *zot shtëpie*. If the brother of the *zot shtëpie* had adult, even married sons, he would in no way have a right to a greater share of common landed property. The situation differed, nevertheless for other property (cf. Stahl 1986).

In Has the father's right as the head of the household to exclude from family property any one of his sons in special cases was recognised but only applied rarely in the distant past.[2] On the other hand, as the head of the household, a father, as opposed to the representation in the *Kanuni i Lekë Dukagjinit* or the *Kanuni i Skënderbeut* is not a *pjesëtar* in the division of landed property (Gjeçovi 1972: 27, Ilia 1993: 92). This was valid even if he was still the head of the household. Nor did the head of household benefit more than his brothers in the division of property; he was a *pjesëtar* with equal rights to his brothers. This is verified by the fact that the death of the head of the household was not a request for the division of a family's property among its members. Fathers had no share on the property due to the fact that they would be living with the youngest brother after property separation among brothers. Even if one son or brother for one reason or another decided not to marry, he did not lose his right to equal share in the property. The same principle is equally applied for those brothers who did not have children or were underage in the time of partition. The property of brothers who did not have any children was divided among his brothers after his death; the brother family that had cared for him during his life enjoyed the right to be the first to choose its share. Even a brother with mental or physical handicaps took equal part in the division of property. He was cared for by the family of one of his brothers, usually with the one caring for the parents. Thus, his share was unified with that of the family he lived with. After his

---

2 The locals narrate that it must have happened in the past but only rarely because such a thing is a great shame for the family that applied such a right.

death, his share was divided *për vëllezër* (among brothers) or it was left to the brother or family that had taken care of him.

The elders or the head of household divided the property in parts and after that the brothers chose shares in turn. The prevalent opinion was that the youngest brother had the right to choose first (see: Nopsca, 1980: 411 - 446). This was a way to support the youngest brother who was least able to benefit in the division of the extended family because he could contribute the least labour. It was stated that this was one of the most important reasons for parents to live with the youngest son. It was also said that the right of the youngest brother to choose first was inherited also by his successors. The brother's then chose in turn from youngest to oldest. If a brother died before the family land was divided, his son would inherit his right to do so; if he was still underage he – or his guardian – would often be given the privilege to choose first.

These rules were applied when a father or the elders carried out the division. If one of the brothers divided the property – and it was often done by the eldest brother – then he took what remained after the rest of his brothers had chosen. The reasoning behind this practice was the realisation of a fair division; the one dividing the property would necessarily get the least favourable parcel. Each parcel would thus be *si për veti* (as if it were for himself).

The family house was usually left to the head of household or to the youngest brother. Cases were cited to me in which the house was kept by an older brother, the youngest being compensated with more or more productive land. In other cases, the fact that the eldest brother inherited the position the head of the household was interpreted as being reason for him to stay in the parental house. With the intention of ensuring fairness and equality among the new households in the property division, brothers who did not get the house were compensated with other goods, mainly stock. In Has land was not part of this compensation as was the case elsewhere (Hasluck 1954: 50). This may have been due to the lack of sufficient agricultural land.

In many cases the new households, although officially separated, continued to live under the same roof. The households were then clearly separated; each of the new families had its own name, economic independence, internal organisation and right of representation in assemblies and in various ceremonies in the community. Each family had its own door, separate garden and path to the street. In the course of the 1990s, as the economic potential of some families increased considerably, a new process for division in agreement with tradition emerged. Either the family house was designed so as to allow each brother his own floor or several houses were built to house each brother. This was financed from their common income and their common labour before the decision was made to officially divide the household. At the moment of division, every brother had his own home.

Another important resource was water, especially in Has, where the water sources are more difficult to access than in other areas. Thus, in the traditional norms regulating the division of the family's property much attention was paid to access to drinking and irrigation water. In many cases it occurred that with the division of property between brothers, one or more of them would not have direct access to a water source. They were thus given the unconditional right to get drinking water from the same source they had used collectively in the past, a right which could not be withheld for any reason. This water was to be accessed using a very clearly defined path, clearly defined so as to avoid argument in the future. The right to drinking water thus acquired, in addition to its juridical and moral character a cultic nature. People believed that those forbidding others access to drinking water would be damned by God in the most extreme way, namely to be left without heirs, *me t'u shkymë hisja* (to tear the inheritance). Even today, springs on family land exist to which many families have common access. Only when new springs or alternative water sources were found could a family lose these rights to get water.

It seems that the brother's system of land or other resources division, as an applied practice, is rooted deep in history, in the time before the emergence of the state and state law. Data collected after the collapse of the communist regime shows that, especially in rural regions such as Has, many of these rules survived communist attacks and the collectivisation process. It is nevertheless difficult to trace this process in detail.

A Story of Plurality: Collectivisation, De-collectivisation and the Kanun

The process of collectivisation began already in 1946 to end towards 1967. In peripheral mountainous regions such as Has, the process of collectivisation took place very late. With collectivisation, private land became the property of co-operatives. To put it bluntly, the year 1967 marked the eradication of private agriculture in Albania (de Waal 1995: 2). According to the new property law, only a parcel of land of no more than one *dönüm* (one-tenth of a hectare) was left to a peasant family to use for subsistence agriculture. In mountainous regions such as Has this allowance was raised to 1.5 *dönüm*.[3] It must be stressed that these were merely use rights and not ownership rights. Peasant families continued to have ownership rights to their houses and outbuildings, stock and draught animals, bees, poultry, smaller livestock. This extent of this property became more and more limited as time went by. It may then be asked how these use rights were passed on from generation to generation? My fieldwork has shown that even during the period of collectivisation, the distribution of usufruct rights to land was realised based on the *kanun*. Houses and other such property also continued to be divided *për vëllezër*. On such an occasion, brothers who had left the parental home to work elsewhere or study were compensated in kind; the house itself then went into the ownership of one of the brothers. Women continued to be excluded from share rights.

The physical collectivisation of the land nevertheless did little to eradicate the memory of ownership among the local population. The various parts of the collectivized land, continued to be known by the names of their former owners, the official names or denominations were ignored, at least in informal settings. In day-to-day use these various parcels, fields and forests were known as *fush Lushi* or *pyll*

[3] Decision of the Council of Ministers, No 27. 03. 1968, article 2

Hamzai (the pasture of Lushi; the forest of Hamza) and so on. Also in the context of social memory, in family narratives, explanations about the size of family property and how it was administered on the basis of the *kanun* abounded. It should be underlined that the social memory of property was more present in nuclear family discussion. People of the region remember that in that time, they feared repercussions if they spoke about private property in the public sphere. Only with trusted people and using a very careful and metaphorical language could matters related to private property be discussed in coffeehouses, the work environment or elsewhere in public.

The *kanun* continued to regulate behaviour in other spheres as well. State law forbade, for example, marriages between blood relations for two generations,[4] the village never arising as a category of exclusion. In Has, however, the village and the brotherhood continued its tradition of exogamy in marriage, demonstrating that de facto, *kanun* was still largely accepted and applied.

After collectivisation, various families, under state regulation, built new houses on parcels of land distributed by it. In delineating these parcels the status of land before collectivization, state law was not taken into consideration, become irrelevant in practical application. Most of these inhabitants did everything that was possible to get permission to build these houses from the expropriated families or former owners. In some case ownership was acquired of the parcel based on the dictates of the *kanun* as well. Here again, the *kanun* took priority over state law, even if this was never made explicit.

The years 1991 and 1992 marked for Albania the beginning of a great transformation in every aspect of social life. The Albanian population faced a deep identity crisis, the whole system of values built over the course of 45 years was overthrown (Saltmarshe 2001: 210). The new political elite was not able to create a relation of trust with its citizens and in regions such as Has, a "return to tradition" was attempted, even though the understanding of this tradition as a whole was "debauched" (Tirta 2005). For the question of de-collectivisation, special importance was laid on what was understood locally as a traditional system of land distribution. In Has collectivised land – agricultural land, pastures and forests – was returned to the expropriated owners in the spring of 1992. The legal basis for de-collectivisation was the *Ligji 'Për Tokën'* (Land Law) of 1991 that recognised the peasant family as an economic unit. The amount of land that a family received from the agricultural co-operatives depended on the number of family members; the system of distribution was known as '*ndarja e tokës për frymë*' (division of land per head). The law was explicit in its non-recognition of specific claims to specific pieces of land based on ownership structures prior to collectivisation. Article 8 of the law claimed that "landed property, its quantity and borders before collectivisation" would not play a role in redistribution.

An important consideration that often is ignored in discussion is the fact that the people's relationship to the land was not only economic but also spiritual, to the extent that the latter often was decisive in attitudes and decision-making processes concerning the land. These spiritual ties are expressed in phrases such as '*këtë tokë*

---

[4] Kodi i familjes, 1982, neni 15

ma ka lanë baba' (this land was left to me by my father), '*e kam brez mas brezi*' (I am its owner generation after generation), '*e kam fitu me gjak*' (I have won it with blood) and so on. These claims are not only a representation of the ties to the land but to the *të parët* (ancestors), a significant emotional and psychological tie. As the locals say, regaining ownership to ancestral land was not only a matter of personal dignity but a moral obligation the ancestors.

Thus, the concrete process of de-collectivisation was faced with a series of problems from the outset, on three counts: 1. The traditional borders of family property units had been massively damaged in the collectivisation period 2. New households had been established without the division of landed property having been realised. 3. Houses had been built on property that did not belong to the families living in those houses.

As mentioned above, the state law was explicit in distancing itself from the pre-collectivization property regimes. If this had remained the case, if property would have been redistributed on this basis, the results would have been harrowing. The Land Law called for commissions to be created that would realise the redistribution of the collectivised land. In a considerable number of cases the local population itself managed to redistribute the land without ever involving the commission. Sometimes the commission distributed a part of the land and the local inhabitants organised the partitioning of the rest. The commissioners lack authority but often played a role in the process – they were left to merely ratify what the locals decided upon. Where inhabitants of the respective region were members of the commissions, their mandate often was realised on the basis of the *kanun*, or at least taking the *kanun* into consideration. One of the most critical issues for the commissioners, as well as for the peasants themselves, was the redefinition and re-establishment of the old boundaries. Elders and other trustworthy people were then asked, as it is prescribed in the *kanun*. If this survey of the social memory remained inconclusive, then an agreement had to be reached by the two parties involved. Once this had been done, the process of property restitution was much simpler. After the boundaries from before collectivisation had been defined, the difficult work begun, in dividing the land among what had in the meantime become a group of families. M. Alia's land, for example, was collectivised in 1967. M. had two sons, Sh. and B. Sh. married and had five sons, B. had only one. In 1991 each of these six grandsons had married and each had founded a family of their own. The land commission had managed to redefine the old borders of M.s land. It had then divided the land into two equal parts, one for Sh. and one for B. who would have each inherited this land from M., if it had not been collectivised. Sh.s *hise e babës* (father's shares) was then divided again into five equal parts, one each for his five sons. B.s son inherited to whole of his father's land, equal to the amount of land redistributed to his five cousins together. All six men, including those who had gaining less land due to this system, were convinced that this form of redistribution was just.

Historical divisions based on the tradition of the *kanun* that had not taken place because of collectivisation were replicated in this system. In some cases, the family groups decided that the state principle of division be applied, although *me kanun* (according to customary law). Even then, they only wanted to receive land that had belonged to their own ancestors. They were convinced that getting someone else's land would not provide them with real pleasure because sooner or later the property would be restituted to the true owner. Men who had left the village or even left the country were included in the redistribution process, often in their absence. This land was then leased out on *kanun* basis, namely on the basis of *gjaja për gjysëm* (for half) (Gjeçovi, 1979: 32). The leaser had to provide the owner half of the harvest. In most cases land was leased to close paternal blood relations. I also heard of cases where a man renounced his claim to land in favour of his brothers. The agreement in each case was made verbally and not recorded in any written document.

Before concluding, briefly I want to mention two difficulties that arose while carrying out the research. The first has to do with the old principle of *nuk ka tokë pa rrugë e pa vijë uji* (there is no land without a road or water access). The situation as pertains to the extent of common goods such as roads was by 1991 quite different from the situation as described in the *kanun* (de Waal 1995: 17). One the one hand, the number of individual plots had grown significantly, on the other hand, agriculture was now mechanised. According to the *kanun*, a road had to be sufficient to allow a pair of oxen or a loaded horse to pass; today the roads were used by automobiles, tractors and combines. There where it was convenient, the old roads were re-established, elsewhere a household would have to cede land that would be used for collective purposes. The solution found in solving this problem were various with more or less success in each case (cf. Voell 2003: 98). In the village of Letaj the following solution was agreed upon: After the land was redistributed, R. and I. Kurpali agreed (verbally) that R. would allow I. and his family members to cross his land with whatever vehicles necessary to harvest their own crops. At the end of the harvest period, I. was obliged to close the path he had made; he was not made liable for any damages that occurred as a result of the passage of his vehicles.

The second difficulty was the situation of families settled on the land of other owners. The beginning of the process of de-collectivisation resulted in a great deal of insecurity. The state was not in a position to protect property rights and enforce the principle of equal redistribution independently of previous ownership regimes. The state itself was dependent of the voluntary application of these principles. The application of the *kanun* was also difficult. According to custom if a family settles on a plot of land and has kindled a *zjarr* (fire) and three days pass by without any claims on the property, then no one has the right to expel them from the plot. According to this tradition, the settled family acquired the rights to the land that was occupied; in the course of time the household was accepted as a village member, and only then the new settler had rights on common property.

In the 1990s the situation was complicated by the fact that the original owners of the property claimed that they had not been free to express their disapproval - the state and its institutions had stood on the way. This was the argument of those landowners who demanded that the squatters leave their houses. In classifying my data from the field on this subject, a solution typology might be established: 1. The original landowner allowed the squatter to vacate the occupied land without asking for any compensation for the use of his property. Such situations were marked in a considerable number of cases by significant disagreement between the two parties. 2. The traditional owner of the land and the squatter agreed that either the latter buy the land or that the former buy the house on the land. In the second case the sale of the house was a simple process that required no official state participation and no written record; the agreement was made verbally and sealed by drinking a coffee together. 3. The third possibility was that land might be exchanged. The original landowner would acquire from the squatter's own property a piece of land of equal value to that on which the squatter's house stood. This solution was dependent of course on the latter having landed property to exchange and this property being in the same or a proximate village. Additionally, this solution was one that only occurred between families that had a very good relationship.

CONCLUSIONS

We might deduce from the above data on Has that landed property in its totality is felt to be in common, it is used and enjoyed by the community, be it a family, a brotherhood or a village as a whole, even if everyone is all too well aware of his own ownership rights. But these rights are seen more as temporary proprietary rights, the land – and other goods – at the same time being the inheritance of a man's son. Talk about property and decisions made about property take place with this fact in mind. A *zot i shtëpisë* is in this sense more of an administrator of his sons' inheritance than an owner of land. Thus, property in Has must be seen in the widest sense as family property, it is not considered property of an individual who can define its destiny according to his own needs and desires. A *zot i shtëpisë* must not even die for his sons to inherit, as this division can take place in his lifetime.

The basic principle in the division of the family's immovable property was that of the equality of all inheriting brothers. In the definition of their respective share, neither their age, their mental or physical competence nor their role in the family, in society or elsewhere was taken into consideration. Every brother was equal on the day of the family property's partitioning.

The *kanun* and traditional practices for the regulation of family property relations in the region of Has, though limited in dimension, have continued to be applied especially in the early years of the postsocialist period, beside and in addition to state practice and state law. This phenomenon of legal plurality was also present during the socialist period (Griffits 1986; Moore 2004; Pospisil 1978: 52-60). Even where a state is stable, it can pass and enforce any number of laws, but it cannot eliminate autonomous or semi-autonomous social fields of various social groups where norms for the regulation of relations within the group, outside the sphere of state law are applied (Moore, 1973, 743). In our case this autonomous field is defined by the various versions of the *kanun* as it was remembered in practice.

Such an observation suggests speaking of a revitalisation of the *kanun's* public life, rather than of the resurrection of its usage, considering that during Albanian state socialism, *kanun* was present in the private realm and used de facto to regulate societal activities of a narrower scope, such as marriage (see also Voell: 2003, 89, de Waal: 2005, 86). The broadening of the *kanun's* fields of application in postsocialism might be due and determined by the following factors. 1. The malfunctioning of postsocialist state law and state institutions and the inappropriateness of laws that were passed. The Land Law for example ignored the social-cultural context in which it was to be applied; it ignored the concepts of inheritance and ancestral land in favour of simple distribution per capita. 2. Even when the state and state institutions functioned, as in the socialist period, where space for the autonomous organisation of social relations remained, the *kanun* was (secretly) applied. 3. The *kanun* is more than a simple law or a juridical tool independent of social practice. It mirrors social relations as a whole, in respect to property as well as the economic and social structure of the community, village and family. The *kanun* is an implicit part of day-to-day life and is applied even where it is not explicitly intended. We might conclude that the survival of the *kanun*, its continued application parallel to state structures reflects its role in distributing socialy perceived and accepted solutions and justice.

BIBLIOGRAPHY

Coon, Carleton S. 1950 The Mountains of giants: An racial and cultural study of the north Albanian Mountain Ghegs. Cambridge: Peabody Museum of American Archeology and Ethnology, Harvard University.

Davis, John 1977 People of the Mediterranean: An essay in comparative anthropology. London, Henley and Boston: Routledge & Kegan Paul.

de Waal, Clarissa 1995 Decollectivisation and total scarcity in High Albania. In: Cambridge Anthropology, Vol 18(1).

de Waal, Clarissa 2005 Albania Today: A portrait of Post-Communist Turbulence London: Tauris .

Dida, Sejdi 1975 Material studimi për disa problem shoqërore nga ana etnografike të famijes, Tiranë, Arkivi i Etnologjisë, Instituti i Antropologjisë kulturore dhe i studimit të artit, fletore nr. 516/23. 71 pages.

Fox, Leonard 1989 Kanuni i Lekë Dukagjinit = The Code of Lekë Dukagjini. New York: Gjonlekaj.

Gjeçovi, Shtjefen 1972 Kanuni i Lekë Dukagjinit. Prishtinë: Rilindja.

Griffits, John 1986 What is legal pluralism. In: Journal of Legal Pluralism. Vol. 24 1-54

Ilia, F. 1993 Kanuni i Skanderbegut, Brescia: La Rose.

Hann, Chris 1993 From Production to property: Decollectivization and Family Land Relationship in Contemporary Hungary, In: Man Vol. 28 pp 299-320.

Hasluck, Margaret 1954 The Unwritten Law in Albania. Cambridge: Cambridge University Press.

Meçi, Xhemal 1996 Kanuni i Lekë Dukagjinit, varianti i Pukës. Tiranë: Çabej.

Meçi, Xhemal 2002 Kanuni i Lekë Dukagjinit në variantin e Mirditës. Tiranë: Geer.

Moore, Sally F. 1973 The Law and Social Change: The Semi-Autonomuos Social Field as an Appropriate Subject of Study. In: Law and Society Review, Vol. 8 pp 719-745.

Moore, Sally F. 2004 Certainties Undone. Fifty Turbulent Years of Legal Anthropology 1949-1999. In: Sally F. Moore (ed.) Law and Anthropology, London: Blackwell pp 343-367.

Nopsca, Franz Baron 1980 Shqipëria: Fiset e malësisë së veriut dhe e drejta zakonore, Tiranë, Arkivi i Etnologjisë, Instituti i Antropologjisë kulturore dhe i studimit të artit.

Pospisil. J. Leopold 1978 Ethnology of Law. San Francisco: Cummings Publishing Company.

Pupovci, Syrja 1967 Kanuni i Lekë Dukagjinit: Burimet, origjina, emni dhe vlefshmenija. Përparimi Nr. 8 pp 965-1015.

Prifti, Bardhyl 1987 Norma kanunore për ndarjen e familjes në Kolonjë. In: Etnografia Shqiptare Vol. 15.

Resta, Partrizia 1996 Un popolo in camino: Migrazioni albanesi in Italia Lecce.

Selenica, Teki 1928 Shqipëria me 1927. Tiranë.
Stahl, Paul H. 1982 Strukturat e vjetra shoqërore shqiptare në kuadrin e shoqërive ballkanike dhe evropiane. In: Kultura Popullore Vol. 2 pp 105-111.
Stahl, Paul H. 1986 Household, Village and Village Confederation in Southeastern Europe. New York: Columbia University Press.
Saltmarshe, Douglas 2001 Identity in Post-Communist Balkan State: An Albanian village study. London: Ashgate.
Tirta, Mark 2003 Etnologjia e Shqiptarëve. Tiranë: Geer.
Voell, Stephane 2003 The Kanun in the City: Albania Customary Law as habitus and its persistence in the suburb of Tirana, Bathore. In: Anthropos 98 pp 85-101.
Zojzi, Rrok 1956 Kanuni i Idriz Sulit, Tiranë, Arkivi i Etnologjisë në IKP, Vol. I.

5. Blood and Seed, Trunk and Hearth: Kinship and Common Origin in southern Albania

Gilles de Rapper

> The Ghegs of Northern Albania present the only true example of a tribal system surviving in Europe until the mid-twentieth century. In those remote valleys with very inadequate communications has survived a group of people whose whole life was organized in terms of kinship and descent. The clan, *fis*, was a group of people all of whom claimed descent from a common male ancestor, who may often have been fictitious (Whitaker 1968: 254).

Studies on the Albanian kinship system and social organisation have focused mainly on northern Albania. Following pioneering work by Edith Durham (Durham 1909: 1928), much attention has been devoted to 'tribal' organisation, which could be observed well into the first half of twentieth century. This organisation was seen by Western scholars as a modern European curiosity, representing a kind of survival from an archaic European past. The central feature of this tribal organisation was the tribe or clan, in Albanian, *fis* (Durham 1909: 20; Daniel 1989: 50).

More recently, some scholars have started to question the 'tribal' characterisation of northern Albanian society, which seemed to them to be the result of both an interest in the exotic within Europe and the uncritical application of anthropological models elaborated in other societies, especially in Africa. Berit Backer thus criticised the lack of theoretical consistency of most works on "so-called Albanian tribal society (Backer 1979: 91-95)," while Albert Doja deplores the fact that most publications on the subject consist of a "compilation anthologique des mêmes données," without any attempt to understand the structural basis of these kinds of social organisations (Doja 1999: 39).

In the media as well as in common representations, tribal and clan organisation has come to be an emblem of Albanian society as a whole taking up Ian Whitaker suggestion to consider recent events in Albanian political history in the general frame of tribal organisation (Whitaker 1968: 282). Today, for instance, organised crime in Albania is generally presented as being clan-organised crime, as are the factions in communist and post-communist political life, which are described as the manifestation of a tribal mentality. Kinship is certainly a resource in political as well as in economic activities, in Albania as elsewhere (cf. Schweitzer 2000). That organised crime and political factions should not be confused with traditional social organisation is, however, revealed in the contemporary tendency in Albania to use the loan word *klan* in the former context instead of *fis*, which remains in use for the latter. From the Albanian point of view, they are two different realities and should be distinguished as such.

The word *fis* is used all over Albania. In southern Albania it is commonly heard with the meaning of 'kin', and it also designates the three generation patrilineage, which is, together with the house (*shpi, shtëpi*), the primary social unit based on kinship. Because of its use as 'tribe' in the common as well as scientific language, working on kinship in southern Albania necessitates some lexical precautions. The same individuals who make daily use of the word *fis* to talk about their close or distant kin are not always prepared to understand what a social anthropologist is doing there: "There are no *fis* here, you should go to the north to study them; that is where they are." I soon realised that the word *fis* was highly polysemic and that the reality it covers in southern Albania could not be understood without taking this polysemy into account.

The purpose of this paper is two-fold: to give an account of kinship and social organisation in less studied southern Albania and, by doing so, to show how local conceptions of kinship and social organisation are embedded in wider representations of society in Albania.

The ethnographic material presented here has been collected during long-term fieldwork conducted in the district of Devoll from June 1995 to September 1996, and in shorter stays in 1998, 1999, 2000 and 2003.

Devoll: General Presentation

Devoll is a district (*rreth*) in southeastern Albania, on the border with Greece. It consists of forty-two villages distributed around its administrative centre, the small town of Bilisht (8000 inhabitants in 1995), which lies on the road between Korçë and the border post of Kapshticë/Kristalopigi.

Most of the villages are situated on both sides of a large and relatively flat valley, in the middle of which flows the river Devoll. This part of the valley is locally called *Fusha*, (the plain) or *Devolli i poshtëm*, (lower-Devoll). The villages are generally located at the foot of low hills or mountains, between agricultural land below and pastures and forests above. A few of them, said to be ancient *çiflig* villages, are located in the middle of the fields. The upper part of the valley, called *Mali* (the mountain) or *Devolli i sipërm* (upper-Devoll), has much less arable land and more pastures and forests and is occupied by villages generally smaller in size.

All villages (*fshat*) are fixed and compact settlements. They consist of at least two neighbourhoods (*lagje*), usually more, lying on both sides of the main street. Around the inhabited part of the village are gardens and small irrigated fields where people grow corn, onions, beans and other vegetables. The more distant fields, which used to be irrigated at the time of the cooperative (before 1991), are in most cases left uncultivated for lack of water and mechanisation.

The population is mainly Albanian-speaking, with the exception of the village of Vërnik, which is inhabited by members of the Macedonian minority. There is no evidence of Greek or Arumanian-speaking populations in most recent history, although some families claim to descend from settlers coming from parts of Greek Macedonia or from pastoral areas in the Pindus range, across the Greek-Albanian border. A few villages on the Greek side of the border had close links with Devoll until 1924 and the exchange of population between Greece and Turkey. These villages were inhabited by Albanian-speaking Muslims who were forced to move to Turkey. Before that time, they used to intermarry with Devoll; Bilisht was their market town.

Most Devollis are Muslims, a minority Orthodox Christians. With the exception of Bilisht, Muslims and Christians live in homogenous villages or, in the case of the few mixed villages, in separate neighbourhoods of the same village. They rarely intermarry and, although quiet and peaceful, their relations are marked by stereotypes and suspicion. As in most parts of Albania, even when the level of religious practice is low, people are nevertheless aware of their religious affiliation and origin (de Rapper 2002).

THE KINSHIP SYSTEM

The two basic units of social organisation are the house (*shpi, shtëpi*) and the patrilineage (*fis*). The *fis* can be defined as a patrilineal descent group and an exogamous unit whose members used to own some property in common.[1] Patrilineal descent is expressed in the concept of blood (*gjak*); all members of the *fis* share the same blood and, through blood, some physical and moral characteristics.

Marriage within blood (*brenda gjakut*) is forbidden. It is also forbidden to marry into the mother's *fis*. A lineage should not take (*marr*) from or give (*jap*) to another lineage to whom it already has a such a relationship. There is however, as in other rural European societies (Zonabend 1981), a tendency not to marry too far off; two lineages are not allowed to intermarry, but it often happens that three lineages favour one another for one or two generations. There is also a tendency to marry within the village or within a small group of villages and, of course, within a religious community. Residence is virilocal. Wives come to live in their husband's household, which is either the husband's paternal house or a new house provided by his father.

Landed property is inherited by sons alone while daughters receive a dowry (*pajë, prikë*) upon marriage. The latter consists of furniture and clothing, but never of land or livestock. Although land is transmitted "by the father's will" (*sipas dëshirës së babait*), as one informant in Miras put it, and he could in theory chose to give land to his daughter as part of the dowry she brings to her husband, "normally only sons receive land" (*si rregull vetëm djemtë*).[2] Each son receives an equal share

[1] After the end of collectivisation (1992), land was returned on a familial basis without taking into account previous lineage property.

[2] According to existing law in Albania, daughters and sons have equal rights to family property. I have never heard, however, of female family members making use of this right. This would not be convenient when women leave their village of origin to live with their husbands in another village. People in general seem reluctant to apply this law. In 1995 a woman from Bilisht explained to me that it was better to share the property "within the family" (*brenda familjes*), i.e. according to the traditional mode, and that making use of the law would be

of property when the household or a part separates (*ndarje*), either upon marriage of the youngest son or upon the death of the father. Every son – except the youngest – is free to leave the house with his share of property upon marriage or shortly after (especially if there is no space in the house for the new couple). According to several informants, cohabitation of two or more brothers in the paternal house long after their marriage and even after the death of the father was more frequent in the past, before the Second World War. The house was then divided into two or more equal parts, each with its own entrance and its own courtyard and kitchen. Each brother, together with his wife and children, formed a separate social unit; the former unity of the paternal house was remembered by means of labelling it a brotherhood (*vëllazëri*). Such situations are rare today, although old houses that were divided for the use of two brothers may still stand in some villages.

This is an instance of how family organisation is perceived by people as evolving; there used to be more solidarity between brothers and between family members in general. Households are said to have been greater in size. "Thirty years ago," said a young man from Bilisht to me, "families in Albania, including Devoll, did not split into small units as they do today. Brothers lived together, even after they were married and had children. Up to 40 people lived in one house." Another man from Bilisht confirmed this claim: "Sons have a duty of mutual aid towards their parents (…). This mutual aid used to extend up to the third cousins."

The youngest son generally remains with his parents and inherits the paternal house (*trung*). His duty is to take care (*yzmet*) of his parents in their old days and he is thus called the 'pillar of the house' (*shtylla e shtëpisë*). A father has the obligation to provide his older sons with a new house or at least with a piece of land (*truall*) on which to build a new house. This is usually done by dividing the *truall* on which the paternal house was built as long as such a division was possible.

As a result, neighbouring houses are generally inhabited by families closely connected by patrilineal ties. They form a *mëhallë*, a group of houses between which solidarity and daily cooperation are expected. As a neighbourhood, it should be distinguished from the *lagje*, which has no such meaning and is more a spatial unit – defined by its position in the village and its topographic features and limits – than a social one.

The village territory is also perceived as changing. According to local discourse, there used to be fewer houses in each neighbourhood, and they used to be separated by gardens, cowsheds and barns. "In 1942," said a man from Miras, "houses were much more distant from one another. There might be only two houses in one neighbourhood. The rest was cultivated land." Today, houses are built very close to one another and gardens have been moved to the village periphery, with the exception of small courtyards (*oborr*) that are used as gardens. The densification of houses is seen as (and probably is) the result of the communist period. Villagers were not allowed to leave their villages and settle in towns, while the population

interpreted by others as a sign of strife within the family and, as such, as a shame (*turp*). At that time, there was little at stake since selling and buying land was then not permitted and family property was generally very small.

kept growing. "This is another consequence of collectivisation," said an old woman from Çipan,

> cowsheds and barns disappeared. Livestock was gathered into large collective cowsheds. Where the sheds and barns used to be, they built houses. That is why today houses are much closer to one another. It is a problem now that private livestock is back.

At the same time, villages were not allowed to expand; space demarked for the construction of houses was separated from arable land by a 'yellow line' (*vija e verdhë*) beyond which it was forbidden to build new houses, despite the pressure of population growth. Since migration, even to a neighbouring village, was forbidden in the communist period, the fragmentation of land inscribed in the devolution system could not be counterbalanced by migration away from the village nor by the buying and selling of vacant plots.

THE LINEAGE AND ITS NORTHERN MIRROR

This description clearly inscribes kinship and family organisation in Devoll within the wider frame of "Balkan patriarchy" (Halpern et al. 1996). It is not an isolated case and shares most of its features with neighbouring areas. As southerners, Devollis nevertheless claim to be different from northern Albanian as regards family organisation. They consider northerners to be much more patriarchal; northern families are marked by 'patriarchalism' (*patriarkalizëm*), which is condemned as a form of 'fanaticism' (*fanatizëm*). This is the case, for instance, for the number of children in a family or the solidarity between brothers and between fathers and sons, which are both said to be higher than in Devoll. The inferior position of women is also frequently stigmatised as something that makes northerners 'fanatics' (*fanatik*): Devollis who have lived in or travelled to northern Albania like to tell stories of how women are kept hidden from foreigners or confined to a role of servant.

All these representations of family life in the north come together with general representations on north and south in which the south and, from the Devollis' point of view, Devoll in particular appear as having 'culture' (*kulturë*) while the north lacks culture and has to acquire it by learning from southerners and imitating them (de Rapper 2004).

At the same time, Devollis look to Europe, and more specifically to neighbouring Greece, as a model of 'culture' that should be imitated and to which they are becoming closer, willing or not. This model, however, bears its own dangers. While northern family organisation is stigmatised as marked by an excessive form of solidarity, 'European' or 'Greek' family is seen as lacking solidarity. Children leave their old parents alone, brothers and sisters fight each other, couples divorce. In contrast to the northern woman, who is damned to be the servant of her husband, Greek women are seen as liberated beyond measure, they spend their time in cafés and bars and forget their family and household duties. The same distinction between lack of modernity and excess of modernity has been noted in Greece. Alexandra Bakalaki describes it as a product of dialectic of modernisation, between the desire to abandon traditional behaviour and the risk of producing "copies non conformes" of modernity (Bakalaki 2005: 318).

This does not mean that everything Devollis perceive about their family organisation is merely a 'socially constructed' reflection of their position within a web of power relations, between a backward north and a modern Greece. I would like here to look at four structural differences between Devolli and northern kinship and social organisation in an attempt to explain this situation: (1) lineage generation depth, (2) segmentary organisation, (3) lineage as political and military institution and (4) patrilinearity.

(1) Although kinship ties are well known and abundantly commented upon by people (the first thing to do when meeting a foreigner is to locate him in terms of kinship), their knowledge is generally limited to three or four generations before ego. I collected genealogies in 48 lineages in the villages of Menkulas, Miras, Sul and Vidohovë. In nearly half of these genealogies (48 percent), informants were able trace their lineage back to their great-grandfather i.e. three generations. In 29 percent of cases they were not able to do even this. In the remaining 23 percent of cases, informants were able to trace their genealogies back four, five or six generations before ego. I found no cases of deeper genealogical knowledge.

Devolli lineage is clearly a three generation lineage, comparable to the Greek *genia* described by Maria Couroucli for Corfu (Couroucli 1985). Although long-term presence in the region can be claimed as a source of prestige, there seems to be no interest in remembering kinship ties beyond three or four generations. Ancestors' collaterals are rapidly forgotten as being separated (*i ndarë*) from the lineage and forming new lineages. "At the beginning of the lineage (*fis*)," said a 70-year-old man from Menkulas, "there were three brothers; Alush, Sali and Alil. Alush was my grandfather. Their father's first name is not known. Their first cousins form another lineage (*soj*)." Actually, there seems to be a vested interest in forgetting distant relationships in order to enable marriages between lineages issuing from the same stem. This shallow memory stands in sharp contrast to the long genealogical lists collected by ethnographers in northern Albania (Durham 1909: 69; Zojzi 1977: 195). There also seems to be no trace of an ancestors' cult in Devoll.

(2) Lineage organisation in northern Albania and Kosovo has often been described as a segmentary system in which a *fis* is divided into several feet or legs (*këmbë*), each starting with one of the founder's sons. Each *këmbë* is divided into several brotherhoods (*vllazni*), which in turn are made up of several bellies (*bark*) and divided into houses (*shpi*). Each level has its own territorial counterpart and its own headman.[3]

Such a description does not fit the situation as observed in Devoll. The *fis* is made up of a certain number of houses, but no intermediary units are recognised

[3] See, i.e., in Daniel 1989: 54. Some authors have used Evans-Pritchard's terminology to describe lineage organisation among Kosovo Albanians: i.e. Backer 1979; Reineck 1991: 43-46.

between these two levels. The word *degë* (branch) is used to refer to a segment of a lineage, but has no influence on the way the lineage actually functions. In fact, when such a branch does begin to have an influence in the eyes of lineage members, it splits and forms a new lineage. The branch takes a new family name, generally based on a close ancestor's first name, and is no longer considered a segment of the original lineage anymore. After one or two generations, members of the two lineages can even intermarry. This was the case, for instance, with one of the largest lineages in Menkulas. The head of one of the branches (he was the son or grandson of the 'founder') chose a new family name, probably in the 1920s, and one of his grandsons later married a third cousin (before World War II) who still had the original family name, but whose father changed it for a new one in 1944 (fig. 1). The woman's brother, from whom I collected the genealogy, did not mention the marriage as a 'third cousin marriage' (which is normally forbidden), but as a regular marriage between two lineages, although he knew very well that both lineages once had the same name and issued from the same ancestor.

Figure 1. Marriage between branches of a lineage

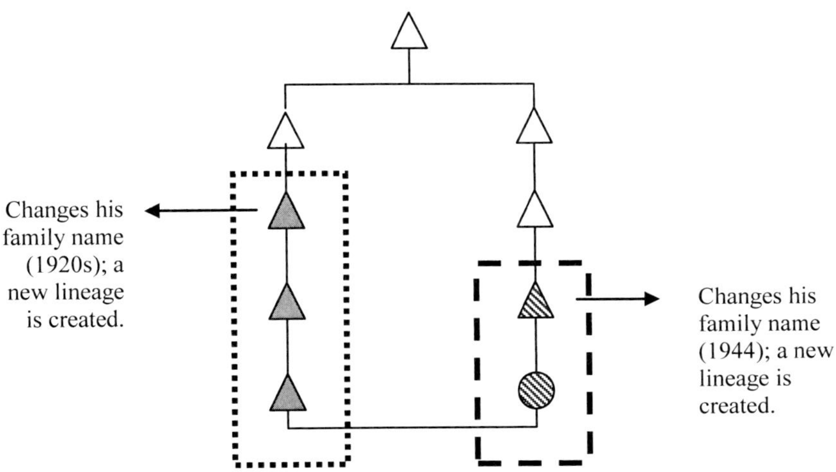

(3) A third feature of the lineage system as described in northern Albania is its existence as a political and military organisation in a specific territory, clearly marked and defended. Although command and military organisation are usually associated with the Ottoman *bayrak* rather than with the Albanian *fis* (Backer 1979: 92-93), the northern Albanian lineage seems also to have had political functions in a bounded territory, as defined in customary law (Doja 1999: 44).

Given the limited genealogical depth of Devolli lineages and the fission process by which new lineages are constantly appearing, the *fis* can hardly be associated with a stable territory larger than a small group of houses and a share of the village's fields, woods and pastures. Indeed, all villages are inhabited by several lineages, and although some of them have a specific relationship to village territory (as the founder of a new neighbourhood, for instance, or as 'old lineages' created a long time ago), none of them claim the village or neighbourhood as its own.

There are no traces of a military organisation, although carrying weapons seems to have been common up to World War II, and the political organisation is communal. Neighbourhoods send an elder (*plak*) to represent them at the village council and elect the village head (*kryeplak*). Different lineages compete to gain access to political functions on the village level, but these political functions are not imbedded in the lineage structure.

(4) Finally, although the Devoll lineage is a patrilineal descent group, as its northern counterpart, it does not exclude recognition of kinship, in terms of blood, through women. The distinction between 'blood' and 'milk' ancestry is not known in Devoll: blood (*gjak*) alone is the principle of kinship, and it runs through male as through female lines. Genealogies are known on the father's side as well as on the mother's, through males as through females, to at least three generations. Thus, for instance, two men from Miras, Abaz and Nesdan present themselves as cousins (*jemi kushërinj*) and add: "we are even cousins on both sides" (*bile jemi kushërinj nga dy anë*). Actually, their mothers are first cousins, while Abaz married Nesdan's patrilateral cross cousin's daughter (fig. 2). This is also the case for Bedri and Elona from Bilisht, who both claim to be related to Sami, mainly through female lines: Sami is Bedri's mother's maternal uncle, and he married the daughter of Elona's mother's maternal uncle (fig. 3). Those two examples reveal the generally precise knowledge of relations through female lines to at least three generations. It probably comes along with the ban on marriage in the mother's lineage: parents have to be located on both sides in order to avoid marrying someone belonging to the same ‚blood'. This stands in contrast to what has been reported for northern Albania on the absence of reckoning of kinship through women (cf. Durham 1909: 21; Coon 1950: 23).

Figure 2. Abaz and Nesdan

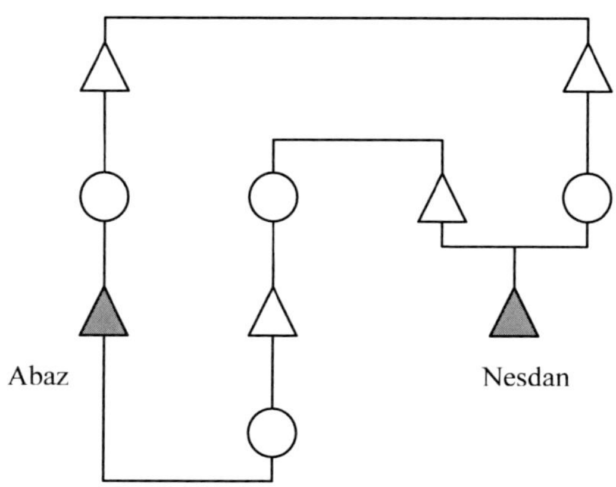

Figure 3. Elona, Bedri and Sami

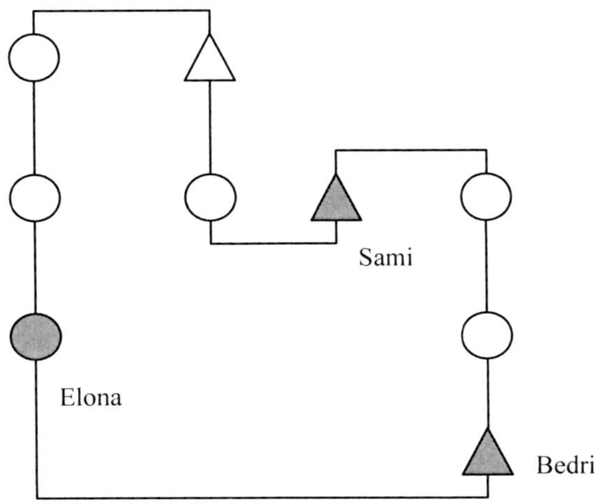

Devollis are thus probably right when they say that their family organisation differs from how it is – or how they think it is – in northern Albania. The clan and tribal image generally associated with northern Albanian society does not apply to Devoll. This does not mean however that we are dealing with two radically different societies. Before coming to the definition and functioning of the Devoll lineage system, it is worth considering a feature that illustrates similarities between northern and southern social organisation.

In Devoll, inhabitants of a given territory (a village, for instance) as well as their lineages, are classified according to their relation to this territory; a result of lineage fission, internal migration and the inheritance system. First come the 'big lineages' (*fiset e mëdhenj*) or 'old lineages' (*fiset e vjetër*), which both claim the longest presence in the village and the role of founders of a neighbourhood after arriving from another region in southern Albania or northern Greece. The *vendali* (locals, from *vend*, meaning country or place) are the ones who have no memory of an external origin and generally form the majority of the population. The most recent arrivals (*i ardhur*), who have only been in the village for one or two generations come last (de Rapper 2000: 458-459).

This categorisation of individuals and lineages on the basis of territory is reminiscent of the system reported for northern Albania. The population of a given territory is said to consist of three different stocks: 'dominants' (*pushtues*), who arrived from another place and conquered the land, 'natives' (*anas*), who were subdued by the conquering newcomers, and finally the most recent arrivals (*të ardhur, ardhacakë*), who are kept in a position of inferiority (Kostallari 1965: 38; Zojzi 1977: 188). Despite the differences of vocabulary and context, the conceptualisation of three distinct categories of people in a given territory appears to be the same in both northern and southeastern Albania.

THE LINEAGE: SEMANTIC HORIZONS

In order to understand what is meant by the term *fis* in Devoll and what it reveals about the kinship system, I suggest exploring three different meanings of the word and looking at other words expressing more or less the same notions in local speech. The three meanings are: (1) the principle of kinship, (2) the descent group and (3) (noble) origin. In this respect, the notions invoked by the word *fis* are in no way unfamiliar in the context of European and Mediterranean societies; they reflect the image of a patrilineal society in which blood is a metaphor for kinship and where belonging to social groups is a function of birth. It is worth noting that the origin of the word itself is not clear. Gustav Meyer first suggested a Modern Greek etymology from *physis* (nature, character) (Meyer 1891: 105). This etymology was later accepted by Eqrem Çabej, who confirms that the term must have been adopted after the eleventh century, but who points out a semantic evolution, especially in the north, from the Latin *gens* to *tribus*, i.e. from a limited descent group to a political organisation based on actual or fictitious common descent (Çabej 1996: 194). This reflects more or less the differences between northern Albanian and Devolli lineages as presented in the previous section. The shift from nature or character to *gens* however, remains unclear. It might indicate that members of a descent group are perceived as sharing common features, both physical and moral, which is, as we shall see, actually the case. It should also be noted that the root *gens* does exist in Albanian in a loan from Byzantine Greek *genea*, which appears in Albanian as *gjini* or *gjiri*, (kin, related) (Çabej 1996: 332-33). As opposed to *fis*, *gjini* does not focus on patrilinearity. It is often associated with *gjak*, (blood); the phrase *gjak e gjini* seems to designate all cognates. It is, however, not used in Devoll.

(1) The word *fis* is first used to express the principle of kinship, the very fact of being kin: *jemi fis* (we are related). At this stage, *fis* does not apply to any descent group in particular, it is not even strictly patrilineal, even though the general patrilineal colouration of the kinship system is more often present than not. In this context, *fis* can be replaced by the word *gjak*: (*nuk*) *jemi gjak* (we are (not) related).

The word *gjak* has been linked with the Slavic root *sok-* (sap) and with other Indo-European words (Çabej 1996: 311-12). In Albanian, apart from the family context, it means a kind of blood sacrifice (it is in this usage a close synonym to *kurban*) and it also means blood feud.

Contrary to examples from other societies, blood as principle of kinship does not come along with other anatomic metaphors; there seems to be no particular conceptualisation of veins. Neither is it associated with other corporal fluids as is the case with kinship concepts in northern Albania. In Devoll, for instance, blood is not opposed to milk. The 'tree of milk' (*lisi i tamblit*) and the 'tree of blood' (*lisi i gjakut*), as they appear in Gjeçovi's customary law (Gjeçovi 1993: 122), are unknown to the Devollis, who use, as do most southerners, the word *qumësht* for milk, instead of *tambël*. Relatives on the mother's side are not called the *lisi i tamblit* in opposition to the *lisi i gjakut* formed by relatives on the father's side.

They are called *fisi i mamasë* (mother's lineage) or *fisi i dajos* (mother's brother's lineage) and they do not differ in nature from relatives on the father's side.

As a principle of kinship, *gjak* and *fis* are exogamous; you have to marry 'outside blood' (*jashtë gjakut, jashtë fisit*). In this context, as already mentioned, relatives on the mother's side belong to the same blood and should not be married. "In order to marry within the village (*brenda fshatit*)," said a man from the Christian village of Qytezë, "three generations must pass on the mother's side, and four on the father's side. Up to third cousins, we are the same lineage (*soj*), we share the same blood (*gjak*), the same family name (*mbiemër*)." Muharem from the Muslim village of Miras, gives the same explanation:

> According to religion, you have to marry outside your lineage (*jashtë fisit*) for five generations. (…) When a man gets married in a lineage, his children, girls and boys, are not allowed to marry in their mother's lineage. The whole mother's lineage is considered maternal uncle (*dajë*).

A new marriage is possible only after four generations have passed, to avoid consanguinity (*bashkëgjakësi*)." The number of generations that have to pass before marriage is possible varies according to informants, generally from three to six.

The point is that contrary to what seems to be the case in northern Albania where, according to Gjeçovi, "blood goes endlessly (Gjeçovi 1993: 122)," blood has its limits in Devoll, which are the limits of collective memory.

> We do not marry within the lineage (*brenda fisit*), within four generations on both sides, more – five or six – when the grandparents are still alive. For the oldest know who is related to whom, they are still there to say: 'those two are related (*i kemi një soj, i kemi një gjak*), they cannot marry!'

Other examples confirm that blood goes as long as you remember it. Even when a common family name makes a common origin probable, it is not a blood relation as long as knowledge of the common ancestor has been lost: "Twenty families share our family name," said a man in Miras, "but they are not related (*nuk janë gjak*). The great-grandfather probably had a brother or a cousin [from whom the other families descend]."

(2) What distinguishes *gjak* from *fis* is that the latter also applies to an actual descent group, identified by a name, by its relations with other similar groups and by its relation to a specific territory. The *fis* name is the lineage members' *mbiemër* (literally: surname) or *llagap*. The identification of a lineage by its name is visible, for instance, in the fact that the number of lineages present in a village is generally expressed as a number of *mbiemër* (pl.: *mbiemra*). Naming is also involved in the act of founding a new lineage; members of the seceding branch chose a new llagap and are then recognised as a group distinct from their old lineage. This new name is generally formed on the basis of the first name or nickname of a common ancestor, which is why it is called *llagap*, a word derived (via Turkish) from the Arabic *lakab* (nickname). In this respect there also exists a kind of 'name exogamy'. People bearing the same family name should ideally not marry, even if the memory of a common origin has been lost. When this does occur, however, people insist on the fact that they are not *fis*, even though they have the same family name. Such is the case in Miras, where

the name of a neighbourhood's dominant lineage was adopted by another lineage living in the same neighbourhood:

> Faik's wife had the same family name as her husband, Muçka, but they are not related (*nuk janë gjak*). Her family used to be called Luke, but they took the name Muçka from the neighbourhood (*lagje*) where they lived at the beginning of communism[4]. Faik married a girl from his neighbourhood and who has the same family name, but who is not of the same lineage (*fis*)."

Each *fis* also has its own history and its elder(s) (*plak, pleq*) who are the bearers of this memory. The lineage history consists of its migration history to the village presently occupied by the *fis*, of settlement and expansion in one of the village neighbourhoods, of separation and fission and the role its members played in events of local or national history worth remembering. Included in this historical memory of the lineage are its relations with the other lineages of the village: who came first, who was more powerful, who was on the right or wrong side during World War II, etc. Connected to this history are also physical and moral features that are defined as lineage rather than individual features. A man is supposed to resemble his male ancestors, whose blood he has inherited. This is also true for career choices. One often hears: "as a lineage, we are merchants (*si fis, jemi në tregti*)" or "my father and grandfather were merchants."

Finally, each *fis* is associated with a specific neighbourhood, even if all its members do not actually live in this neighbourhood. In all these contexts the word *fis* cannot be replaced by *gjak*: a *gjak* has no name, no history and no territory. As a descent group, *fis* can be replaced, with some restrictions, by other words including *farefis*, *racë* or *soj*, all meaning 'a community based on common origin' or 'a group of people existing and acting as descendants of a common ancestor'.

The word *farefis* is clearly a compound of *farë* and *fis*. In Devoll, *farë* is used alone with the meaning of species or kind and also seed. It is, however, used in other parts of Albania as well as in some regions of Greece and among the Arumanians with the meaning of a more or less extended descent group, from a household to a lineage and to a gathering of several lineages or tribes (Çabej 1996: 142-45). Despite this generally accepted etymology, in Devoll the word is sometimes understood as being formed on the adverb *fare*, meaning entirely, totally or completely, and the word *fis*, giving the latter a wider extension: *farefis* is then the entire *fis*, it is, as one informant put it, something like *fis*, but broader (*më i zgjeruar*). Indeed, the uses of *farefis* reveal a much less patrilineal conception of kin. It is not a synonym for blood (*gjak*) and includes all relatives on the father's as well as on the mother's side.[5]

The word *racë* (race) denotes a large group of people having a common origin. It is frequently used as a synonym for nation (*komb*). One can hear talk of 'the Albanian race' (*raca shqiptare*) or of 'the Greek race' (*raca greke*) in the sense of

---

[4] After World War II and the communist rise to power, some families that had fought on the wrong side or belonged to lineages categorised by the communists as belonging to the opposition changed their surname in order to avoid political stigmatisation. This may have been the case here.

[5] In scholarly language, kinship as a field of social relations is expressed by the words *farefis* and *farefisni*; kinship system is sistem *farefisnor*. *Farefis*, unlike *fis*, has no tribal connotation.

nation. Both words also apply to religious communities, Christian and Muslim, as they are generally perceived as natural communities to whom one belongs by birth rather than by choice. It is not uncommon to hear about the 'nation of the Turks' (*kombi turk*), i.e. Muslims, or about the 'Christian race' (*raca e krishterë*), i.e. Christians. Both the nation and religious communities are conceived of as blood communities. This meaning is found in the kinship context to express common origin and the blood community of several lineages. In the village of Sinicë, for instance, one informant explained the links between three lineages saying that "the *fis* Guta and Damo come from the Panos, they are the same *racë*, the same *fis*."[6] As such the word *racë* is reminiscent of the use of the Greek term *ratsa* for a group of lineages (*genia*) who share the same last name without being able to trace their links back to a known common ancestor (Couroucli 1985: 68). As we have seen, however, in Devoll such relations between lineages are not considered; there is no word, for instance, for the different lineages who share the same family name, and a *racë*, contrary to a *fis*, is not identified by a common name. In the kinship context, the word *racë* is also used to stress the size of a family or lineage and to insist on their numerical importance. On the return of her brother from migration in Greece, where he had spent the last five years, a women from the village of Miras described how she had spent the whole afternoon at her parents' house, where the whole family was gathering for the occasion: "Children were running everywhere," she explained, "you could hardly go from one room to the other. Actually, I hardly saw my brother at all! The race was gathered (*ishte mbledhur raca*); he came back for the first time in three years." Clearly, the exceptional value of the event and its manifestation call for the use of *racë* rather than *fis*. A *fis* might be small or large, while a *racë* is a multitude.

The last word used to designate a group of people related by blood is *soj*. It comes from Turkish *soy* (literally: bone) and means a patrilineage in opposition to the flesh (Gokalp 1987: 83-84). It is in use in Greek (cf. du Boulay 1984) as well as in South Slavic (cf. Stahl 1979). Generally speaking, in Devoll, *soj* is interpreted and used as a synonym for *fis*. Like *fis*, *soj* is based on blood, has a limited genealogical depth and is identified by a name: "up to the third cousins, we are one *soj*, we share the same blood (*gjak*) and we have the same family name (*mbiemër*)." Like *fis*, *soj* is also the bearer of moral values attributed to its members. The compounds *sojli* and *sojsez*, borrowed from the Turkish, are thus synonyms for *pe fisi* (of lineage origin) and *pa fisi* (without lineage), which expresses nobility and respectability or the lack thereof.

The Macedonians of Devoll, who live in the village of Vërnik, make use of the words *soj* and *fis* with the meaning of family or kinship. However, they consider *fis* to be an Albanian loan, while *soj* sounds more Macedonian to them. The contrast between the exteriority of *fis* and interiority of *soj* also appears in the way Albanian Devollis use both words. Indeed, despite their often equivalent uses, *fis* and *soj* are two different things, or rather, two different aspects of the same reality. For instance, one will never hear that a village consists of a certain number of *soj* (the word is hardly ever used in the plural), but always that it is made up of several *fis*

[6] Note the two meanings of *fis* in the same sentence.

(pl.: *fise*). In order to identify a stranger, one possible question would be '*pe ç'fisi është ky*?' (from which *fis* is he?); in this case, *soj* has little chance of being used. On the other hand, *soj* is used in contexts where the descent group is conceived in its more practical and concrete dimensions, as a subsistence or work community. For instance, members of the lineage who are appealed to regularly in domestic or agriculture work or occasionally for the preparation of family events such as weddings or funerals are said to belong to the same *soj*. In this respect, *soj* is an expression of lineage solidarity and mutual help. It has less to do with identity and common origin than with manifestations of identity and common origin. If *fis* is an outward community, always considered in relation and opposition to other *fis*, *soj* is an inward community, it is the intimate facet of the lineage.

(3) Finally, each *fis* has its own history and, in most cases, a known origin, even if it is not far removed. Its origin is generally linked with the appearance of the *fis* name (*llagap, mbiemër*) and with its settlement on its *truall* or in the house still occupied by members of the *fis*.

In this context, *fis* is often heard together with the word *trung*. Deriving from the Latin *truncus*, the word means a tree trunk or a stump. In a kinship context, it designates the married couple – usually the speaker's grandparents or great-grandparents in the male line – who are the origin of the lineage (*fis*) or of the blood (*gjak*). Male children of this couple form the beginning of the branches (*degë*) which themselves divide in a process of ramification (*degëzim*). As one informant put it: "the grandfather and grandmother are the trunk, then come the branches (*gjyshi dhe gjyshja janë trungu, pastaj janë degët*)." It may also be heard that the trunk represents the farthest known ancestor and that each of his sons form the beginning of the main branches. The phrase familial trunk (*trungu familjar*) means a married couple with children, a potential new lineage.

The word *trung* also applies to a building, namely the oldest house in a neighbourhood, the one which was built and inhabited by the common ancestor. In this context, one can hear a specific house being referred to as the *trung* of the *fis* and of the *lagje* in which it stands. As houses in general are destroyed and rebuilt every two or three generations in order to gain in size and comfort, it often occurs that the house designated *trung* is not the actual house built by the ancestor but the one which stands on the same plot (*truall*) and which was passed down through the youngest sons.

Lands that one inherits as member of a lineage (paternal lands) are said to come 'from the lineage, as trunk' (*nga fisi, si trung*), they come not only from the father but from the common ancestor of the *fis* who first took possession of these lands.

If every married couple is a potential *trung*, the birth of a son and the beginning of a new branch make it a real *trung*, for the birth of a son is required to ensure that the house will carry on. "When a son is born to you," said a young father in the village of Miras, "the trunk does not die out *(trungu nuku shuhet*), it continues to have flames (*flagë*) and smoke (*tym*)." In this case, the tree image of a *trung* with its branches is mixed with another metaphor of common origin, the one of the hearth with its ever burning fire. The *trung* is also what is burning and what should not be extinguished. The image of the fire is invoked as the place of common origin, the lineage is identified with an original fire (*zjarr*). "A *fis*," said an elder from Miras, "is one blood (*një gjak*), they are the ones who come from the same fire (*pe një zjarri*)." Together with fire comes the reference to the hearth (*oxhak*) and fireplace (*vatër*) where the fire is burning. The metaphor of the hearth also invokes another aspect of fire, not only as primeval fire, but also as a place of common life and commensality. The censuses of the Ottoman era were made on the basis of the household, understood as a group of people living and eating around the same hearth; in other parts of the Balkans, the smallest social units were thus designated using words meaning hearth or smoke (Cvijic 1918: 225). Today, in Devoll, the size and relative importance of villages are still expressed in terms of numbers of houses (*shpi*) or smokes (*tym*), while the use of the word *oxhak* is maintained as a metaphor of common origin. Indeed, the fact that the house is generally inherited in the same blood means that it often constitutes the very place of common origin; the fire that is still burning in the fireplace is the same as the one that was burning when the grandfather owned the house and which was lit upon the birth of a son. Hence the phrase 'a son in the house opens the chimney' (*kur ke djalë në shpi, u hap oxhaku*).

Finally, the words *oxhak* and *fis* are used to express a sense of nobility and excellence attached to some important lineages. The phrases pe *oxhaku* (from the fireplace) and *pe fisi* (from the lineage) mean 'of good lineage' or 'of high birth'. When parents begin to think about marrying their sons, they consider potential brides and look for information about their lineages: are they from a good lineage (*nga fisi i mire*) or from the fireplace (*pe oxhaku*)? Already in the 17th century, Latin *nobilis* and *nobilitas* were translated in Albanian as *fissnich* and *fissnichia*, which are today *fisnik* and *fisnikëri* all derivatives of *fis* (Bardhi 1932: 66). To sum up the good things that make the 'honour of the house' (*nder i shpisë*), an informant from the village of Menkulas used the phrase "oak wood [in the fireplace] and a woman of high birth" (*dru pe lisi, grua pe fisi*).

CONCLUSION

This review of the various meanings of the word *fis* in Devoll thus reveals that it designates more than simply a lineage. Although the lineage observed is a relatively limited descent group composed of people descending through the male line from a common grandfather or great-grandfather, the word *fis* is also used for more abstract concepts such as kinship and common origin.

The comparison I have drawn between northern and southern lineage systems had a single purpose, namely to point out the structural differences between the two systems and initiate an examination of the southern Albanian lineage concept. One of the main differences is that the southern system is perpetuated via fission rather than via a segmentary principle. New lineages are created by fission and engage in intermarriage as exogamous units whose common origin is forgotten or at least made irrelevant. In a way, the system tends to transform parents into allies.

Although not effective in marriage arrangements, the concepts of kinship and common origin beyond the lineage are also expressed in the word *fis*. There are, however, contexts in which these concepts become relevant; the recognition of kinship is not only a matter of perpetuation of social units via a marriage and devolution system, it is also dependant of the use of kinship as a social resource. It is interesting, for example, to look at what becomes of the lines between kin and non-kin in the political context of 'class struggle' (*lufta e klasave*) as understood during the communist period (de Rapper 2006). People frequently refer to it as a principle according to which political stigmatisation of an individual automatically extended to their whole *fis*: "If you did something wrong towards the Party, your whole *fis* was punished." This is another example of how family and kinship organisation are embedded into wider representations of society, parallel to how Devollis perceive themselves as southerners in opposition to northerners.

BIBLIOGRAPHY

Backer, Berit 1979 Behind the Stone Walls. Changing household organization among the Albanians in Yugoslavia. Oslo: PRIO-Publications.

Bakalaki, Alexandra 2005 L'envie, moteur de l'imitation. Ethnologie française Vol. 35(2) pp. 317-327.

Bardhi, Frang 1932 Dictionarium latino-epiroticum (1635), édité par Mario Roques Paris: Paul Guethner.

Çabej, Eqrem 1996 Studime etimologjike në fushë të shqipes, vëll. IV (DH-J) Tirana: ASHSH.

Coon, Carleton S. 1950 The Mountains of Giants: a Racial and Cultural Study of the North Albanian Mountain Ghegs Cambridge, (Mass.): Peabody Museum of American Archeology and Ethnology.

Couroucli, Maria 1985 Lignage, dot et héritage In: Colette Piault (ed.) Famille et biens en Grèce et à Chypre Paris: L'Harmattan pp. 67-93.

Cvijic, Jovan 1918 La péninsule balkanique Paris: A. Colin.

Daniel, Odile 1989 Montagnes tribales et coutumiers In: L'Ethnographie Vol. 106 pp. 43-74.

de Rapper, Gilles 2000 Entre masculin et féminin. La vierge jurée, l'héritière et le gendre à la maison In: L'Homme 154-155 pp. 457-466.

de Rapper, Gilles 2002 Espace et religion: chrétiens et musulmans en Albanie du Sud. Etudes balkaniques. In: Cahiers Pierre Belon Vol. 9 pp. 17-39.

de Rapper, Gilles 2004 Les Guègues et les Tosques existent-ils? L'opposition Nord/Sud en Albanie et ses interprétations. In: Espace, Populations, Sociétés Vol. 3 pp. 625-640.

de Rapper, Gilles 2006 La 'biographie': parenté incontrôlable et souillure politique dans l'Albanie communiste et post-communiste In: European Journal of Turkish Studies Vol. 4 http://www.ejts.org/document565.html.

Doja, Albert 1999 Morphologie traditionnelle de la société albanaise In: Social Anthropology Vol. 7(1) pp. 37-55.

du Boulay, Juliet 1984 The Blood: Symbolic Relationships Between Descent, Marriage, Incest Prohibitions and Spiritual Kinship in Greece In: Man Vol. 19(4) pp. 533-556.

Durham, M. Edith 1909 High Albania London: Edward Arnold.

Durham, M. Edith 1928 Some Tribal Origins Laws and Customs of the Balkans London: George Allen and Unwin.

Gjeçovi, Shtjefën 1993 Kanuni i Lekë Dukagjinit Tirana: Albinform.

Gokalp, Altan 1987 "Le Dit de l'os et du clan". De l'ordre segmentaire oghouz au village anatolien In: L'Homme Vol. 102 pp. 80-98.

Halpern, Joel M., Karl Kaser and Richard Wagner 1996 Patriarchy in the Balkans: Temporal and Cross-Cultural Approaches. The History of the Family Vol. 1(4) pp. 425-442.

Kostallari, Androkli 1965 Contribution à l'histoire des recherches onomastiques dans le domaine de l'albanais In: Studia Albanica Vol. 2(1) pp. 32-54.

Meyer, Gustav 1891 Etymologisches Wörterbuch der albanesichen Sprache Strasburg: Karl J. Trübner.

Reineck, Janet Susan 1991 The Past as Refuge: Gender, Migration, and Ideology Among the Kosova Albanians. Ph.D. Dissertation submitted to the Faculty of of Arts, University of California at Berkeley.

Schweitzer, Peter P. (ed.) 2000 Dividends of Kinship London and New York: Routledge

Stahl, Paul H. 1979 Sociétés traditionnelles balkaniques. Contribution à l'étude des structures sociales Paris: EHESS.

Whitaker, Ian 1968 Tribal Structure and National Politics in Albania, 1910-1950 In: I.M. Lewis (ed.) History and Social Anthropology London: Tavistock pp. 253-293.

Zojzi, Rrok 1977 Survivances de l'ordre du fis dans quelques micro-régions de l'Albanie In: La Conférence nationale des études ethnographiques, 28-30 juin 1976 Tirana: ASHSH pp. 185-206.

Zonabend, Françoise 1981 Le très proche et le pas trop loin. Réflexions sur l'organisation du champ matrimonial des sociétés à structures de parenté complexes In: Ethnologie française Vol. 11(4) pp. 311-318.

6. Education and the Integration of the Province of Gjirokastër in interwar Albania

Nathalie Clayer

During the Ottoman period, the regions that were later included in the Prefecture of Gjirokastër had been both under the influence of Greek and Ottoman cultures and had produced numerous elites, among the Christians as well as among the Muslims. In the late Ottoman Empire, a dense network of Christian (Greek) primary schools developed in the region, with centres in Ioannina, Istanbul and Athens. In order to counter its influence, the Ottoman authorities decided in the 1880s to reinforce and renewed their own network of schools, centred on Ioannina and Istanbul.

In interwar Albania, in the first phase of the state-building process in this new independent country, the question of education was generally of particular importance, but it was even more important in this southern Albanian province, placed under Albanian administration in 1920 after a seven year Greek and Italian occupation. In this paper I want to examine this issue of education in southern Albania in presenting firstly how the state authorities saw the issue and developed their policy on the matter. Then, in a second part, I will analyse how the local actors saw the education issue and how they behaved in that field. In the last part I will consider a specific issue, namely that of the existence of a lyceum in Gjirokastër, which developed to become the heart of a debate between the political authorities and the local intellectuals.

The View from the State

Education: a tool for the nationalisation of society

Like in other countries, officials and politicians in inter-war Albania saw education as being crucial for the building of the state and the nation. Consequently they wanted to control the school network directly, to develop and to use it for their own purposes. This wish was all the more strong because they felt that the Ottoman system had permitted 'foreign propaganda' (i.e. the diffusion of Greek, Romanian, Italian and other national ideas) to develop through school networks. In 1922, the Minister of Education, using this argument, wrote to the Prime Minister that because primary education was particularly important, it was necessary to control the primary schools, their teachers, their financial support and their hygiene (Kaso 2003: 28). Another prominent aspect of state policy concerning education was its secularisation, since religion had an important place in the various school networks of the Ottoman period and the clergy was seen as having been an important channel for the mentioned 'foreign propaganda' (Peters 2003: 38-39; Gogaj 2004: 95-97, 124-127).

Southern Albania, and particularly the Prefecture of Gjirokastër, was a sensitive region from this point of view, since the most wide-spread educational network there at the end of the Ottoman rule was that of the 'Greek schools', serving the Orthodox Christian population. Since the Albanian government recognised the rights of minorities as a member of the League of Nation in October 1921, these Greek schools were legalised, but only in Greek-speaking villages, and could continue to function or reopen (those that had been closed during the Italian occupation of 1916-1920). From the point of view of the state, the existence of Greek schools (of varied status and with private or publicly financed teachers)[1] represented a problem for the integration of the 'Greek-speaking minority' and more generally for the integration of the Orthodox Christians. They were the only non-Albanian schools remaining in the region after Albanian state schools (henceforth for Muslims and Christians alike) had replaced the 'Ottoman schools' in Muslim villages and the 'Greek schools' in Christian villages, while Aromanian (Kostelanik 1996) and Italian schools had been closed.[2] Furthermore the Greek schools remained much more frequented than the Albanian schools. In 1922 for example, in the Prefecture of Gjirokastër there were ninety three 'Albanian schools' with only 3855 pupils, while there were thirty two 'Greek schools,' with 2297 pupils (Mema and Shahu 2001: 232).[3] And the Greek school network frequented by children from the region also extended across the border into Greek territory (Gogaj 2004: 98; Clayer 2004: 165).

During the 1920s and 1930s the successive governments made efforts to control the existing schools, even the Greek ones, which were slowly 'Albanised' with the introduction of the teaching of the Albanian language, the progressive substitution of Greek by Albanian as teaching language and the obligation that the teachers know Albanian until they were completely nationalised in 1933, when all private schools were closed down in the country (Clayer 2004: 161-162). As an example of these measures, we can take the order given in August 1932 by the Minister of the Interior to the Minister of Education to henceforth replace the local teachers, official and private, in Greek-speaking villages with non-local teachers so as to avoid the

---

[1] All 'Greek schools' were taken under Albanian authority in 1920. As of 1923, Greek villages were again granted the right to open privately funded schools and to fund additional teachers in state schools. The Albanian authorities nevertheless suspected that the funding for these private schools and teachers to come from Greece. Between 1933 (nationalisation of education in the whole country) and 1935, the remaining Greek schools were transformed into state schools; in September 1935 they became all private schools again, funded by the villages themselves and/or Greek institutions.

[2] As we will see below, an Italian technical school opened in Gjirokastër in the interwar period.

[3] The Greek-speaking population represented only around a quarter of the total population of the province (*Arkivi Qëndror i Shtetit* (AQSh), Tirana, F. 152 (*Ministria e Punëve të Brendëshme*), v. 1924, d. 146/2, fl. 36). In 1924, the population of the Prefecture amounted to 125,000 inhabitants, that is, 15 percent of the total population. A slight majority was Orthodox Christian and of these a slight majority was Greek-speaking. Around 4,000 Christian Orthodox were Aromanians (Mema and Shahu 2001: 30-33). The number of schools varied a great deal during the interwar period, particularly the Greek schools, but proportionally, the school network seems to have remained denser in the Christian (both Greek and Albanian) villages.

development of "the anti-national propaganda supported by the Greek state." The Minister of Education answered that the Ministry had appointed non-local teachers trained at the teachers' training college in Elbasan.[4] As a result of the opinion of the International Court of The Hague in favour of the Greek minority in 1935, however, the private Greek schools could reopen and function more freely than before (Clayer 2004:162).

The quantitative limitations of education policy

Apart from this indirect international intervention into Albanian policy, the Albanian governments had to cope with important internal shortcomings in implementing their educational policy. They were sometimes forced to close down schools because of financial limitations. In 1922, for example, eighteen schools were closed in the province of Gjirokastër (Mema and Shahu 2001: 232). Especially at the beginning of the 1920s, teachers and school buildings were lacking, particularly in mountainous areas, and communication problems also limited the impact of the school network (Kaso 2003: 11). In the region of Kurvelesh (northwest of Gjirokastër) for example, primary schools were few, as in other predominantly Muslim areas in the Sub-Prefectures of Tepelenë and Përmet. Of course this was also a sign of the lack of interest, or the lack of means on the part of the local population for the development of education, since, as we will see later, like during the Ottoman period, school buildings were often built by the village community itself and philanthropy continued to play a major role in the education system. Philanthropy was even encouraged by the authorities, since the state was unable to face the situation alone.

As for secondary and tertiary education, it was limited to one or two secondary establishments in Gjirokastër, and children were obliged to continue their education outside the province (in Korçë, Tiranë or Shkodër) or even abroad, notably in Greece, but this only concerned a very small minority. According to statistics from 1924, 260 students from the region of Gjirokastër were studying abroad, of which 234 were being financed by family alone, nineteen had an Albanian and seven a Greek state scholarship (Kaso 2003: 43). With time the number of state scholarships increased, but their distribution was problematic since nepotism, which also existed for the appointment of teachers, was widespread (Kaso 2003: 103). In April 1927, *Demokratia* (n°100: 2), the newspaper published in Gjirokastër, denounced the fact that scholarships were being given to close relations of parliamentary deputies.[5]

---

[4] AQSh, F. 195 (*Ministria e Arsimit*), v. 1932, d. 110, fl. 80-81. Petro Marko (2000: 99) mentions the arrival of these teachers trained in Elbasan.

[5] In October 1930, *Demokratia* (n°270: 2) reported that the Minister of Education had had the courage to repeal the scholarships of the sons of rich parents, especially the sons of Ministers and Members of Parliament.

The qualitative limitations of education policy

But problems were not only quantitative, they were also qualitative. Indeed, the reality of the development of education on the ground was the complex result of policies decided centrally by different actors (the Ministry of Education, the Ministry of the Interior, the Council of Ministers, etc.) and the activities of officials at different levels, policies and activities that were often in conflict. To give an example, we can take the problem that occurred in 1928 in the region of Konispol concerning a Greek school. According to a letter from the Prefect of Gjirokastër addressed to the Inspector, this school had been closed down by order of the Sub-Prefect who had been informed by the local Director of Schools that the teachers had not presented the requested documentation. The Prefect ordered the immediate reopening of the school and demanded that schools not be closed according to such a procedure (Kaso 2003: 143).

The problems in establishing a harmonised educational system was also due to the fact that the authorities were obliged to build a system out of heterogeneous pieces. In particular, the teachers had extremely different profiles and qualifications. Petro Marko, a well-known Albanian poet from Dhërmi (Himarë) and for a time teacher in the Greek village of Dhuvjan in Dropull (south of Gjirokastër), describes this situation describing his two colleagues, one a Muslim from the region of Sarandë who was a graduate of the teachers' training school of Elbasan and the other a Greek-speaker from Dropull who had studied at the Christian Orthodox religious school in Vella (in Greece, north of Ioannina) (Marko 2000: 99). In a list of thirty three teachers working in the district of Gjirokastër drawn up in 1925 we can see that some of them only had a primary school education while others had been to a secondary school (Ottoman-Turkish, Greek, etc.) Some had at least gone to a higher school and few had finished. Only a minority was trained in a teachers' training school, and only one had studied two years at the Athens University (Kaso 2003: 57-58). Twelve years later the teaching staff was much more homogeneous. For example, among the active teachers in the districts of Delvinë, Sarandë and Konispol, almost the half had graduated from the teachers' training schools of Elbasan and, to a lesser extent, Korçë. About ten Christian teachers had finished a teachers' training school or a secondary school in Greece, while other teachers had been to a secondary school in Albania (Kaso 2003a: 354-356).

These teachers, situated at the bottom of the education system, were in a position, sometimes at the same time, to be the most fervent promoters of the nationalisation of society and potential political opponents of the regime. In 1928, for example, the director of the boarding school in Sarandë suggested to the Ministry that it order the local police to punish Albanians who were caught speaking Greek in the town, explaining that he had himself condemned such behaviour in meetings where he had some authority.[6] Petro Marko explained that as a teacher in the Dropull he removed the icons from the classroom, replacing them with portraits of Ismail Qemal, Skanderbeg and King Zog because it was a 'state school.' He also tried to convince the pupils and the villagers that, although a 'minority,' they had to study

[6] AQSh, F. 195, v. 1929, d. 7, fl. 151.

the Albanian language because their fatherland was Albania (Marko 2000: 99, 104-106).[7] In this sphere, teachers (or school inspectors) sometimes went even further than the central authorities desired. In the inspection reports teachers were judged not only on their abilities as educators but also on their patriotism (cf. Kaso 2003: 124-130).

As educated people, (often young) teachers began to occupy an important place in the social and political life of society. Under the leadership of the Avni Rustemi,[8] some of them created in 1921 a professional association called the *Lidhja e Mësuesve* (League of Teachers)[9] in the region of Gjirokastër. Their goal was to defend the profession, to develop education in the country and co-operate with other associations, in particular the federation *Atdheu* (Fatherland) in promoting the democratic unity of the Albanian people. Like Avni Rustemi, some of them even took an active part in politics, which made them suspect for the authorities. In January 1925, the school inspector provided the Ministry with a list of teachers who participated to the 'most recent revolt' (i.e. the June Revolution of 1924 against the Zog government) in the regions of Gjirokastër and Përmet.[10] In the same way, after a secret organisation was discovered in 1933, the local authorities were asked to draw up a list of suspects among the teaching staff. Then, investigations were made. Some teachers were cleared, others remained suspect and the Prefect proposed to transfer them to the north of the country, because they were from Gjirokastër and had local connections. Whereas the Minister of the Interior agreed with this idea, the Minister of Education thought that if they were dangerous, they were so everywhere and consequently it was necessary to dismiss them from any teaching function.[11]

THE VIEW FROM THE LOCAL POPULATION

Adapting to local specificities

We have seen that teachers and school inspectors were in a central position to realise the nationalisation of society. When they were native to the province in which they worked they could also be more flexible than the central authorities, adapting education policy to local specificities. For instance, in 1921, despite the wish to Albanise the education system, the local school inspector thought that it was important to continue teaching religion in the Greek language in

[7] He nevertheless found "fanatical" the local officials who castigated the villagers who greeted one another saying *kalimera* (hello in Greek) instead of *mirëdita* (in Albanian).

[8] Avni Rustemi was from Libohovë. He was born in 1895 and studied at a *rüshdiye* and at the teachers' training school in Elbasan before beginning to teach in different places. Later he went to Italy to study. In 1920, he murdered Esad Pasha Toptani in Paris. He was himself victim of an assassination attempt in 1924, which led to the 'June Revolution'.

[9] This association existed at least until 1924 (Mema and Shahu 2001: 202-204).

[10] AQSh, F. 195, v. 1925, d. 96, fl. 4.

[11] AQSh, F. 152, v. 1933, fl. 15-17.

order to keep the Christian Orthodox children in the Albanian schools (Kaso 2003: 18). In 1929, when the government was developing a project to open a boarding school for Greek-speaking children in Labovë (in the region of Rrezë, northeast of Gjirokastër), Branko Merxhani, a contributor to the local newspaper but also a deputy school inspector, wrote in a report for the Minister that this idea had not been well received by the local Albanian Christians from Rrezë, Zagori and Lunxhëri and that it would be better to accept children from the Albanian-speaking villages of these areas in the future school. The inspector, however, intervened against what he considered an attempt by Branko Merxhani to interfere in the Greek-speaking teaching and, as a matter of fact, the project was never realised.[12]

Choices made from below

Beyond the diverse positions of the local officials involved in the structuring of education, the local population at large also had its own views, its own interests and its own strategies concerning education choices. At the beginning of 1921, the school inspector in Gjirokastër noted the varied interests the local population had in education. At that time two kinds of schools existed: Albanian and Greek ones. However, interest for the Albanian schools was very limited, on the part of both Christians and Muslims. The former wanted teaching to be in Greek because of their Greek culture, while the latter had no real interest at all in education or for sending their children to school. According to the inspector, Greek villages hastened to demand the opening of schools, whereas the Albanian-speaking villages were indifferent or could not be heard since the law stipulated a minimum of 40 children and their villages were too small (Kaso 2003: 16-18). That is why, proportionally, the number of Greek schools was much higher than that of the Albanian ones.

In the following years there were repeated reports on children not being sent to school on the part of Albanian parents and the attempts to fine them (Kaso 2003: 132, 133-134).[13] According to *Demokratia* (n°287: p.3), illiteracy was still considerably widespread in the province in 1931. In the town of Gjirokastër, young craftsmen were almost all illiterate. In the whole country, 60 percent of children between six and thirteen years-of-age did not go to school; only 300 primary schools existed for 2,500 villages. In the Prefecture of Gjirokastër, however, not only the non-frequenting of schools by (generally Muslim) children was a problem, as we have seen; there was also the problem of the fact that Christian families (generally Greek-speaking but sometimes also Albanian-speaking) preferred to send their children to boarding schools in Greece where the Greek government had set up a network of schools for just that purpose.

However systematically interpreting the frequenting of schools in Greece as a rejection of the system proposed by the Albanian state would be false. Of course,

[12] AQSh, F. 195, v. 1919, d. 390, fl. 8-12.

[13] In 1921 a law was passed that made primary education compulsory for children between seven and twelve years-of-age, but it was not really enforced.

for some parents this was certainly a reaction against Albanian policy. For others however, the problem was the level of the schooling, which they felt not to be sufficient in Albania. For some it could simply have been a question of convenience. The choice was not necessarily ideological; tradition, family and friendship networks, as well as other conditions were all determining factors, as we can see in the example of Dhimitër Beduli. Born in July 1914 in the Greek-speaking village of Skore in the northern Pogon region east of Gjirokastër that was incorporated into the Albanian state in 1920, the young Dhimitër first went to the village school. Then, when he was twelve years old, he had to go away either to work or study, as was tradition (not to go away was socially depreciating). It was no longer possible to send him to Istanbul as had been the case previously and he was not qualified to get a Greek scholarship for one of the boarding schools founded on the other side of the border, since his grandfather, who was a teacher, had collaborated with the Albanian authorities. He could not get a scholarship from the Albanian government either. The only solution for the family was to accept the help of an aunt whose husband was from Poliçan (a nearby village) and had a friend, a pharmacist, living in Athens. In 1925 Dhimitër Beduli left Skore for Athens, where he worked in the pharmacy and studied in the lyceum. Graduating in 1930, he then studied theology in Romania thanks to a recommendation by two fellow villagers to the High Council of the Albanian Orthodox Church. Back in Albania in 1934, Dhimitër Beduli was to become an architect of the Albanisation of the Orthodox Church in Albania (Beduli 1999: 27-39).

Intellectual capital: a resource for some families

For many Christian families, but also for some urban Muslim families from Gjirokastër and Libohovë, investing in intellectual capital had for decades been an economic and social strategy. The Prefecture was well known for its elites, both Muslim (Clayer 2006) and Christian. The number of graduates from diverse universities native to the province was quite significant, as can be seen in the lists drawn up by the Albanian administration in the 1920s.[14] Muslim families with a high status continued to invest in this kind of capital and in doing so often sent their children farther abroad to complete their higher education, especially to Italy and France, but also to Germany or Austria.[15] The local newspaper, *Demokratia*, often reported on their return to the province on the occasion of the summer holidays or at the end of their studies (for example n°162: 1; n° 190: 1; n°412: 2; n°413: 2; n° 418: 3; n°564: 2; n° 586: 2; n°607: 3).[16] Whereas some of these students had received a state scholarship (such as

[14] AQSh, F. 195, v. 1926, d. 104; F. 294 (Prefektura e Gjirokastrës), pa vit, d. 871, fl. 11

[15] AQSh, F. 195, v. 1922, d. 31, fl. 1-2; v. 1936, d. 263, 6, 7, 185-189, 196.

[16] In August 1932 the newspaper announced the death of Vehap Ciu, a graduate of the Agronomy Institute in Montpellier, and mentioned the eulogy held by Enver Hoxha in the name of all his friends, during the burial ceremony held in Gjirokastër (*Demokratia*, n°342: 2). Enver Hoxha, the future leader of communist Albania was born in 1908 in Gjirokastër. He studied in Gjirokastër in the newly opened lyceum in 1923. When the lyceum was closed in 1928 he went to the French lyceum in Korçë. In 1930 he received a state scholarship and went to

the well-known linguist Eqrem Çabej, son of the former *cadi* of Durrës), many were supported financially by their own families.

At a lower level, a significant number of young Muslims went to the Italian technical school on Corfu, which provided training in accounting and commerce. In October 1930 they numbered more than sixty, many of them coming from the province of Gjirokastër, but also from the Prefectures of Vlorë and Korçë as well as from central Albania. In summer 1932 most of the graduates were Albanians, Muslims as well as Christians, from the province of Gjirokastër (*Demokratia*, n° 270: 2, 4 and n°339: 1). As far as the Orthodox Christians are concerned, Greece was naturally a more frequent choice for secondary and tertiary studies (and even primary school, as we have seen). In 1930 there were twenty four students from Albania (all of them Orthodox) at the University of Athens, the majority of them from the province of Gjirokastër. Only two of them had an Albanian scholarship.[17] In 1937 there were 112 Orthodox Christians (again generally native of Gjirokastër) studying in Greece, more often than not medicine or law.[18] Apart from Greece, Orthodox Christian students could be found studying in Italy, in France, in Austria and even in Istanbul.[19]

SECONDARY STUDIES IN ALBANIA

The case of secondary studies is far more interesting than that of primary education (which was compulsory) and that of tertiary education which was necessarily to be done abroad. In inter-war Albania, there existed only a few state secondary schools (among them the lyceums of Korçë, Tirana and Shkodër and for a time Gjirokastër, an American technical school in Tirana, an agricultural school in Lushnjë, Jesuit and Franciscan lyceums in Shkodër and a teachers' training school in Elbasan). It seems that these establishments attracted an ever increasing number of young people from Gjirokastër and surroundings, for various reasons, and contributed to the integration of provincial society to the Albanian state.

Particularly the teachers' training schools in Elbasan became a frequent passage for the integration of young students from the province into the national education system. These students were generally born into middle or low status families. For them, becoming a teacher was a means of social climbing and secured a small income in a period of economic insecurity. In many Muslim families from Gjirokastër, but also from the small town of Libohovë and from the village of Fterrë

Montpellier to study biology. After three years he moved to Paris, where he registered at the School of Political Sciences. He then worked one year at the Albanian embassy in Brussels before returning to Albania – without a degree (Asllani 2003: 212).

[17] AQSh, F. 195, v. 1930, d. 103, fl. 58-59.

[18] AQSh, F. 195, v. 1936, d. 263, fl. 208-210.

[19] AQSh, F. 195, v. 1936, d. 263, fl. 5-6, 166, 189-187, 196.

(west of Gjirokastër), boys were sent to this establishment, especially in the 1930s, when the economic situation became even more acute.[20]

Orthodox Christians also began to frequent these secondary schools, but apparently less often. Otherwise *Demokratia* would have not reported so meticulously in September 1930 that the doctors Nathanaili and Labovitiadi as well as the teacher Vidhuri had decided to send their sons to the lyceum of Korçë, financing it themselves, despite the fact that one of the boys had already studied in Athens for three years (*Demokratia*, n°269: 2). At the beginning of the 1930s a young Christian from the village of Kakos (in Lunxhëri, an Albanian-speaking region) applied for a scholarship to study at the new teachers' training school in Gjirokastër, arguing that he was the first in the region to apply for such a thing.[21] Shortly before, even Greek-speaking families in the region of Delvinë were beginning to apply for Albanian scholarships for their sons to study in secondary schools in Albania, such as the teachers' training school in Elbasan, the lyceum in Korçë or the American technical school in Tirana. In 1931, for example, there were five Greek-speaking scholarship-holders enrolled in the teachers' school in Gjirokastër.[22] We can assume that they were from families with a low income or with a good resource network in Albania.

THE QUESTION OF THE LYCEUM, OR TWO WAYS OF BUILDING THE NATION, FROM THE CENTRE AND FROM THE PERIPHERY

To better understand the interplay between the different dynamics contributing to the development of the provincial school network and beyond that to the nation-building process, it is interesting to analyse more in detail the question of the lyceum of Gjirokastër.

A short-lived lyceum

The idea of founding a secondary school in Gjirokastër came first from local schoolteachers, at a time when the centralisation of the state was not proving very effective. The above-mentioned *Lidhja e Mësuesve* (League of teachers) began in 1921 to agitate in favour of founding a 'Western' school in order to professionally train a new generation. Based on its close ties to the diaspora in the United States[23], its members thought to open a mixed American-Albanian high school. An American Protestant missionary, Professor E. Jones from the Board of the Methodist Church in New York, came to Gjirokastër for that purpose, but the attempt failed because of the lack of support on the part of the

---

[20] Cf. http://fterra2.tripod.com/id8.html; newspaper Libohova (Tirana, since 2002).
[21] AQSh, F. 195, v. 1931, d. 93, fl. 172
[22] AQSh, F. 152, v. 1925, d. 215, fl. 8 ; F. 195, v. 1931, d. 93, fl. 18.
[23] Many migrants from the province, Christians as well as Muslims, lived in the United States.

local population and the national government (Mema and Shahu 2001: 234-235; Asllani 2003: 70-71).[24]

Two years later the local authorities, having been persuaded that it would be a good means to counter 'negative propaganda,' welcomed the idea and succeeded in convincing the government in Tirana. Local administrators in Gjirokastër underlined in their reports that there was a discrepancy between the poor conditions offered by the state in the field of education and the demands of the population. They added that the prohibition of the Greek language (the former teaching language in Christian schools) in state schools pushed many parents to send their children to study in Greece. Faced with this problem, some local civil servants thought that a solution could be the opening of a lyceum where a European language like French would be used beside Albanian in order to compete with Greek.[25]. In the summer of 1923, the Albanian Parliament voted to found a French-Albanian lyceum in Gjirokastër, which opened that October, with French and Albanian teachers and around forty students (Asllani 2003: 71).

However, the new institution was to have a short life. Firstly, it was not complete and had only six classes. To finish their studies, students would have to go to the French lyceum in Korçë. The establishment only had a technical and administrative director for the first year. The curriculum was never completed and the lyceum was closed in 1928 to be replaced by a technical school and later, in January 1931, by a teachers' training school (*Demokratia*, n°117: 2; n°273: 2; n°355: 2; n°368: 2; n°388: 1).[26] The lyceum of Gjirokastër was reopened at the beginning of the 1935-36 school year, but the central authorities continued to put a question mark over it. In September 1938 a new law made provisions for only three lyceums in the country (in Korçë, Tirana and Shkodër) and the transformation of the lyceum in Gjirokastër into a technical school, since technical education was in future to be favoured (*Demokratia*, n°619: 1,3; n°622: 1). This decision was apparently never implemented.[27]

In fact, the issue reveals quite acutely the problem of the place of the province within the Albanian state and the tension existing between different points of view, that of the central authorities, that of the local authorities and that of young local intellectuals concerned with the nation-building process.

---

[24] American missionaries had opened several prestigious schools in the Ottoman Empire such as the Robert College in Istanbul. They had already opened Albanian schools at the end of the Ottoman period (for instance a girl's school in Korçë) and were already involved in the founding of other schools in Albania (in 1926 they opened an American school in Kavajë, while the American Red Cross opened a technical school in Tirana in 1921).

[25] AQSh, F. 195, viti 1923, d. 66, fl. 162.

[26] AQSh, F. 195, v. 1929, d. 66. When the lyceum was closed, around fifty students went to the lyceum of Korçë (Asllani 2003: 71). In June 1932, the government planned to transfer the teachers' training school to Qestorat (Lunxhëri) (*Demokratia*, n°333 : 1).

[27] The lyceum seems to have continued to exist during the Italian (1939-1943) and the German (1943-1944) occupations, as well as during the early socialist period.

The question of the lyceum as seen from the centre

Seen from Tirana, the lyceum in Gjirokastër was only one secondary school among others in an integrated national education system, the functioning of which was severely hindered by financial shortages.[28] In such a context, the establishment in Gjirokastër seems to have been less important than the three other lyceums.[29]

This does not mean that the Albanian central authorities were trying to marginalise the province of Gjirokastër. The idea to open a technical school or a teacher's training school (as implemented in January 1931) rather than a lyceum was perhaps better for the state-building process in the region. A lyceum tended to address the elites whereas a teachers' training school would attract many more pupils of more modest extraction from areas that had not been well integrated until then, such as the mountainous region of Kurvelesh.[30]

Besides, it is clear that the central authorities were also very sensitive to the particular situation of this frontier province where an important Greek minority was living and where they saw the dangerous development of what they called 'Greek propaganda' against the 'interests of the state'. The sudden change in Tirana's policy in 1935 and the decision to reopen the lyceum is to be seen, I believe, as a consequence of the reopening of the Greek private schools, which had been closed by the Albanian state in 1933.

Indeed, the nationalisation of the school system introduced through a change in the Albanian Constitution in April 1933 was fraught with consequences for the province, even if the Italian and Catholic schools of central and northern Albania had been in fact the main target of the reform (Gogaj 2004: 100-105). In the autumn of 1933 the few private schools remaining could not open, the privately funded teachers in state schools located in Greek-speaking villages were dismissed and a new programme with fewer Greek-language courses (at least initially) was initiated. But with the start of the next school year Albanian schools were boycotted in certain villages while petitions were sent to the League of Nations by diverse Hellenic organisations, asking for the reopening of the Greek schools. The opinion in favour of the Greek minority made by the International Court of Justice in The Hague obliged the Albanian government to back down in 1935. The Greek schools reopened in the province of Gjirokastër for the 1935-36 school year (Clayer 2004).

---

[28] Early in the life of the lyceum the Prefect wrote a report saying that the Ministry of Education had not sent the necessary education materials and that the French teachers had only been offered unfurnished residences. The Minister of Education replied to the Ministry of the Interior by accusing the local population of indifference and the Prefecture of lacking initiative (AQSh, F. 152, v. 1924, d. 275).

[29] According to *Demokratia* (n° 259: 2), the Ministry argued that the budget was not large enough to fund a fourth lyceum and that the other three lyceums already had 700 students. These were nevertheless not a sufficient reasons, so the newspaper's publishers, for not opening the lyceum in Gjirokastër.

[30] Safet Butka, the director of the teachers' training school, wrote in a report in 1934 that most of the pupils who had a scholarship were from the poor regions of Tepelenë and Kurvelesh or from the irredente region of Çamëria in Greece (Butka 2003: 93).

The decision to reopen the lyceum in Gjirokastër at the same time cannot be a coincidence. It shows how Tirana's authorities were sensitive to the peculiar problem posed by the province of Gjirokastër, the building process of a Greek minority and the danger it represented. However, this sensitivity seems to have been weaker than that of people working and living in the province itself.

The question of the lyceum seen from the province

The local authorities had often put forward in their reports arguments in favour of a lyceum. In 1932 for example, the new Prefect, Qazim Bodinaku, evaluated the situation in the province and underlined the presence of an important Greek-speaking population along the border as a main problem. Among these people, the men were living and working abroad and ensuring an 'urban' lifestyle for their families. According to him, it was a population that had no Albanian national feeling, that had its own teachers, and could, albeit illegally,[31] send its children to boarding schools established by the Greek state for just this purpose on the other side of the border. Among the solutions proposed by the Prefect was the opening of a lyceum in Gjirokastër, in order to discourage Greece for the Greek-speaking, as well as (Albanian) Christian boys to go to these schools in Greece.[32]

It is possible that the Prefect's point of view was inspired by his contacts with intellectual circles in Gjirokastër. Indeed, as the content of the local newspaper testifies,[33] a small group of people involved in the nation-building process was regularly advocating the opening of a lyceum or improving its functioning. Their argumentation had two dimensions, the first was that presented by the Prefect, the second concerned the position of the province within the Albanian state.

Like the Prefect, this group saw in the building of boarding schools along the border in Greece and their attraction for students from the province a danger for the region but also for the Albanian nation as a whole. The opening of a lyceum was aimed at drawing children away from the boarding schools in Ioannina, Corfou or Voshtina, which had been built up, according to them, to counter the lyceum of Gjirokastër when the latter existed. That is why they were criticising the government's policy, which they saw as lagging behind the Greek state's policy. In August 1929, the editors of *Demokratia* underlined that Greece was closing high schools everywhere except in Epirus, even keeping the school in Voshtina, which was little more than a village, because Greece understood where its own interest lay. References to Greece were made in the young journalists' criticism of the rich provincial notables who were not reacting to the absence of a local lyceum. Instead, these notables were sending their children to the lyceum of Korçë, and ignored

---

[31] Illegal because they crossed the border without a passport, and infringed the law that forbade the acceptance of foreign scholarships.

[32] AQSh, F. 294, v. 1932, d. 580.

[33] The following discussion relies on various articles published in the newspaper (*Demokratia*, n°54: 2; n°73: 1; n°108: 2; n°117: 2; n°118: 1; n°162: 1; n°172: 1; n°173: 1-2; n°175: 2; n°184: 2; n°185: 2-3; n°203: 3; n°218: 1; n°233: p. 3; n°264: 1 and 4 ; n°267: p. 2; n°269: p. 1; n°273: 1 and 4; n°291: 2; n°319: 1; n°326: 1; n°622: 1 and 2.

demands for them to be more charitable, after the model of the 'rich Greek men' in the region during the Ottoman period.

For the editors of *Demokratia*, the lyceum would thus be a tool to fight Greek cultural propaganda. They considered a technical school, which trained carpenters and blacksmiths, or a teachers' training school, as inappropriate for this purpose. Indeed, they saw culture as the key to dominion in the region. Without a lyceum, the "alien element," which had an historical past and a strong culture supported from abroad, would inevitably dominate. Although they pointed out the fact that many Albanians were also sending their children to Greece, they also developed in this respect a specific discourse on the issue of minorities. Quoting Gustave le Bon, who wrote that the famous "principe des nationalités" had plunged Europe into anarchy, they underlined the problem of the arbitrary nature of borders in the Balkans and the mixture of races. Under such conditions, avoiding the development of a "state within the state" was only possible through the implementation of the principle according to which every people living in Albania had only one way out: "becoming and being Albanian, and only Albanian." Granting a special status, even a minimal one, to "allogenous people" could be dangerous and lead to the creation of tiny states: "after language, comes the school, after the school the Church, after the Church representation in Parliament", wrote the journalist Jorgji Meksi in *Demokratia*. The defence of the lyceum or of the boarding school in Sarandë[34] in that border region had thus "not only a cultural, but also a political and national mission."

However, in the discourse of the local intellectuals, the demand for a lyceum was not only related to a general view of the nation-building process and the issue of minorities. It was also linked to the specific place of the province within the nation and the state and finally to the question of their own position. Indeed, in their argumentation they propagated the "first place of the province" in the cultural domain. This leading position was not only due to the huge number of cadis and civil servants native of the province serving the late Ottoman Empire, but also because of the present intelligentsia born in the region and educated in Greek and Turkish schools, or more recently in Albanian and West European establishments. For the group of *Demokratia* authors these educated people had played an important role in the "liberation of the country", and they should continue to be the spearheads of the "civilising mission" and "the fight for the synchronising of the life of the whole nation."

Branko Merxhani and his fellow editors were themselves the promoters of an intellectual movement called *neo-Shqiptarismi* (neo-Albanianism), which emerged in Gjirokastër at the end of the 1920s. Reinterpreting different elements of the positivism of Gustav Lebon, the regime of Mussolini or that of Mustafa Qemal, they wanted to educate the people and reform Albanian society. Thus, their claim that impeding the opening of a lyceum was a sign of disdain for the intelligentsia of

[34] This establishment opened in 1928. In 1932 it housed 47 boarders, most of them *Çams*. There were also 93 Albanian and Greek-speaking day pupils. In October 1933 the Ministry decided to close this school but it appears that this never happened (*Demokratia*, n°341: 1; n°406: 1).

the province reveals their wish to defend their own social and political position as provincial intellectuals, especially in the field of the nation-building process.

This centre/periphery issue appears even more explicitly when they accuse the central governments of curtailing the intellectual potential of the southern provinces: "Gjirokastër, the country of cadis and civil servants, and of the highest number of academics, remains without a lyceum!" They even threatened not to pay taxes anymore if nothing was done in the province and accused the deputies and provincial notables who had influence in the capital of doing nothing for the Prefecture and of being traitors.[35] What is striking is that the young intellectuals from Gjirokastër considered this cultural superiority as being biological and due to their position of proximity to the Greeks (who were nevertheless menacing the Albanian nation with their culture.) Indeed they claimed that the local intelligentsia was sophisticated because it found itself at the crossroad between the Albanian and Greek races.

Lastly, they had also an argument of an economic nature. They considered the absence of a lyceum as detrimental to the provincial economy which was traditionally dependent on emigration and civil service. Emigration was continuing, especially to Romania, Turkey, Egypt and America,[36] but it was no longer the source of revenue it had once been, and regions like Lunxhëri were considerably impoverished. If culture, which was the other resource of the province, were to die, Gjirokastër would also die, the editors of *Demokratia* argued.

CONCLUSION

This article has not intended to examine in detail the question of education in inter-war Gjirokastër region; further research is needed before this can be done. It aimed rather at showing how this question can reveal many social and political issues, as I have already done in another study concerning the making of the Greek minority during the inter-war period (Clayer 2004).

Alongside the army and, in a different way, religious institutions, school was certainly one of the most important means for the state to nationalise society, although other methods were also implemented to "educate" beyond the school system. The political authorities ordered the communal officials to hold public conferences and the religious officials to preach and organise conferences on different issues, such as patriotism, social relations, education and relations with administrations, agriculture and health (Dizdari 1935; Clayer 2008).

The prefecture of Gjirokastër was perceived as a sensitive province by the state because of its Greek-speaking population and the fear of real or imagined "Greek propaganda". As a result, in a way, the Albanisation policy was often concerned

---

[35] The deputy Javer Hurshit answered that he was elected to work for all the country and not just for the province.

[36] They did not mention emigration to Greece, which was the most important country of emigration for the region.

more with the Greek-speaking (and more generally the Christian) villages, where the existing school network was denser, than with Albanian-speaking Muslim villages. But as we have seen, the nation-building process as it developed in the province was, as elsewhere, both the result of state constraints and the interest of the local people (Noiriel 2001: 130). In this border region the interest of most families lay in surviving in a period of economic crisis. In doing so they applied personal networks that at that time were only partially oriented on the Albanian state. Through emigration and other economic activities, these networks had many nodes, within and outside of Albania (and especially in Greece).

However, the school issue shows that choices were often different for Christians and Muslims, because the 'constraints' exerted by the Albanian state (but also by the neighbouring Greek state) differed and because the personal or group priorities were of extremely different natures.[37] These aspects need to be examined in more detail in the future. Indeed, young Albanians experienced a quite different situation in the 1930s with an intensified economic crises, the stabilisation of the Albanian state, growing Italian influence and the emergence of the communist ideology, especially among students.

As we have seen, constraints and interests were different for the different social groups of provincial society. The existence of a lyceum in Gjirokastër was important above all in the eyes of the local intellectuals. The families making up the traditional local elite simply continued to send their children elsewhere to study. For the new local intellectuals, the debate was first a question of their own status within the new state and its intellectual elite. It was also a cultural-political issue, but with a slightly different meaning from that for the central authorities due to specific social mechanisms of the nation-building at its border (Sahlins 1989; Anderson 1996; Donnan-Hastings and Wilson 1998). Their claim to be intellectually superior because of an hybrid (Albanian and Greek) racial origin, despite their fight against Greek culture, is particularly revealing in this respect.

[37] The 'constraints' exerted by the Albanian state concerning education were compulsory primary education, the theoretical impossibility to send children to schools abroad with a foreign scholarship, the banning of Greek-language education, except for the Greek-speakers, and even for the latter the imposition of an increasingly Albanised teaching. The constraints exerted by the Greek state consisted for example in distribution of scholarships only to families who did not accept the Albanian educational system and were not involved in Albanian politics

CHRONOLOGY

1920	Prefecture of Gjirokastër placed under Albanian administration
Oct. 1921	Recognition of minority rights by the Albanian government at the League of Nations
1922	Closing of 18 schools in the Prefecture of Gjirokastër for financial reasons
mid 1923	Decision by the Albanian Parliament to open a French lyceum in Gjirokastër
June 1924	'Revolution'; collapse of Zog's government and formation of a government under Fan Noli
Dec. 1924	Zog's return to power
1928	Closing of the lyceum, replaced by a technical school
Jan. 1931	Opening of a teacher's training school in Gjirokastër
April 1933	Change in the Constitution for the nationalisation of Education
April 1935	Opinion of the International Court of the Hague in favour of the Greek minority
Sept. 1935	Reopening of Greek private schools; reopening of the lyceum
April 1939	Italian occupation of Albania

BIBLIOGRAPHY

Anderson, Malcolm 1996 Frontiers: Territory and State Formation in the Modern World, Oxford: Polity Press.

Asllani, Uran 2003 Studentët shqiptare të Francës dhe veprimtaria e tyre, Tiranë: Ilar.

Beduli, Kristofor (ed.) 1999 Dhimitër Beduli, Tiranë, Botim i Kishës Orthodhokse Autoqefale të Shqipërisë.

Butka, Uran (ed.) 2003 Safet Butka, Tiranë: Maluka.

Clayer, Nathalie 2007 Frontière politique, frontière ethnique et État-nation. L'exemple de la région-frontière albano-grecque dans l'entre-deux-guerres. In: Dušan Nećak (éd.), Meje v jugovzhodni Evropi : Kultura in politika od XVIII. Do XXI. Stoletja/Borders in Southeastern Europe: Culture and Politics between the 18th and 21st Century, Historia, 7, Ljubljana pp 159-176.

Clayer, Nathalie 2006 Investing in the intellectual capital: The kadı of Gjirokastër and Libohova and their descendants. In: Proceedings of the second international symposium on Islamic Civilisation in the Balkans, Tirana, Albania, 4-7 December 2003, Istanbul: IRCICA pp 115-124.

Clayer Nathalie 2008 Behind the veil. The reform of Islam in inter-war Albania or the search for a 'modern' and 'European' Islam. In: Nathalie Clayer and Eric Germain (eds.), Islam in Inter-War Europe, London: Hurst pp 128-155.

Donnan-Hastings and Thomas Wilson (eds.) 1998 Border Identities: Nation and State at International Frontiers, Cambridge: Cambridge University Press.
Gogaj, Iljaz 2004 Mirash Ivanaj. Personalitet i shquar i universit shqiptar, Tiranë: Erik Botime.
Kaso, Mehmet 2003 Arsimi në Sarandë, Delvinë e Konispol, Tiranë: Geer.
Kostelanik, David 1996 Minorities and Minority Language Education in Inter-War Albania. In: East European Quarterly, 30(1) pp 75-96.
Marko, Petro 2000 Intervistë me vetveten (retë dhe gurët), Tiranë: Omsca.
Mema, Bektash and Ajet Shahu 2001 Prefektura e Gjirokastrës 1920-1924, Berat: Jonalda.
Noiriel, Gérard 2001 Etat, nation et immigration. Vers une histoire du pouvoir, Paris: Belin.
Peters, Markus 2003 Geschichte der Katholischen Kirche in Albanien 1919-1993, Wiesbaden: Otto Harrassowitz.
Sahlins, Peter 1989 Boundaries: The Making of France and Spain in the Pyrenees, Berkeley: University of California Press.

7. German-speaking Travel Writers in Interwar Albania

Andreas Hemming

This paper represents a first step in a larger project on the role and reception of foreign representations of Albania and Albanians in contemporary Albania. The goal is to examine a specific phase in the tradition of travel writing on Albania, to delineate who went to Albania under what circumstances and with what intentions, and to analyse what they wrote about these experiences.

We are first struck by a paradox. On the one hand, a discussion of the genre of travel writing in Albania has not found its way into a single longer monograph of note;[1] on the other, Albania is worth an entry in an encyclopaedia on the Literature of Travel and Exploration (Minta 2003). There the Western European interest in Albania as more than one of the many transit country to the Holy Land, as was the case in the Middle Ages, is tied directly to the establishment of Ali Pasha's semi-independent court in Ioannina in 1809 and the interest this 'Napoleon of the Balkans' awoke in the countries of Western Europe. Ali Pasha's most prominent guest was likely Lord Byron, who in his desire to meet Ali Pasha resulted in him venturing into what is now southern Albania to do so. The result was that "Byron's fantasy of Albania, as one of the world's wild places, [became] the mainstay of most English travel writing about the country ever since (Minta 2003: 10)." Byron's fascination was documented in the memoirs of his travel companion John Cam Hobhouse (1813) and, of course, in his epic Child Harold's Pilgrimage, published in 1812 (Byron 1918). This stereotype continues to haunt Albania (cf. de Loos 2000 for a prominent contemporary example); it is also a core reason why Albania was and continues to be of interest to Western European travellers.

In the course of the 19th century the centre of interest in Albania shifted from the English-speaking to the German and Italian-speaking part of the continent. "The writing," it can be argued, "becomes much more informed, less driven by a fantasy of the remote (Minta 2003: 10)." The interest in Albania shifts from pure exoticism and acquires an irredentist political character. Italy and Austro-Hungary would spend a good half a century competing with one another and with other stake-holders for influence in this disputed part of post-Vienna Congress Europe.

With the turn of the 20th century begins, Stephen Minta continues, "the golden age of Albanian travel writing (Minta 2003:10)," which will end with Enver Hoxha's accession to power. Minta conveniently ignores the fact that writers continued to travel socialist Albania and report on their findings (i.e. for example Ehrenburg 1947; Seliger 1960; Myrdal and Kessle 1976). But is not the point here.

---

[1] Lindita Arapi provides a brief introductory overview of the history of travel writing in Albania and attempts a preliminary classification before continuing to the core of her analysis (Arapi 2005: 21-41; see also Skëndo 1999).

The historical focus of this article is on Minta's golden age and the position of German-speaking travellers and writers of the interwar period have in it.

THE SCHOLAR AND THE INTELLECTUAL IN THE WEIMAR REPUBLIC AND REPUBLICAN AUSTRIAN

A discussion of German and Austrian travel writing must begin with the state of writing, of scholarship and literature as such, in the Weimar Republic and in republican Austria; it is hardly possible to understand the former, if the situation of the latter is not clear. It need hardly be said that the literary and scholarly scene in Germany was in a state of upheaval in post-World War I, post-November Revolution Germany. But much of this was self-inflicted pain. Infected by extreme Wilhelmine hubris (Hammerstein 1999: 23), the scientific and scholarly community in Germany broke all ties with the international scientific community when World War I broke out in 1914, declaring itself solidary with the nation and the army. The Treaty of Versailles cemented this break, formally terminating all scientific ties between German and foreign institutions (cf. Marsch 1994: 35-39). The massive inflation that followed in the early 1920s resulted in the explosion of costs for personnel as well as in expenses for foreign literature and journals and did its part to cast German scholarship into a serious crisis that took many years and the investment of many million Reichmarks to escape (Marsch 1994).

German anthropology specifically, was – understandably enough – even more dependent on this international scene than other disciplines; and it was up to that time a formidable player in said scene,

> launch[ing] some of the of world's largest anthropological expeditions; ... a powerful presence at international conferences [and] found[ing] a number of internationally recognized periodicals (Bunzl and Penny 2003: 5)

in the period up to the war. But it

> never recovered from World War I. The war led to the loss of the German colonies, destroyed the funding sources of German ethnology, and eradicated the international networks German scholars had built up over the previous four decades (ibid: 7).

The desolate (financial) situation may best be described by the anthropologist Theodor Koch-Grünberg in a letter to his publisher in 1923:

> I admit a degree of shame to have to take up your offer of reimbursing me these expenses. What have we come to in Germany as a result of this abominable war! Sometimes I feel to be imprisoned (cited in Kraus 2004: 483).[2]

The consequences of this depression and the political and social upheavals of the early 1920s was escapism – for example, in the ivory tower of science for

---

[2] All translations are my own.

science' sake – or ideological polarisation: either the system as such was questioned or the fault was seen as coming from outside. Scholars and writers found themselves forced to take sides; the manifold literary and artistic movements that emerged in this period were direct or indirect responses to the political climate or a vain attempt to escape (Beutin et al. 1994: 364).

The new economic situation must also be considered. Literature and the publishing industry were suddenly transformed. Literature (and scholarship) had become a product in a market and thus subject to all the demands of such an industry: "The author became increasingly dependent on a to him foreign and impervious system of production and distribution that… saw art exclusively as a consumer good (Beutin et al. 1994: 345)."

The contradictions that resulted were central to Walter Benjamin's critique as articulated in his The Author as Producer (1970, orig. 1934) or in The Work of Art in the Age of its Technological Reproducibility (2008, orig. 1936).

The market was changing, large publishing houses were emerging and either buying out the competition or forcing it into bankruptcy. These large media empires, like the Ullstein or Hugenberg corporations, were bourgeois, right-wing conservative and in time became increasingly anti-Semitic, anti-democratic and anti-intellectual. They had the power to dictate authors how and about what to write. The influence of democratic, liberal and socialist media was minimal. More importantly, a remarkable number of "revolutionary themes" – to use Benjamin's words – were assimilated and even appropriated by the "bourgeois apparatus of production and publication... without seriously placing its own existence or the existence of the class that possesses them into question (Benjamin 1970: 87)." Authors were forced to make their way in this environment, one that can best be described as marked by "alienation" and various attempts to overcome it (cf. Beutin et al. 1994: 365-368).

It is difficult to say anything concrete at all about the situation in republican Austria, where two of the authors to be discussed here originate. An increased – both political and public – interest in the Balkans emerged in the Dual Monarchy with the occupation and, finally, the annexation of Bosnia in 1908. Austrian Volkskunde in the Balkans experienced a boom in the course of World War I and the occupation of good parts of region between 1915 and 1918. Scholarship went hand-in-hand with military occupation and adminsitration (Marchetti 2007). That having been said, the examination of the scholarly tradition of this period has with the exception of the odd institutional history (i.e. Hittmair and Hunger 1997; Pusman 1991) barely gone past the stage of sketches (Eberhart 1998) and overviews (Gruber 1998). Christian Häußer for his part argues that the intensive interest and analysis of the occupied territories in the Balkans by the Austrian Volkskunde and the concomitant collaboration – if not collusion – with the military and political administration was an attempt "to gain recognition by the state and in doing so realise a footing as a (university) science (Häußer 2005: 5; cf. Marchetti 2007)." And Austrian Volkskunde having claimed scholarly hegemony in the region (cf. Krauss 1885)[3], the demise of the Dual Monarchy with World War I, so it follows, can be seen as the demise of Austrian scholarship in the region, a point verified by Gruber (1998: 211-212). Indicative is the fate of the Balkan-Abteilung of the Museum für österreichische Volkskunde, which had to do without becoming,

> as envisioned in 1917, the 'scientific centre for the study of all Balkan countries', but (until well into the 1950s) a curiosity of past greatness (Häußer 2005: 3; cf. also Gruber 1998: 210-211).

The sad fate of the Ethnographic Museum in Kitsee, where the collection was exiled to after World War II is indicative of the peripheral status this sphere of scholarship has in Austria today.

Approaching the genre of Austrian travel writing from the perspective of a history of literature proves equally frustrating. Again, when the Austrian literary tradition is examined, especially in this period, it is described not in its own terms but as a rump of German literature. In a survey of the state of scholarship on this sector, Ernst Fischer describes the need to meet this deficit (Fischer 1985). Little has been done to improve the situation in the two decades that have since passed. Fischer does make more than clear in his essay that the literary traditions in Austria at this time were marked by the "competition and conflict between the political poles (Fischer 1985: 183)," each faction with its own literature. Like in Germany, people were forced to take sides.

ALBANIA IN THE 1920S AND 1930S

The situation in Albania in the 1920s and 1930s was as multifarious as the situation in Weimar Germany and republican Austria, if for completely different reasons. While officially and independent state since 1912, few if any functioning state structures had been established even a decade later. It was only in 1920, for example, that Tirana was named capital (cf. Shkodra 1994; Aliaj et al. 2003); the country's official borders were only delineated in the course of the 1920s as well (cf. Giles 1930). State structures existed on paper and served as points of reference for international partners of various kinds, but their efficacy depended more on the charisma of who was in charge than on any form of institutionalised monopoly on power. Ministries, offices, (para-)military commands and titles, these structures were much more the currency with which various Albanian 'strongmen' (cf. Fischer 2007) bought the loyalty of their allies and subalterns. In the course of the early 1920s the Mati chieftain Ahmed Bey Zogolli (later: Ahmed Zogu; and even later: King Zog) proved the most

[3] Austrian anthropology – *Völkerkunde* – never even considered laying a claim to scholarship in the region, its dean, Pater Wilhelm Schmidt, being more interested in other issues elsewhere. Representatives of the disciplines of *Volkskunde* and *Völkerkunde* were not on good terms in Austria in any case, the Catholic Schmidt playing a significant role, for example, in preventing his *Volkskunde* counterpart – and Protestant – Michael Haberlandt from being offered a chair at the University of Vienna (cf. Marchand 1993: 309).

successful in this struggle for political supremacy. By early 1925 he had taken a tight hold of the reins of power in Albania and managed to not let them go until his most powerful benefactor Mussolini – the Mephistopheles to his Faust – decided that he had had enough and integrated Albania completely into the Italian Empire in 1939 (on the rise and fall of Ahmed Zogu see Fischer 1984; Schmidt-Neke 1987; Tomes 2003).

In many ways a child of international diplomacy, the Treaty of Versailles and the League of Nations, it is remarkable how many foreign specialists of one kind or another were involved in the attempt to establish a functioning Western state in Albania in this period. Joseph Swire (cf. Swire 1937) is probably the best known of them in the English-speaking world. The country attracted any number of adventurers, speculators and swashbucklers. Three of them will be discussed in the following.

WRITING ALBANIA IN THE INTERWAR YEARS

Richard Busch-Zantner

Richard Busch-Zantner (1911-1942) travelled through Albania as a youth on an annual basis from 1927-1930 in the accompaniment of his mother (and possibly once again in the late 1930s, although this cannot be verified). Each visit lasted from a few days to a few weeks and was generally a part of a more extensive tour of the Western Balkans region (for details see Kühne 1991). Busch-Zantner appears to have begun writing very early, initially for the local press. He began studying geography in Munich in 1930 and later in Erlangen and promptly began submitting articles to geographic and other journals, his first publication of this nature appearing in 1931 (cf. the bibliography in Kühne 1991: 128-32). His interests were broad and beside his articles on various, primarily economic, issues in Albania (Busch-Zantner 1931, 1932a, 1932b, 1933, 1935, 1938/39 1939b, 1940a, 1940b), he published throughout the 1930s until his death in 1942 on Bulgaria, Greece, Southeastern Europe in general, colonial studies and riverine shipping. His only longer monograph on Albania, Albanien. Neues Land im Imperium (1939a) is the focus of the following deliberation.

As the title of the Busch-Zantner's monograph discloses, Albania is discussed here in the context of the Anschluss to the fascist Italian Empire, Busch-Zantner himself making his intentions clear in his (in part prophetic) Forward:

> The situation today is such that we can no longer be ignorant of Albania… because it has become part of the *Imperium Romanum*, with which we do not only have close political but also close military ties. Italy's concerns are thus our concerns (Busch-Zantner 1939a: 5).

This brief excerpt already hints at Busch-Zantner's politics, Ingo Kühne wording it diplomatically:

> The situation of the time as conditioned by axis policies and Busch-Zantner's personal political position, which as opposed to his earlier politically more sovereign opinion saw him drift into the wake of National Socialist ideology, had the effect that recent

> events – more or less since 1938 – were described less objectively than previous periods (Kühne 1991: 25).

A close reading of the text allows for a more damning conclusion: Albanian history as a whole and not only the last two years are represented from a teleological perspective, the Italian invasion of 7 April 1939 casting its shadow on all events leading up to it as an inevitable and sole logical conclusion. Another consideration that might have been in the back of Busch-Zantner's mind in writing the book is that the most recent volume of this comprehensive scope written on Albania that he was aware of, Stephan Ronart's Albanien von heute (1933), was already more than five years old.[4]

The 218 page volume is divided into four sections, the first, the 40 page introduction, providing a geographical and in the broadest sense ethnographic overview of the country. Today, Busch-Zantner is revered in the geographical disciplines as an early and influential figure in the establishment of the subdiscipline of social geography (specifically Busch-Zantner 1937). This introduction is exemplary in this respect: Busch-Zantner sees the substance of the term 'Albania' as a combination of three factors

> that allow one to read a community's every political expression: the nation [orig.: Volk] as the biological result of Creation, the social structure of the nation as the origin and skeleton of its efficacy as a community and, finally, the space in which this nation lives as a frame and stage for these processes (Busch-Zantner 1939a: 9).

The rest of the section is written in this spirit: political developments are seen as a factor of geographical and sociological a priori. Power structures are interpreted as an outgrowth of Ottoman policy, specifically: feudal property relations and the existence of a small class of powerful landowning families, the principle equality of all Muslims independent of their ethnic origins and the priority of Islam over other categories as a factor in identification. He ends his socio-geographic introduction with a brief description of Albania's four most prominent religions,[5] the four paragraphs on the *Bektashi* being more or less a literal transcription of previously published thoughts on the issue (Busch-Zantner 1932b).

The second section titled the Way to Empire represents the largest part of the book, covering the history of Albania from the situation at the outbreak of World War I until that fateful Easter Sunday morning of 1939, when Italian troops landed in Durrës to formally occupy Albania. It is an unremarkable summary of this 25 year period, a fusing of press material, above all sources from Belgrade and Prague (Busch-Zantner 1939a: 108), literature available at the time and his own personal experiences. Busch-Zantner is nevertheless very reserved in exhibiting the latter openly, even as anecdotes. This would have clearly been contrary to his very sober perception of scholarly writing, as evidenced not only here but in the rest of his

[4] Joseph Swire's King Zog's Albania was published in 1937 but Busch-Zantner was clearly not aware of its existence.

[5] "Other religions are not represented. Albania does not have and never had a Jewish problem, independent of how one sees the issue, either as a racial or 'merely' a religious issue (Busch-Zantner 1939a: 38)."

publications. He allows himself to be drawn out of this reserved position only once, when he describes the emerging cult of personality around the figure of Ahmed Zogu:

> It is remarkable... how the initials AZ are becoming a kind of symbol of the state... Skanderbeg's helmet – Albania's crown – is being shown increasingly in association with these initials. In his public appearances the President is also becoming more conspicuous: he no longer dresses in the conservative black suit and top hat of a republican head of state; instead he appears in a white silk uniform and a tall, white kalpak with a long heron-feather and intricate lacing; his bodyguards... are dressed in blood red uniforms with black lacing (Busch-Zantner 1939a: 96).

The impressionable Busch-Zantner was there, he saw it himself:

> On this 7 August, in which every foreigner was forcibly expelled from Scutari, the author was able not only to remain in Scutari but to drive out to meet the President in Mamuras, where he made a midday stop. The author remembers with interest above all the numerous, publically displayed portraits with the then still cryptic inscription 'The President and Prince (Mbret)[sic] of the Country' (Busch-Zantner 1939a: 96).

Although packaged in a sober 'remembers with interest', the fascination, the excitement felt by the then 16-year-old Busch-Zantner rings through, reminiscent of Heinrich Mann's monarchy-drunk Patrioteer (1921).

This is of course an isolated episode, but it reveals what for many might have been at the core of their fascination with Albania, a fascination with the pageantry of a bygone era. However fascinated he in fact was by this display, Busch-Zantner spends a significant amount of time later deconstructing it, highlighting the corruption and waste behind it, a post hoc justification of fascist intervention:

> The collapse [sic] in 1939 showed that the prominent public appearances of the family members of the dynasty were bought at great financial expense that had to be carried either by the penniless and itself very modest population or the Italians (Busch-Zantner 1939a: 116).

Zogu himself was among the most corrupt in his court:

> Emigrants have claimed repeatedly that Zogu took bribes for political decisions... that certain oil and above all lumbering concessions were sold more than once is common knowledge (Busch-Zantner 1939a: 116-117).

Is any more justification for the Italian invasion necessary, for, as Busch-Zantner titled this section of his narrative, the neutralisation of the Albanian problem?

In the short third section of the book, Busch-Zantner summarises the changed political situation for the Axis powers and Albania's economic potential as part of the Italian Empire. He begins nevertheless with a deriding response to the indignation in the rest of Europe:

> The "great democracies" protest by means of publishing unfriendly articles that above all claim that Italy has infringed natural laws of ethnic order, against [international] law and against morality. These arguments are completely without substance (Busch-Zantner 1939a: 157).

This, it appears, is the central reason for writing the book. It is not, as Busch-Zantner suggests in his opening words, a description of and introduction to a new part of the Italian Empire, it is not a book whose major intention is the information of a population about a country and its people, but an apology, a justification of Italian aggression.

Hugo Adolf Bernatzik

Hugo Adolf Bernatzik (1897-1953) is a both colourful and controversial figure in Austrian scholarship, the child of an upper-class Viennese family – his father was a law professor – who came to academia relatively late in life. He spent much of the 1920s travelling across what in times past was the Austro-Hungarian Empire. This was in many ways a form of flight, from death (his older brother having been killed in the war in 1916, his father passing away in 1919 and his first wife in 1924), from failing business enterprises and from the shaken remains of Imperial Austrian society (cf. Byer 1999: 22-23, 29, 31).

> The hunt, the pursuit of a fleeting moment with the camera, the confrontation with ever more foreign and dangerous living conditions... ever more breath-taking experiences at ever greater distances, to supersede and thus triumph over the social alienation at home (Byer 1999: 29)

became an obsession.

Bernatzik was stationed in Albania during World War I and had gotten to know the pelican colonies in the swamps there. These were among the last colonies of their kind in continental Europe. The passionate ornithologist and hunter thus organised an expedition to observe and photograph these birds in their natural habitat – the swamps of coastal Albania – before they fell victim to modernisation, namely the draining of the swamps and their controlled irrigation (Bernatzik 1930, Byer 1999: 20, 33-34). The result was a narrow volume titled Riesenpelikane und ihre Kinder, published in 1930. The more ethnographic volume, Albanien - Europas vergessenes Land, published like its sister volume for the first time in 1930 and renamed Albanien, Land der Skipetaren in its second and third editions in 1932 and 1937 must be seen as a side effect of this endeavour, even if it proved to be the larger and on the whole more successful of the two books.[6]

The second, renamed 1932 edition of Bernatizik's work is still only a modest 148 pages, including 105 photographs. The text, interspersed with the first 17 of these photographs is limited to the first 63 pages. Reading the text and examining the photographs, it becomes quite clear that Albania and the people of Albania are only of secondary importance to the author, who clearly positions himself at the centre of events. Where Bush-Zantner hardly ever emerges as the personal guide to events in Albania, Bernatzik himself dominates the narrative. Bernatzik writes in his three page introduction about all the myths about Albania that are rampant in the rest of Europe and that he would like to do away with, to then set the stage for his own self-apotheosis: Albania has for centuries been a closed, inaccessible part of the world, unexplored by Western scholars, he writes. And those Westerners who have come to Albania, immune to sentimentality or of moralising demands, are in the

[6] It is also the only one of the three books being reviewed here to have been translated into Albanian, even if only recently (Bernatzik 2003).

process of blindly destroying the local way of life. Scholarship had done what it could to preserve what was being destroyed, but "a breath of life must supplement the 'material,' give life and, in turn, truth. And this is the modest goal of this volume (Bernatzik 1932: 9)." He continues:

> I have wandered across this country with the camera and have recorded the land and the people as I encountered them. The goal was not a systematic study or a classification based on class or race (Bernatzik 1932: 9).

This is a claim to an unadulterated truth, verified by the reality of his photographs, a common attitude of the time. "Thus it should be a salvaging of the truth and of reason. If this should to a degree be successful, it will be recompense enough for much drudgery and sacrifice (Bernatzik 1932: 9)."

That having been said, it takes Bernatzik three chapters until he first introduces the reader to the residents of the country he has decided to travel to. Beside an anonymous *bey* who allows him access to his lands and three well-meaning but essentially incompetent servants, the only human being in the narrative – a narrative that at its core is one of the primordial conflict between man and his environment – is the author himself. This is a third of the text: in the first chapter Bernatzik describes the local geography; in the second he narrates his attempts to photograph night-active jackals, the above-mentioned pelicans and falcons as well as a nearly fatal encounter with a poisonous snake. The third chapter is in its entirety the heroic description of the again nearly fatal exploration of a mountain cave – on eight pages Bernatzik describes how he entered the cave and, losing his balance and falling, loses both his lantern and his lifeline. He emerges into daylight nineteen harrowing hours later to wake his sleeping servants "who had despaired ever seeing me again, but in their Muslim impassiveness waited for me nevertheless (Bernatzik 1932: 32)."

Only then does the first Albanian make a personal appearance, a northern Albanian chieftain, who invites the traveller into his house and home to share the little he has with his guest. This is a dying culture, Bernatzik argues, evident in the high heels worn by the dancing Vlach women, a sign of the Albanian's willingness to adopt what they sees as practical:

> obvious benefits they adopt at once and with great vigour… (but) this otherwise so clever and adaptable nation will not survive any form of civilisation, any sudden dislocation (Bernatzik 1932:34).

Bernatzik's language is straightforward and direct, he tends to romanticism and to the heroic over-dramatisation of his own person.[7] This book, like many others in this period of his career, was written with his next expedition in mind (cf. Byer 1999: 32-34). Its sale would help finance it, its success convince his sponsor's – primary among them suppliers of expensive camera equipment – to support him.

---

[7] This is not the place to go into the conflicts Bernatzik was drawn into in his later career as a professional anthropologist; an awareness of his difficult personality and his self-absorption is nevertheless conducive to understanding his work (cf. Byer 1999).

The photographs in Albanien, Land der Skipetaren are the most remarkable and by far the best part of the book, a contemporary reviewer putting it as follows:

> [Bernatzik] has... a pleasant and vivid, if somewhat florid style. The chief attraction of his book lies in the 105 photographs, including pictures of landscape, architecture, the people and the wildlife. These include some of the most interesting and beautiful photographs which the reviewer has ever seen. It is impossible to praise too highly either their technical achievement or their artistic quality (C.A.M. 1932: 724).

This is a rare form of praise for a scholarly journal. But at what cost are these photographs made? What is irritating for the contemporary anthropologist is the absolute lack of respect Bernatzik shows for his subjects, photographing them when they clearly do not consent (i.e. figures 8, 74, and 51-52).[8] In a later publication Bernatzik even suggests making a blind to photograph the locals in action "like in wildlife photography (Bernatzik 1947: 34)." This attitude can be attributed, as one will, to the zeitgeist of the time, to ivory tower ignorance or to Bernatzik's own arrogance.

But to return to the text of the book: Bernatzik does have a riveting style of writing; and if he does not have a photograph, he will describe one:

> The goatskin on which the father thrones more than he sits, the smoky patina of the ceiling beams, the open hearth and the black cauldron, the ancient furniture in the dark corners, the colourful dress and the inherited silver jewellery; this all breaths unity and self-confidence. The shining eyes and the weapons an arm's length away are signs of an untamed ferocity that can be atoned by blood alone, assuming a practical sense for gold has not been appeased. An Albanian's honour... cannot be paid for in gold (Bernatzik 1932: 33).

In this sense the text allows the reader to come very close to the lives of the people and to their life situation. Bernatzik's perceptive eye sees all and his descriptive (if florid) style paints a vivid picture. His arrogance and his own idiosyncrasies – among other things insisting on living in a tent instead of accepting local hospitality – surely kept him from seeing a great deal more. He was even at this time the quintessential participant observer.

But as historical and as chronological as Busch-Zantner is, so ahistorical and so timeless is Bernatzik. No travel route becomes apparent. He makes no reference at all that might fix this collage of impressions and experiences in time and space. A list could be made of where he was – and above all where he was not – and his descriptions of annual festivities provide a certain frame for the specialist, but this is beyond the average reader. Only in his afterword does he go into current events and the current situation, which he perceives as miserable, malaria and mismanagement laming a country with a great deal of natural and human potential. And as quickly as Bernatzik appears to comment, so quickly does he disappear, to hide behind the objective camera and his irony. He likes the Albanians, respects them and laments their turn to civilisation. But at the same time he does all he can to show their flaws, to make fun of them, to disparage them in their backwardness, devoting a whole unflattering chapter to 'real' Albanian anecdotes. He makes it all too clear that he does not want to get too close.

---

[8] Wallisch could be accused of the same thing (cf. Wallisch 1931: 36).

Friedrich Wallisch

Friedrich Wallisch (1890-1969) probably knew Albania the best of the three authors being discussed here. He was a journalist before World War I and was in Albania in 1914 to report on Prince von Wied's brief regency (cf. Heaton-Armstrong 2005). After the war he studied medicine in Vienna, but appears never to have worked in the profession. He continued to write, publishing his works in various small publishing houses. Much of this literary work – poetry, lyricism, biography and novels – was for the most part a romantic memorial to the Austrian-Hungarian Empire. His writing on the Balkans and on Albania in particular was also extensive (Wallisch 1914, 1917, 1928, 1931, 1940). He was well connected in Albania and goes out of his way to describe his encounters with the King, the King's mother and sisters and other social commitments in Tirana "with leading personalities (Wallish 1931: 82)." A romantic monarchist, Wallisch found in Albania in the late 1920s what he lost in Austria in 1918.

Neuland Albanien (1931) is structured as the documentation of a several weeks long tour of the country. True to his own claim that "one must always be able to compare the present with the past (Wallisch 1931: 8)" the author shifts back and forth between 1914 and 1930, between narrative, contextualising aside and anecdote. This works very well – Wallisch is a brilliant storyteller. And although he is in essence as self-absorbed as Bernatzik,[9] he is much more discreet, seeking his fame not in tales of heroism but in the company he keeps. The book is divided into 10 chapters tracing the travel route from Durrës to Tirana, Shkodër and back, to Korca and across the southern plateau to Tepelena and Vlora, south to Saranda and via Berat back to Durrës.

An experienced Albania specialist who, as opposed to Bernatzik and Busch-Zantner, I suspect spoke at least a minimum of Albanian (all three authors are very unclear about their own linguistic competence), he is closer to the people and more ethnographic in his descriptions. But this does not mean he is any more sympathetic towards them, quite the contrary. He is not above the prejudices of the time, especially when it comes to the Gypsies:

> There are no doubt too many travelling Gypsies in Albania. In the past they were fewer but today they are coming over from southern Serbia. It is a mistake that they are not prevented from doing so (Wallisch 1931: 76).

Although more positive towards the Albanians, he does speak down to them in a typically imperial manner:

> The Albanian is sly but at the same time naive… it is a piece of truly oriental naiveté and misplaced craftiness that today many an Albanian merchant, especially of the older generation, will think: Anyone who comes to my country must have a particular interest in my goods and thus I must demand more for them. Thus it is that in Bari or Triest he will often ask for less for the same treasures than at home in Skutari or Durrazo (Wallisch 1930: 71-72).

---

[9] Speaking of the young Albanian accompanying them, he writes: "needless to say, he never tried to show us any Potemkin villages… the attempt would have been in vain. I was sticking my nose deep into Albanian pots when he was a mere child (Wallisch 1931: 35)."

His paternalistic conclusion is that "if one ignores this misplaced craftiness, which is so naive that it cannot seriously compromise a European businessman (Wallisch 1930: 72), the Albanian merchant is an honest fellow.

CONCLUSION

Comparing these three disparate writers on Albania, a journalist-publisher, an adventurer-photographer and a student geographer, the differences could not be more dramatic. They have in common only their upper middle-class backgrounds and a certain degree of wealth that made their travels possible. Busch-Zantner is significantly younger and impressionable in a completely different way than his older, war weary colleagues. While the traumatic experience and aftermath of World War I dominated the perspectives of the Austrians Wallisch and Bernatzik, the former looking for a revival of the pageantry of the Dual Monarchy, the latter looking to escape its ruins, Busch-Zantner – twenty years younger and writing almost a decade later – was already caught up in the whirlwind of its National Socialist reincarnation. He is in that respect more openly political, his report a teleological vindication of contemporary politics. He would become a victim of the very politics he so supported: drafted into the Wehrmacht, he would die on the Eastern Front aged a mere 32. Wallisch – the Austrian royalist and socialite – is just as conservative, even if he is more discreet in his politics. Bernatzik – self-absorbed – can probably be best described as apolitical, an indifference and lack of deference to existing structures that would contribute to his own tragic fate (cf. Beyr 1999). While all three were in Albania repeatedly, Bernatzik stands out as having the least knowledge of the situation on the ground – and as being not the least bit interested in it. The contextual information available to date makes it impossible to comment on his preparation in this respect; he makes no references to the literature in the text. But again, it must be kept in mind that his travel volume was a side effect of his actual ornithological interests. Wallisch, the oldest of the three, clearly has the most insight into the country, while Busch-Zantner, drew most of his information from the newspaper reports that he and others like him produced.

Well-educated, the three authors may each be defined as intellectuals, each in their own way. None was involved at the time in any serious literary or scholarly circles, although the data on Wallisch is too haphazard to be certain. If one presumes to understand literary genres as mind-sets reflecting social phenomenon then Bernatzik and Wallisch's position might best be reflected in Stefan Zweig's romantic nostalgia:

> When I attempt to find a simple formula for the period in which I grew up, prior to the First World War, I hope that I convey its fullness by calling it the Golden Age of Security… This feeling of security was the most eagerly-sought after possession of millions, the common ideal of life. Only the possession of this security made life seem worthwhile, and constantly widening circles desired their share of this costly treasure (Zweig 1946: 1).

Life in what was left of the great Danube Monarchy – politically unstable, suddenly of marginal international influence and without any of the pomp and pageantry of empire – could not be anything else but a pale shadow of what had been before. Albania was a refuge where one could escape the sad realities of interwar Vienna, a projection screen for nostalgic fantasies.

A mere seven years old at the end of World War I and hardly a candidate for the nostalgia of empire as Zweig described it, Busch-Zantner is nevertheless in search of a fantasy as well, although a forward-looking one. Living in Weimar Germany, as politically unstable and free of imperial pomp as republican Austria, he does not bemoan lost empire: in Albania he celebrates, as it would turn out, a fatal return to empire.

No longer the victim of a Byronian fantasy of an untamed wildness, between the two World Wars Albania emerged as a projection screen for any number of disaffected Europeans, a miniature of either a great European past – or of a grand European future.

BIBLIOGRAPHY

Aliaj, Besnik, Keida Lulo and Genc Myftiu (eds.) 2003 Tirana. The Challenge of Urban Development, Tirana: cetis.

Arapi, Lindita 2005 Wie Albanien albanische wurde. Rekonstruktionen eines Albanienbildes. Marburg: Tectum.

Benjamin, Walter 1970 The Author as Producer. In: New Left Review, Vol I/62 pp 83-96.

Benjamin, Walter 2008 The Work of Art in the Age of its technological Reproducibility and other Writings on Media, Cambridge (Mass.): Harvard University Press.

Bernatzik, Hugo A. 1930 Riesenpelikane und ihre Kinder. Mit Beiträgen von Adolf Heilborn und Hans Weiss. Vienna: L.W. Seidel & Sohn.

Bernatzik, Hugo A. 1932 Albanien. Das Land der Skipetaren (2nd edition), Vienna: L.W. Seidel & Sohn.

Bernatzik, Hugo A. (ed.) 1947 Afrika: Handbuch der angewandten Völkerkunde, 2 Vols. Innsbruck: Wagner'sche Universitätsbuchdruckerei.

Bernatzik, Hugo A. 2003 Shqipëria. Vendi i Shqiptarëve (trans. Taulant Hatia). Tirana: Shtëpia Botuese Uegen.

Beutin, Wolfgang et al. 1994 Deutsche Literaturgeschichte. Von den Anfängen bis zur Gegenwart (5th revised edition). Stuttgart and Weimar: J.B. Metzler Verlag.

Bunzel, Matti and H. Glenn Penny 2003 Introduction: Rethinking German Anthropology Colonialism and Race. In: H. Glenn Penny and Matti Bunzl (eds.) Worldly Provincialism. German Anthropology in the Age of Empire. Ann Arbor: University of Michigan Press pp 1-30.

Busch-Zantner, Richard 1931 Zur Siedlungsgeographie Südwest-Albaniens. In: Mitteilungen der Geographischen Gesellschaft München, Vol. 24 pp 309-316.

Busch-Zantner, Richard 1932a Senkungsseen in Albanien. In: Mitteilungen der Geographischen Gesellschaft Wien, Vol. 75 pp 166-171.

Busch-Zantner, Richard 1932b Die Sekte der Bektaschi in Albanien. In: Petermanns Geographische Mitteilungen, Vol. 78 pp 245.

Busch-Zantner, Richard 1933 Beiträge zur Wirtschaftsgeographie Albaniens. In: Erde und Wirtschaft, Vol. 7 pp 8-18.

Busch-Zantner, Richard 1935 Agrarreform und Agrarverfassung in Albanien. In: Bericht über Landwirtschaft, Vol. 20 (1) pp 87-109.

Busch-Zantner, Richard 1937 Ordnung der anthropogenen Faktoren. In: Petermanns Geographische Mitteilungen, Vol. 83 pp 138-141.

Busch-Zantner, Richard 1938/39. Ländliche Siedlung in Albanien, In: Archiv für Wanderungswesen und Auslandskunde, Vol. 10 pp 34-36.

Busch-Zantner, Richard 1939a Albanien. Neues Land im Imperium. Leipzig: Wilhelm Goldmann Verlag.

Busch-Zantner, Richard 1939b Italien, Albanien und Achmed Zogu, In: Deutscher Lebensraum, Vol. 6 pp 194-197.

Busch-Zantner, Richard 1940a Probleme des albanischen Volkstums, In. Volkstum im Südosten, Vol. 17 pp 212-217.

Busch-Zantner, Richard 1940b Ein Jahr faschistischer Wirtschaftspolitik in Albanien, In: Der Vierjahresplan, Vol. 4 pp 472-473.

Byer, Doris 1999 Der Fall Hugo A. Bernatzik. Ein Leben zwischen Ethnologie und Öffentlichkeit 1897-1953. Cologne, Weimar and Vienna: Böhlau Verlag.

Byron, Lord 1918 Childe Harold's Pilgrimage, Cambridge: University of Cambridge Press

C.A.M. 1932 Review of Hugo Adolf Bernatzik, Albanien. Das Land der Skipetaren. In: International Affairs, Vol. 11(5) p 724.

Eberhart, Helmut 1998 Von Ami Boué zu Hugo Adolf Bernatzik. Skizzen zur Geschichte der österreichischen Ethnographie in Albanien vor 1938, In: Österreichische Zeitschrift für Volkskunde, Vol. 52(101) pp 9-34.

Ehrenburg, Ilja 1947 Auf den Strassen Europas. Reportagen. Berlin: Verlag Volk und Welt.

Fischer, Bernd J. 1984 King Zog and the Struggle for Stability in Albania. Boulder (CO): East European Monographs.

Fischer, Bernd J. (ed.) 2005 Balkan Strongmen. Dictators and Authoritarian Rulers of South Eastern Europe, London: Hurst.

Fischer, Ernst 1985 Literatur und Ideologie in Österreich 1918-1938. Forschungsstand und Forschungsperspectiven, In: Wolfgang Frühwald, Georg Jäger and Alveto Martino (eds.) Internationales Archiv für Sozialgeschichte der deutschen Literatur, 1. Sonderheft, pp 183-252.

Giles, Frank 1930 Boundary Work in the Balkans. In: The Geographical Journal, Vol. 75(4) pp 300-310.

Gruber, Siegfried 1998 Austrian Contributions to the Ethnological Knowledge of the Balkans since 1850. In: Ethnologia Balkanica, Vol. 2 pp 209-224.

Hammerstein, Notker 1999 Die Deutsche Forschungsgemeinschaft in der Weimarer Republik und im Dritten Reich. Wissenschaftspolitik in Republik und Diktatur 1920-1945. Munich: C.H. Beck.

Häußer, Christian 2005 „Balkan-Expeditionen" und Össterrechiche Volkskunde. Zur Erkundung des „Fremden" und zur „Erfindung" einer Wissenschaft in Österreich-Ungarn. In: Kakanien Revisited www.kakanien.ac.at/beitr/materialien/MHaeusser1.pdf

Heaton-Armstrong, Duncan 2005 The Six Month Kingdom: Albania 1914, London: I.B. Tauris.

Hittmair, Otto and Herbert Hunger 1997 Akademie der Wissenschaften. Entwicklung einer österreichischen Forschungsinstitution. Denkschrift der Gesamtakademie. Vienna: ÖAW.

Hobhouse, John Cam 1813 A Journey through Albania, and other Provinces of Turkey in Europe and Asia, to Constantinople, during the Years 1809-1810. London: Cawthorn.

Kraus, Michael 2004 Bildungsbürger.im Urwald. Die Deutsche ethnologische Amazonienforschung (1884-1929). Marburg: Curupira.

Krauss, Friedrich Solomo 1885 Ueber seine Reise in Bosnien und der Herzegowina. In: Mitteilungen der Anthropologischen Gesellschaft in Wien, Vol. 15 pp 84-87.

Kühne, Ingo 1991 Richard Busch-Zantners Beitrag zur Landeskunde Albaniens, In: Hans Becker, (ed.) Jüngere Fortschritte der regionalgeographischen Kenntnis über Albanien. Beiträge des Herbert-Louis-Gedächtnissymposiums (Bamberger Geographische Schriften Vol. 10), Bamberg: Fach Geographie an der Universität Bamberg pp 11-26.

de Loo, Tessa 2000. Der Traumpalast. Eine Reiseerzählung. Munich: C. Bertelsmann.

Marchand, Suzanne 2003 Priests among the Pygmies: Wilhelm Schmidt and the Counter-Reformation in Austrian Ethnology, In: H. Glenn Penny and Matti Bunzl (eds.) Worldly

Provincialism. German Anthropology in the Age of Empire, Ann Arbor: University of Michigan Press pp 283-316.

Marchetti, Christian 2007 Scientists with Guns. On the ethnographic exploration of the Balkans by Austrian-Hungarian Scientists before and during World War I. In: Ab Imperio, Vol. 1 pp 1-25.

Marsch, Ulrich 1994 Notgemeinschaft der Deutschen Wissenschaft. Gründung und frühe Geschichte 1920-1925 (Münchener Studien zur neueren und neusten Geschichten Vol. 10) Frankfurt a.M.: Peter Lang.

Mann, Heinrich 1921 The Patrioteer, New York: Harcourt Brace.

Minta, Stephen 2003 Albania, In: Jennifer Speake (ed.) Literature of Travel and Exploration. An Encyclopedia Vol. 1, New York and London: Fitzroy Dearborn pp 9-11.

Myrdal, Jan and Gun Kessle 1976 Albania Defiant. New York and London: Monthly Review Press.

Pusman, Karl 1991 Die Wiener Anthropologische Gesellschaft in der ersten Hälfte des 20. Jahrhunderts. Ein Beitrag zur Wissenschaftsgeschichte auf Wiener Boden unter besonderer Berücksichtigung der Ethnologie. (Dissertation, University of Vienna).

Ronart, Stephan 1933 Albanien von heute. Vienna: Edition Pays et Peuple.

Schmidt-Neke, Michael 1987 Entstehung und Ausbau der Königsdiktatur in Albanien (1912-1939). Regierungsbildungen, Herrschaftsweise und Machteliten in einem jungen Balkanstaat, Munich: R. Oldenbourg Verlag.

Seliger, Kurt 1960 Albanien. Land der Adlersöhne. Leipzig: VEB F.A. Brockhaus Verlag.

Shkodra, Zija 1994 Tirana - Capital City of Albania. In: Harald Heppner (ed.) Hauptstädte in Südosteuropa, Vienna: Böhlau Verlag pp 133-147.

Skëndo, Lumo 1999 Udhëtarët e huaj në Shqipëri. Tirana.

Swire, Joseph 1937 King Zog's Albania, London: Robert Hale and Company.

Tomes, Jason 2003 King Zog. Self-Made Monarch of Albania, Phoenix Hill: Sutton Publishing.

Wallisch, Friedrich 1914 Der Adler des Skanderbeg: albanische Briefe aus dem Frühjahr 1914, Vienna: J.Eberle.

Wallisch, Friedrich 1917 Die Pforte zum Orient: unser Friedenswerk in Serbien, Innsbruck: Tyrolia.

Wallisch, Friedrich 1928 Der Atem des Balkans. Vom Leben und Sterben des Balkanmenschen. Leipzig: Dieterich'sche Verlagsbuchhandlung.

Wallisch, Friedrich 1931 Neuland Albanien. Stuttgart: Franckh'sche Verlagsbuchhandlung.

Wallisch, Friedrich 1940 Albanian und seine Postwertzeichen. Vienna: Verlag für Fachliteratur.

Zweig, Stefan 1946 The World of Yesterday, New York: Viking Press.

8. Roma Communities in Elbasan

Gerda Dalipaj

Official sources indicate that there are currently 2622 registered Roma[1] living in the city of Elbasan, settled in three well distinguished areas, in the centre, periphery and extreme periphery of the city. The Roma communicate internal differences in terms of tribal origin, the date of their settlement, standard of living, way of conducting trade and the way they represent themselves. While the Roma have been subject to continuous change and adaptation vis-à-vis the society in which they live, they have also made sure to manifest their distinctiveness in the city.

This paper intends to provide a general description of Roma life in the city of Elbasan in the course of the 20th century in terms of the broader society in which they have been living. The paper also touches on 1. Why the city of Elbasan has come to be a preferred place of habitation for the Roma; 2. Communist politics towards the Roma and their reactions to the regime; 3. Roma migration and trade after 1990, and 4. New social stratification and representation. The paper is based on fieldwork carried out systematically since July 2005 and an intensive review of the sparse literature.[2]

The lack of documents on Roma life in Albania does make this a difficult enterprise. The Roma working in cultural projects funded by non-governmental initiatives in Elbasan are few and isolated, and the NGO reports are either fragmented or include a significant number of positive stereotypes reminiscent of Okely's argument that the images and information we have of the Roma tend to inform more on greater society than on the Roma themselves (Okely 2002: 10). Fieldwork among the Roma is also a particular challenge; Roma enjoy confusing a stranger with the overwhelming contradictions in their reports. It is thus essential to spend a great deal of time establishing oneself in Roma community and to return again and again to the same topic. Finally, the Albanian Roma communities themselves have been involved in vehement debates on how they wish to definition themselves as a group or whether they desire to be considered an ethnic minority or simply a cultural one. The Albanian state officially considers the Roma community

---

[1] According to documents in the possession of the Roma Youth Community Centre in Rrapishta. This number should be taken with care since traditionally, Roma communities in Elbasan had problems with their legal registration, especially Roma of the extreme periphery, where fluxes in population still take place.

[2] Most literature was written after 1990 and deals with issues, among others, of human rights, the role of the state vis-à-vis the Roma, criminality, mentality, integration and education. Writing on the Albanian Roma is limited to two Roma newspapers, *Ylli i Karvanit* and *Ditët tona* and in a rare article in other newspapers, the Journal of Gypsy Lore Society, a dozen books in English or other languages on Roma life in Europe and Balkans and a few reports by the Albanian Amaro Drom Union and other NGOs.

to be equivalent to other ethnic groups, recognising their concomitant rights under the Constitution.

THE ROMA IN ALBANIA

According to the Albanian Human Rights Group (AHRG), the existence of Roma in Albania can be traced back to 1635 (AHRG 2004: 89) and may have been present in Albania even since the 12th and 13th centuries, coinciding with significant Roma migration movements in Europe (AHRG 2004: 89). Hasluck traces the Roma presence to 1604 (Hasluck 1938: 49). Roma arrived in Albania from two directions, from the south, to settle in Korça, Bilisht, Pogradec, Elbasan, Berat, Lushnja, Vlora, Tirana and Fushë-Kruja, and later from the east, settling in Shkodra, Kukës, Milot, Dibër and Mat (AHRG 2004: 89).

According to Ottoman registries from 1523, there were 374 Roma families living in Albania at that time (AHRG 2004: 89) and Hasluck reports in 1938 that these nomads hardly numbered 2,000 individuals in all of Albania (Hasluck 1938: 50). In the absence of official census figures, the data on the exact number of Roma in Albania can only be approximate. While data provided by some foreign demographers indicate that ca. 100,000 Roma live in Albania today, the International Helsinki Federation for Human Rights (IHFHR) on the other hand reports that this number is around 30,000 (IHFHR 2001: 17) while the Albanian Amaro-Drom Union maintains that the number should be closer 150,000 (Leci 2000: 27). This huge divergence confirms once again the lack of a clear picture of the Roma population in Albania.

The Roma communities in Albania preserved their own language in the absence of Roma-language schoolbooks, which are only a recent introduction, so few of them know how to write it. Today the Roma communities in Albania are ideally divided into four main tribes: Herli, Meçkar, Kurtof and Çergar. The Herli are represented by non-Roma as aggressive and impulsive. They are found in Elbasan, Korça, Pogradec, Bilisht, Tirana and a few in Fushë-Kruja. Also they are known for trading horses and as such have been in continuous movement throughout Albania as merchants. The Herli are also known as Karbuxhi among the Meçkar. The Meçkar are known as farmers. These are the only Roma who are permanently settled and are not periodically or continuously on the move. They settled in Myzeqe, Berat and Vlora. This tribe is also known for its affluence and relatively high level of formal education.[3] The Kurtof are quintessential nomads who, so the stereotype, still live in tents in temporary camps. They are known for their refusal to subject to the official establishment in Albania in terms of registration and education. The Çergar are known for their skills in astrology, magic and fortune-telling and can be found in Shkodër, Milot, Durrës and Tiranë. Widespread legends

[3] The president of the Albanian Amaro-Drom Union is Skënder Veliu, is a Meçkar with university degrees in agronomy and law.

about the Çergar have emerged with time, such as that they kidnap white (that is, Albanian) children and drink their blood. During my time among Roma communities of Elbasan, I discovered that the term Çergar is sometimes used as a derogative among other Roma to indicate individuals of born of mixed Roma and 'Egyptian' marriages.[4]

THE ROMA IN ELBASAN DURING THE TWENTIETH CENTURY

The district of Elbasan entails a territory of 1338 km^2 and a population of almost 270,000 inhabitants. It is located in the centre of Albania, linking the north with the south. Historically is known for its role as a station on the via Egnatia. The city of Elbasan, with a population of 123,209 inhabitants is made up of five boroughs. It has experienced a great deal of demographic growth in the last decade, a result of the fall of the communist regime in 1990, a fact confirmed in the Project Report of Elbasan Municipality for the City General Regulative Plan (CGRP) in April 2005. The continuous migration to the city is mainly due to the difficult socio-economic situation in the rural areas of the Elbasan district in a situation where there is no state control of illegal settlement.

The Roma in Elbasan are distinguished from other minority groups. In the consciousness of white hand[5] people, they were nomads who lived in tents and spoke Romani. In Elbasan, the Roma have been called (and still are called) *Arixhi* (f. *Arixheshka*), meaning 'bear men'. According to Margaret Hasluck, both 'Egyptians' and Roma were found in Central Albania before 1604, as revealed in Turkish fermans in the possession of Lef Nosi of Elbasan (Hasluck 1938: 49). Roma activities in Elbasan included trading horses, begging, artisanry and other skilled trades. According to Hasluck, four or five Romani-speaking nomad families had long been settled in the neighbouring villages of Bujgjës and Jagodina, and other nomad families had settled in Meraja e Gjatë and Bejlik, in a separate *stan* (colony) from the sedentary Roma and did not intermarry with the sedentary 'Egyptians' (Hasluck 1938: 53)[6]. Hasluck also reports that the nomads used to go about in their own dress, that their tents were of the simplest type, with quilts and straw mats as their only bedding. They spoke fluent Albanian and any other

[4] Various popular forms of the term 'Egyptian' are commonly used in Albania to identify sedentary Roma, distinguishing them from other Roma. For example, in Korça Egyptians are called *evgjitë* and Roma are called *kurbetë*, meaning nomads. In Elbasan, Egyptians are called *jevq* while Roma are called *arixhi*, meaning "bear man". In Shkodra, Egyptians are called *magjypë*, while Roma are called *gabelë*. All these terms are, according to Hasluck, variations on the word Egyptian (Hasluck 1938: 50).

[5] The term white hand is common jargon among the Roma in Elbasan to identify 'white' non-Roma. I rarely came across the word *gadji* during my fieldwork, which seems in the past to have been in common use to identify non-Roma. This shift in Romany everyday jargon may represent a shift from a mostly culturally-based concept of "the other" such as the word *gadji* conveys, to a racial one like white hand.

[6] Even today, Roma see 'Egyptians' as inferiors and intermarriage between them is almost impossible.

language that they commonly encountered. They were seen by Albanians as untrustworthy people *i pafe* (without religion).[7]

According to my interviews, the Roma have lived the city of Elbasan as semi-nomads since the 19th century in a quarter known today as *Kinezët*. Once on the periphery, due to the continuous growth of the city and changes in points of reference and differing conceptions of space, the area is today interpreted to be near the centre and belongs to the first borough. Roma still inhabit this quarter and are recognised by other Roma and Albanians alike to be very old inhabitants of Elbasan.[8] They have very good incomes and represent the Roma elite in Elbasan. The old houses in the quarter were in accordance with the style of traditional Elbasani houses. Descendants of these old Roma families remember their forefathers and compete with one another in recapitulating their genealogies. They belong to the Herli and as such were merchants and migrated seasonally. Migration began in the spring and ended by late autumn, when they returned to their houses in Elbasan. Some Roma report to remember the graves of their ancestors, others say that the tradition of ceremonial burial in a cemetery was adopted later, substituting the tradition of burying the deceased there where they died. Elbasan was also a stop for many migrant Roma colonie that set up their tents especially on the banks of the Shkumbin River and the Manazdere Stream. Some older Roma reported to have housed migrant Roma families in their houses during the winter. Most houses in the quarter were nevertheless demolished by the end of the 1950s to make place for a pedagogical high school college and other public buildings, the owners being granted small plots in Rrapishta as compensation. Rrapishta is an area found on the extreme periphery of the city near the Manazdere, where transmigrant Roma often set up their camps.

Judith Okely points out that the choice to live near industrialised and inhabited areas are indicative of the Romany way of life (Okely 2002: 43). The city of Elbasan was a good choice because of its position in the centre of Albania, linking the north and the south. This location favoured seasonal migration throughout Albania and abroad. Large trade fairs essential for Romany traders used to be held in Elbasan and present-day Roma consider these trade fairs as the main reason why their forefathers chose to settle in Elbasan.[9] These settled Roma also provided a point of entry and a place to stay for other Roma visiting the fairs. According to Zija Shkodra, periodical trade fairs were established very early in Elbasan. He counts three important trade fairs, one of which, the trade fair of Shinjoni, is documented to have taken place as early as the 14th century, that were frequented by visitors from, among other places, Kavaja, Dibra, Tirana, Korça, Ohrid and Manastiri (Shkodra 1984: 217-218). According to fieldwork notes taken by Bardhosh Gaçe (and archived in the Institute of Folk Culture, Tirana) the trade fairs in Elbasan took place at least until 1908. Convenient climatic conditions and the

---

[7] The proverb Arixhinjtë s'kanë as din, as iman (the Roma have neither religion nor faith) is popular even today. This nevertheless contradicts my observations of Roma observances of religious feast days, especially Shën Gjergj (St. George's).

[8] Some of these Roma have old documents showing how long the houses have been in their ownership.

[9] According to Safet R., descendant of one of oldest Roma families in Elbasan.

confluence of the Shkumbin, Zaranika and Manazdere,[10] were also favourable factors attracting Roma migrants. Mark Tirta nevertheless does not count Elbasan to those cities most affected by emigration at the turn of the 20th century (Tirta 2003: 165-166).

Society in Elbasan was characterised by a relatively family-centred and closed way of life with clear boundaries to other communities. This situation facilitated the selling of products from abroad. The Elbasani take a long time to accept outsiders and even today, migrants of the third generation are still not considered native despite generally harmonious living conditions. But despite the aversion towards newcomers to the city, Elbasan is characterised by gentleness and generosity as indicated in many Elbasani proverbs.[11] Traditionally, they never threatened a beggar but were more than generous, which was also attractive for Roma who earned a living as beggars. As such, the Roma-Albanian coexistence in the city was marked by mutual indifference and sporadic contact.

The situation of the Roma after the establishment of the communist dictatorship

The Roma community was much affected by the policies and politics of the communist dictatorship. They were forced to settle and register, were forced into regular employment, into military service and administration structures. They were also the subject of new myths, propagated through the media and literature.

As a result of settlement politics, many Roma settled permanently in the region of Myzeqe, Korça and Tirana. As mentioned, at the end of 1950s many Roma who had long been residents of Elbasan were granted small plots of land in Rrapishta as compensation for losing their houses in the centre. Rrapishta was marked by a grove of plane trees, dreadful and far away from city; even today, despite the growth of the city, it remains on the extreme periphery. There the Roma built new houses in the style of their old, demolished ones. The settlement initiative resulted in the Roma being registered, although no record of their being Roma was kept. This, and the fact that Roma surnames are as a rule identical with those of Muslim Albanians, makes it difficult to reconstruct the Roma population of Elbasan at this time. The Roma found themselves subject to the controls of the state, including the quarter's *këshilli popullor* (people's councils). Every village and quarter in communist Albania had its *këshilli popullor*, which oversaw the running of the area under its mandate and was manned by the only party in power. Roma were often also party members; the head of the *këshilli popullor* of Rrapishta was a Roma[12] and many of its members were Roma.

---

[10] The Roma preferred to camp near rivers and streams; among their favourites were the Shkumbin (in Elbasan) and the Vjosa (in Vlora), especially during late autumn and winter.

[11] Such as Elbasani asht' vend i butë (Elbasan is gentle place) or Tokë e butë, mot i butë, njerëz t'butë (Gentle land, gentle climate, gentle people).

[12] Namely Esat S. a civil service driver. He received a half a standard wage for this work. He resigned in 1985, and having married a Kosovo woman, began to trade across the border.

If residents of the quarter were unemployed, a job was proposed by the *këshilli popullor*. If this suggestion was refused, strong reprisals were the rule. Many Roma were fined or imprisoned. Roma I interviewed reported that working under these strict controls was the most difficult part of living under the regime, but was better than being imprisoned, which was the worst thing that could happen to a Roma, a fact that is indicative of their love of freedom and space. For instance, Safet R. reports that he used to work in a co-operative and in a train station. This was very hard for him, but he accepted it and was sure that this was a better fate than that of his father, who was imprisoned many times as a result of his rebellious attitude towards the work assigned to him by the state. He also said that Rrapishta was a kind of paradise for him. The area was stigmatised and run down, but strangers used to stay away, even the police, who once had one of their vans destroyed by the Roma living there. Safet R. could wander the quarter without restriction or plaguing demands from the authorities.

The Roma were employed primarily in three sectors. The first of these was with the NSHN (State Construction Enterprise) as transport workers, travelling from place to place aboard a lorry in groups of four or five. They were also employed in the forestry industry. In Elbasan the cherry trees on Krraba were planted by Roma, as were the olive trees of Vidhas and the pine trees of Krrasta e Madhe, Shushica and Qafbull. Finally, the Roma were also employed in the trades and as artisans, working as basket weavers and musicians. They also taught basket-making. Assuming they were registered, Roma men were also subject to the usual two years of military service and continue to be so today (Leci 2000: 28);[13] again, no record of their being Roma was made. Needless to say, military service was not well-liked by the Roma men. In most cases Roma were not treated like non-Roma when they were called to complete their military service. The Herli Roma of Elbasan were often assigned duties related to stockbreeding and animal care. They were also assigned to play in the army's orchestras. Others were assigned to do service on the borders.

In the areas where I conducted researched, the Roma proudly recall the quasi-mythic story of Gani Misha - the rebel, which they relate with much feeling. Gani came from Berat to Elbasan and refused to work or to serve in the military. He was imprisoned many times, only to be let go or escape. One time, the police encircled and caught him, but again, he profited from their lack of attention and escaped again. Although in handcuffs, he hid five or seven hours in the cold water, breathing through a reed straw, until the police went away. The Roma insist, "Gani was a real Roma, he had an unyielding soul." Generally, the Roma were represented in the media as faithful and trustworthy, illiterate but sincere and full of hope.[14]

[13] The Kurtof Roma are an exception and were able to maintain their nomadic lifestyle. They were thus not all registered and thus not all conscripted into the military. After 1991 the weak state was no longer in a position to register or conscript everyone and many Roma in Elbasan could avoid military service.

[14] Specifically in representations of Roma participation in the National Liberation War. One Roma, Sabri Mile, even rose to become a brigade commissar; cf. Leci 2000.

ROMA ENTREPRENEURSHIP

Judith Okely points out that the Roma refusal to accept regular and stable work is a direct result of their identity (Okely 2002: 46). Despite the controls, the Roma of Elbasan found room for entrepreneurship. Their illegal business enterprises included the making and selling of baskets. During work in the forest, the man would also do the work of his wife (or wives),[15] who would spend the time collecting materials for making the baskets that were then sold illegally in the nearby villages or were sold to the state for cash. Today, the Roma both of the centre and the periphery experience their identification with basket-making as somewhat embarrassing since new forms of self-representation and identity have emerged or been emphasised after 1990.

Tinkering[16] was another illegal activity. Roma took aluminium, plastics, glass and other raw materials to make baking pans, sieves and other vessels that they sold in the villages. The materials were taken either directly from the workplace or in collaboration with other workers and supervisors, who then shared in the profit. Thread and cloth was also traded, the material being acquired in the same manner. Glass and plastic were made by primitive means into beads or other decorative objects. Begging was also practised outside of the Roma community. Sherif Sh. recounted that during community labour in the forest, he sent his three wives to beg for food. In this case he worked for four. Trading horses was also illegal, but almost all Roma in Elbasan have conducted horse trading, especially in the remote villages. According to field notes taken by Bardhosh Gaçe, the Roma of Llakatund in Vlora conducted horse trading with Macedonia from 1952 to 1967 and the Roma of Elbasan have reported to have conducted horse trading with the Roma of Vlora throughout the dictatorship.

Beyond the borders

Goods from outside Albania were circulated and traded in Elbasan (such as brand name and digital watches, brand name clothes etc.) as a result of Roma connections. The common way to acquire these goods was to make a deal with drivers who regularly travelled abroad. These then smuggled these goods and sold them via trustworthy Roma for cash and/or other goods (such as oil ration coupons). Another way of acquiring these goods was via Roma living abroad who came to visit their relatives in Albania. Considering the observation they were subject to, great care had to be taken and they regularly waited three or four months before selling their goods or they sold them in remote areas. When they were caught, they were imprisoned, such as the case of Servet A. from Elbasan, who was found guilty of selling foreign watches.

---

[15] Polygamy is illegal but still practiced unofficially; Kujtim S. had 4 wives and 31 children. Today his three surviving wives (one died in emigration to Greece) live in separate houses.

[16] This is not a very common profession among the Roma of Elbasan.

Not only did the Roma come into the possession of forbidden goods from abroad, they also exported objects of interest, often via the port of Durrës. Safet R. relates how he searched the country for gold coins or jewellery to export by means of established connections via Durrës. The Roma also claim that in the waning years of the communist dictatorship they were able to cross the border to Yugoslavia and Greece to trade. While these claims need to be considered with care, the Roma clearly had knowledge of illicit routes to and from Albania. Both Roma and the official authorities verified that after 1990, Roma were very confident illegal migrants; many non-Roma attached themselves to Roma groups when crossing the border to Greece.

Understanding Roma entrepreneurship within a dictatorial system

Eastern European Roma never really bought into the system of socialism and instead were excellent in black and grey market activities; the public sphere of socialist life was never of great concern for them, neither economically nor symbolically (Marian-Bălaşa 2004: 216). Although others perceived them as peripheral to day-to-day Albanian life, the Roma themselves were conscious of the insufficiencies and predilections of greater society and thus adopted a key position in the exchange between the urban and the rural, the centre and the more far-off areas of communist Albania in which society was closed and the movement of the population strictly controlled. The extreme poverty under the cruel dictatorship made people adapt, helping oneself to so-called common property became a part of life, as such a virtue and not condemnable, at least in public opinion. The informal economy was ever-present in the 1980s; people augmented their meagre wages by means of the exchange of goods stolen from common property.

The Roma, although illiterate, had a broad knowledge of non-Roma habitus. They knew what was needed and how to get it, all the while managing the necessary interaction with the authorities on their own terms. The Roma were able to project the image that would in a particular case help them the most, and it is from this perspective that the withdrawn Romany lifestyle should be understood.

During the dictatorial regime they used to present themselves as ignorant and aggressive. The widely recognised fact that Roma were illiterate seems to have justified their 'lack of knowledge' about the normal course of things in a dictatorship. For example, Sherif Sh. reports that once, the police stopped him on the way to trade in a remote village. The horses he intended to trade were all loaded with goods, but since the whole family was there, this did not appear to be too problematic. The police initially wanted to confiscate the baskets and beads, but Sherif and his family appeared to be very poor, illiterate and humble and they allowed them to go. The stigma of Roma aggressiveness and impulsiveness assured a necessary distance from 'the normal course of things' and consequently, room to prepare for trade. The Roma were also able to get the attention of non-Roma when necessary, for example when this was profitable or to avoid attracting attention if this was the better course. This approach is reflected in the reaction of non-Roma when asked about the way the Roma lived, or merely about the way they had conducted trade during the communist period. With the exception of those who lived in the direct neighbourhood of Roma, the rest of society seems to have had no knowledge of Roma activities. The naïve but significant response of one of my non-Roma informants in Elbasan, Skënder D., is typical: "the Roma seemed not to exist; you knew they were around, but you would only become aware of their presence when they came to your door and begged."

THE ROMA AFTER THE COLLAPSE OF THE REGIME

After 1990, Albania opened up to the world after being the most isolated society in Europe. The transformation from a centrally planned to a market economy and from a totalitarian communist regime to a democratic system is continuing and has left much confusion in its wake: extreme poverty, a difficult economic and a social situation resulting in extreme migration movements. Criminality and quick money, the chance to build houses illegally or with documents acquired through bribery emerged. New phenomena appeared under the veil of tradition and lost traditions rematerialised. New values and mentalities emerged or became manifested within Albanian society.

In the following I will delineate the effects this system change had on Roma migration and trade, the core of Roma identity and way of life. As such, these changes convey the changes within the Roma community in Elbasan and at the same time affect the ever-present points of contact between Roma and non-Roma. Three kinds of migration emerged among the Roma of Elbasan after 1990, migration within Albania, seasonal migration and emigration.

Migration within Albania, movements in search of better living conditions, resulted in new Roma settlements in Rrapishta and in a new quarter called Stadiumi locally. Stadiumi is at the periphery of the city although much closer to the centre than Rrapishta. Once a farm, it was first settled by Roma shortly after 1990.[17] The houses were built without permits and are not conform to city planning standards. In general, Roma families who have settled here are from families of Elbasani Roma origin. Other Roma have also settled in Rrapishta and Stadiumi, migrating from Pogradec or Berat and do not necessarily belong to the Herli tribe.

Seasonal migration is much affected by new conceptions of space brought about by the introduction of new technologies. Judith Okely points out that motorisation has furthered nomadism (Okely 2002: 45). Even for the Roma of Elbasan, owning a means of transport maked it easier to traverse long distances, shortened periods away from home, increased the frequency of travel and assured control over a larger territory. The Roma of the extreme periphery (i.e. Rrapishta) maintain the tradition of seasonal migration as a family, the woman and children being considered working arms. This seasonal migration begins in the spring and ends in

[17] This is not only a Roma phenomenon. Many families from rural areas have moved to the cities in search of better living conditions and have settled close to members of their old communities (cf. Voell, this volume, for a case study).

late autumn with destinations including Peshkopia, Mirdita, Kukës and Bajram Curri in the north, Myzeqe in the south and, of course, Tirana. The Roma of the periphery move at irregular intervals, following the trading and market days in Albanian cities, towns or villages to come back the same day or in a few days. The children often stay at home. The Roma of the centre tend to trade abroad with Germany or Italy buying inexpensive or out of fashion clothes. Another line of trade is with Turkey and the United Arab Emirates. Recently, a clothing trade has emerged with China. These migrants usually work alone.

Emigration is also common among Roma in Elbasan. While local migration is more prominent among older individuals, emigration, especially to Greece, is the métier of the young and the youth. The extreme periphery (Rrapishta) and less the periphery (Stadiumi) are affected most by such movements. Migration may last years and parents, when asked, are adamant that their children will return to Albania. Usually the emigrants work as *palaxhi* (gatherers) in recycling or they simply beg.

Judith Okely stresses in her work the dependence of Roma on the economy at large and of their need for an intact relationship with greater society, their detailed knowledge of the social environment and openness to change (Okely 2002: 41). Roma links to the fate of non-Roma have continued in the 1990s; the often risk-laden opportunities have, if anything, multiplied. The 1990s were characterised by the influx of goods from abroad. One sphere of Roma activity disappeared only to be replaced by new ways of earning a living in congruence with the needs and lifestyles of the rest of society. Beside traditional occasional and self-employment, some Romany traders established large enterprises, which represent a so called "big boom of Romany trade," such as ADEMI Ltd., which won the tender to deliver police uniforms for the district of Elbasan. Roma continue to earn their living through begging, recycling, basket-weaving sporadic construction work, music, petty trade and enterprise. Elbasan represents for the Roma a hub for goods coming from abroad; from here they are redistributed to more rural areas.

The Roma are also present in used clothing markets (known as *gabi* or *xhiku*, derivatives of the terms *gabelë* and *arixhi*), which are improvised and run down. These markets in Stadiumi and Rrapishta occupy an area 3400 m^2 and 800 m^2 respectively, of a total market area in Elbasan of 19,100 m^2. Trading used clothes is considered one of the most profitable spheres of Roma activity in Elbasan.

As opposed to the established Roma community living in the centre, Stadiumi and Rrapishta are identified by the city as a problem primarily because of the illegal housing and inadequate infrastructure. It has repeatedly been discussed, if the informal markets should not be shut down. Thus it is impossible to talk of long term strategies among the Roma; most of their activities are characterised by the speed in which they come into being, relatively small investments and generally broad scope.

New stratification and self-representation

Roma life after 1990 is also marked by changes in the way Roma deal with one another and with non-Roma. Expanded Roma migration and the boom of Romany trade have made room for new forms of stratification and self-representation. Due to the significant migration to – and very rarely out of – Elbasan, contact between different Roma tribes and clans or Roma of different geographical background has increased. Among the 'native' Roma of Elbasan, a need for stronger differentiation from newcomers appeared. Combined with the preference to collaborate in business with close relatives, a clear stratification based on wealth, tribal an kin origin and settlement history emerged. A more varied Roma culture began to appear in Elbasan society and more possibilities for contact arose. As mentioned, the 'native' Roma of Elbasan are *Herli*. Those who arrived in Elbasan after 1990 had to accept the predominance of the *Herli* communities, who stress their position as native and as the most noble Roma tribe, which, they say, follow a patriarchal, authoritative and rigorous lifestyle, reifying these values as the 'real thing'. They do not like to be identified as nomads and explain that huge differences exist between their own and other, 'lesser' Roma tribes, their community and other Roma communities, focusing on language differences, hygiene ideals, clothing and communication-skills with the white hands. Some of them also stress their Roma values and traditions, the trading of horses, the significance of personal freedom and their impulsiveness. In interviews, Roma explain that those Roma found in the centre and periphery of the city are 'pure Herli' while in the extreme periphery the tribes are mixed and some still conduct an 'ignoble nomadic lifestyle.' The worst that could happen to these 'pure Herli' families is marriage with a Kurtof.

Nevertheless, despite all their claims to the contrary, the Herli still have to deal regularly with other Roma groups. Safet R., a Herli who in the past traded in Vlora, used to seek protection and a place to sleep among the Kurtof. But he would never marry his daughter to a Kurtof, his excuse being that they have problems with hygiene. But he is hopeful: "Only a few Kurtof Roma live in Elbasan and as time passes they become more like us (like the Herli)".

Beside tribal origin, geographical origin is also a basis for stratification. Statements such as "We are from Korça and a Korça Roma is indistinguishable from a white hand," stress the good hygiene, clothing and emancipation of Roma from Korça. A Roma man from Korça confidently conveyed to me that they (the Roma from Korça) will always be as different from the Roma of Elbasan as day is different from night, and even after two hundred years, they will still be different. At a meeting of Roma representatives of the periphery with a parliamentary candidate before the 2005 elections is also exemplary. The Roma representatives had already agreed to contribute to the candidate's campaign, but only if their Roma neighbours of Korça origin were excluded, calling themselves "authentic Elbasani Roma".

Stratification based on wealth is an important consideration when marriages are planned. Although the number of mixed marriages is slowly increasing, clear restrictions continue to be made on the choice of partners. Police authorities in Elbasan reported on the trouble a rich Roma family from Tirana had, whose daughter eloped with a poor Roma boy from Elbasan. The bride's family would in no way accept this and arrived en masse from Tirana; they made a scene that could only be resolved through police intervention. Although both families belonged to the same tribe, the bride's family still considered their daughter's marriage with a poor Roma from Elbasan an offence and as such they managed to finally take the young woman back to Tirana, despite the fact that she was already married.

The status of a Roma family is often represented in the number of floors their houses have; "many Gypsies who made money abroad, sometimes through dishonest means, invested that money in to the construction of impressive mansions (the nowadays infamous "Gypsy palaces"), which were less for comfort than for vanity, and which had many unnecessary facilities (Marian-Bălaşa 2004: 198)." This phenomenon is also present among the Roma of Elbasan. Such investments gain in importance with the extreme stratification among Roma in Elbasan. It nevertheless reveals the anxiety and uncertainty that has emerged as a result of the changes the community is passing through; the competition and need to be compared with others also serves as a way to be part of a group, assuring belonging.

CONSIDERATIONS ON ROMA REPRESENTATION

The non-Roma inhabitants of Elbasan see the Roma as a group of people, who live pursuing their ‚own nature', deviant from that of the majority. Marriage at a young age, impulsiveness, the liking of music and dancing, heavy jewellery and colourful dress are associated with the Roma.[18] Having experienced a Marxist evolutionary ideology for more than 40 years, Albanians in general have difficulty with concepts that do not fit such evolutionary approaches. Roma nomadism is interpreted as primeval and primitive, unhygienic and inhuman. The stereotypes that Roma live in tents and even if they are sedentary still do not live in houses, eat together from a common pot and marry within the blood line predominate and serve to re-enforce the Marxist logic. The fact that all peripheral quarters in Elbasan are characterised by infrastructure problems or are far away from political attention is ignored when Roma are described as living on the periphery or are at the margins of political interest. The same is true when a Roma's poor appearance leads to them being understood as beggars or when their irregular work or marginal professions are interpreted as ignoble despite the fact that they bring a good income.

After 1990, Albanians had the chance to make free choices regarding education, which was followed by an overemphasis of formal education; having a diploma of some kind became an obsession.[19] In such a situation, Roma deficits in formal education are commonly interpreted as an inadequacy or as an inability to learn. But formal education is not seen as particularly important in Roma communities in Elbasan; and the lack of education and irregular schooling does not necessarily mean ignorance (Okely 2002: 46). The Roma earn a satisfactory living without it. In most of NGO reports, this lack of formal education is almost always attributed to external factors rather than to Romany values. Romany children are still educated in Romany terms, meaning they learn the skills required to achieve the desired success in petty-trade. This does not mean of course, that no Roma aspire to provide their

[18] Roma are often described as 'close to nature', 'unmanageable' or as having a 'savage instinct.'
[19] This obsession gave way to corruption in formal education structures.

children with formal education, some do and admit it in private. Roma attitudes towards education, for young girls[20] but also for boys, are rooted in a fear of deviation should children be permitted to be away from home alone for a long time. The system of formal education has itself been passing through a transitional crisis. The inclusion of Roma in a peaceful environment in heterogeneous classrooms has been of little concern. Additionally, the cycle of how Roma are represented and how non-Roma reflect on this, leads to 'deprived' Roma children facing discrimination and neglect in schools.

The Roma are still commonly interpreted as being rebellious, aggressive, incorrigible and menacing. This image contradicts the facts such as those collected by the police in Elbasan. According to the authorities, Roma communities are in no way more dangerous and problematic than other quarters; crime rates among Roma communities in Elbasan are even the lowest in comparison to other communities. The authorities' approach is to "let Roma go their own way." The authorities justify their approach with the fact that most Roma conflicts are solved internally by traditional Roma means. Thus, although conflicts are as common as anywhere else, they are resolved without outside intervention. These conflicts and their resolution follow a typical scenario. They begin with the women arguing before the men get involved and finally the elders meet to come to a resolution. Certain conflicts even end with a consolidation wedding among the parties involved. This tradition of the scenery quarrel is still vividly apparent among the Roma and is seen as a part of Roma identity. A Roma informant used to say that his only dream was to make two films, one on a Roma wedding and one on a Roma quarrel.

Aggression towards non-Roma usually remains latent and serves as a marker of distance. As a whole the Roma value their position apart. The police see little risk of Roma involvement in large scale organised crime due to their general reluctance to co-operate economically with non-Roma. The Roma remain a community "in themselves".[21]

CONCLUSIONS

This paper has aimed to provide an overview of Roma life in Albania and especially in Elbasan and the ongoing changes these Roma communities have experienced. While several NGO initiatives have focused on the plight of the Roma in Albania after 1990, they remain very few and isolated, and more importantly, are characterised by their activist nature and a prominent lack of

[20] According to almost all NGO reports viewed, marriage is the most often named reason for young girls to leave school. Although this may be true in some cases, in my experience, most Roma girls left school long before getting married.

[21] Which does not mean that they are not sometimes involved in criminal activities. As mentioned previously, the Roma are experienced in border crossing activities, which may include the transport of illicit goods in co-operation with Greek Roma.

concrete knowledge about these communities.[22] Despite their stated intention to challenge and change stereotypes, NGO reports often unintentionally do just the opposite and reify the stereotypes, blaming exclusive environments, Roma mentality, Roma self-representation and so on for the problems in the community. The truth is that Roma communities, in Elbasan as elsewhere, are extremely dynamic and extremely heterogeneous. Having settled in three well distinguishable quarters in the centre, periphery and extreme periphery of Elbasan, these communities are highly differentiated. And they are intrinsically tied to the greater community. As such, to speak of Roma isolation is nonsense. They have survived as a distinct community only because they have actively promoted this distinctiveness. The vital Roma values of freedom and space, which have been frequently translated as defiance or animosity vis-à-vis greater society, are not symptoms of isolationism. On the contrary, Roma in Elbasan have always felt themselves to be part of and taken part in greater society. This status is sometimes individually initiated, sometimes explicit or socially recognised and sometimes inconspicuous or concealed. The upheavals experienced by Albanian society at large are also reflected in the way the Roma trade and move, designate themselves and others and interrelate with them or organise their own communities. Exploring the Roma community within and in interaction with greater society is vital for understanding their situation.

BIBLIOGRAPHY

Albanian Human Rights Group 2004 Minorities: the Present and the Future. Report of AHRG on the Situation of Minorities in Albania, Tirana: GSHDNJ.

Hann, Chris 2003 Is Balkan Civil Society an Oxymoron? From Königsberg to Sarajevo, via Przemyśl In: Ethnologia Balkanica, Vol. 7 pp 63-78.

Hasluck, Margaret 1938 The Gypsies of Albania In: Journal of the Gypsy Lore Society, Vol. 17(2) pp 48-61.

IHFHR (International Helsinki Federation for Human Rights) 2001 Human Rights in the OSCE Region, Protection of Ethnic Minorities.

Kajsiu B., A. Bumci and A. Rakipi 2002 Albania - A Weak Democracy, A Weak State: Report on the State of Democracy in Albania Tirana: Albanian Institute for International Studies.

Leci, E. 2000 Kontributi i Rromëve të Shqipërisë në problemet e mbrojtjes In: Rromët në vendin e tyre, Qendra Mesdhetare, Tirana: ALWO pp 26-30.

Marian-Bălaşa, Marin 2004 Romany Music and Gypsy Criminality In: Ethnologia Balkanica, Vol. 8 pp 195-225.

Okely, Judith 2002 Ciganët shtegtarë Tirana: Dituria

---

[22] The Albanian Institute for International Studies criticises the NGO sector in general as reflecting "international rather than local priorities. As such they have been unable to speak for and on behalf of the general public and also unable to bring any substantial pressure to bear on government policies" (Kajsiu et al. 2002). "An anthropological approach to 'civil society'" by contrast, so Chris Hann, "can avoid ethnocentric bias by concentrating on social relations and core meanings in the everyday life-worlds of the people we study (Hann 2003: 64)."

Shkodra, Zija 1984 Qyteti shqiptar gjatë Rilindjes Kombëtare Tirana: ASHSH.
Tirta, Mark 2003 Etnologjia e Shqiptarëve Tirana: GEER.

9. "THE SMILING DAUGHTERS." TRADITIONAL CLAN STRUCTURES AND CUSTOMARY LAW IN POSTSOCIALIST ALBANIA.

STÉPHANE VOELL

On 15 November 2001 I was sitting with an Albanian colleague[1] in the guest room of a family from the northern Albanian region Dibra. The family had migrated to Bathore, a suburb of the capital Tirana from the north several years previously. The head of the house was recommended to us by some of his neighbours because he was familiar with the northern Albanian customary law *kanun*. Our host invited us to sit in the guest room; next to our host sat his two daughters. On the coffee table lay a new copy of the *kanun*. Slowly and thoughtful the head of the house answered our questions concerning the practice of the customary law in the suburb. We asked him what the younger generation, specifically his children, thought of the *kanun*. Our host answered like so many other interviewees in the previous days of our research in Bathore: of course he educated his children according to the *kanun* and taught them its rules accurately. Despite numerous social changes in Albania in the last years, he continued, the northern Albanian youth and especially his children still knew about the importance of their own cultural traditions. This also touched on how the children were to be married. The head of the house reiterated that a young woman, according to the *kanun*, did not have the right to decide about who she would marry. This was to be done by her father or her brothers. At the least, women were not allowed to become engaged without the explicit consent of her family.

We asked our host what would happen if one of his children would marry without asking his consent. His daughters suddenly looked very interested. Our host spoke of his son, who graduated university and came home together with a young woman that he had gotten to know at university. But both did not forget their roots, said the head of the house, and they both asked their families to consent to an

---

[1] The research in Bathore would not have been possible without the help of Xhovalin Tarazhi. Bledar Kondi helped me while doing research in the north of the country. My fieldwork (cf. Voell 2003; 2004) in Albania in the years 2000-2002 was sponsored by the German Academic Exchange Service DAAD (Doktorandenstipendium im Rahmen des gemeinsamen Hochschulsonderprogramms III von Bund und Ländern; http://www.daad.de); the trip in 2003 was partly financed by the Südosteuropa-Gesellschaft, Munich (http://www.suedosteuropa-gesellschaft.com). Research was done primarily in Shkodra, Puka and Bathore. I mainly conducted semi-directed interviews with elders, heads of brotherhoods and fis, mediators and family heads. Much of my research was done in little conversations, reading articles in newspapers and programmes on television. In Tirana I carried out interviews with lawyers, anthropologists and representatives of conflict resolution NGOs.

engagement. Despite their modern university education, both his son and his fiancée respected the *kanun*, said the father.

We asked him again how he would react in respect to his daughters: what would have been his reaction if they would not have asked his consent to get engaged and marry? After a short period of consideration he answered us just as thoughtfully as during the rest of the interview that this would be a violation of family honour and that in such a case he would have to proceed to the ultimate penalty. He did not speak of his children directly; rather, he spoke in an abstract form. We expected such a statement because we had heard similar accounts previously in Bathore, but we were not prepared for the reactions of our host's daughters, also because they had not said a word up to that point of the interview. The two daughters were smiling broadly and clearly had to hold themselves back so as not to laugh out loud. "There you have your answer," said my colleague in English. The head of the house did not look in any way concerned and either did not notice or not want to notice his smiling daughters.

A hasty interpretation of this anecdote could be that the customary law *kanun* is possibly still a well-known collection of norms and rules but that in contemporary Albania it does not have any repercussions in society anymore. But it would be more accurate to say that the *kanun* should not only be understood as a collection of abstract rules but also as an expression of a specific social field. A central aspect of the field are the patriarchal clan structures (*fis*). The anecdote of the smiling daughters already indicates that within the traditional family structures long-established power relations are crumbling. In this article I will describe the persistence of the social field of the *kanun* as exemplified in kinship relations in northern Albania and with migrants from the north in Bathore. I will discuss how patriarchal, segmentary and specific economic traditional structures and ideologies are still today important aspects of Albanian society, but which likewise are being questioned, mainly due to economic influences. The *fis* and its segments are not the prime frame of references for social action anymore. But traditional kinship relations are maintained in part in present-day Albania and through their persistence there also persist social and economic structures with which customary law *kanun* need to put into relation.

FROM *KANUN* TO KINSHIP STRUCTURE

A large handicap in the discussion of the present day relevance of the *kanun* is the fact that when in academic and similar discourses it is asked whether or not traditional rules are still valid, this is often only understood in relation to written versions of the *kanun*. These texts, among them the prominent compilation *Kanuni i Lekë Dukagjinit* by Shtjefën Gjeçov, have or had only little to do with the real practice of law. The Albanian Franciscan Gjeçov (1874-1929)[2] collected rules and norms of the *kanun* in different communities in northern Albania, which at the time was under Ottoman rule. A compilation of his ethnographic work was published posthumously in 1933 under the title of *Kanuni i Lekë Dukagjinit*. A new edition of this book can be bought today in any random bookshop in Albania.[3] But this version of the *kanun* is problematic as a source for the practise of law, which can be said of any other version of the *kanun* as well:[4] First, the book has to be considered as a political statement, an answer to the often heard claim that Albania was inhabited by lawless and unorganised primitives. Gjeçov showed the people in northern Albania as living within a highly differentiated society structure. Today doubts have been raised if such a form of social organisation ever existed (Krastev 2000: 202). Second, Gjeçov collated rules from various regions and from different times into one text (Fox 1989a: 118; Ivanova 1960). Third, the book is structured similar to a 'classic' code of law, with articles and paragraphs. The law was clearly supposed to be valorised in book form but has in this form only limited significance for the real practice of the rules (Voell 2004: 46-49). Therefore, the written versions of the *kanun* describe only insufficiently its past and actual practice. Furthermore, the *kanun* as a book that one is presented in many households in northern Albania is of little importance, i.e. the book itself is not used as a work of reference to look up the exact wording of a particular article. The book is not read, nobody refers directly to certain pages and no children seem to learn directly from it. The *kanun* as a book is, rather, an artefact that is pointed to and which is presented in a prominent place in the house.

The local law *kanun* cannot be found in the written and abstract articles of the *Kanuni i Lekë Dukagjinit*. But actual social practice is just as difficult to find in the rules scholars are presented in interviews. This is not a usual phenomenon. The legal anthropologist Franz von Benda-Beckmann reports of a similar phenomenon in the presentation of the customary law *adat* in Sumatra. The people in the villages presented their *adat* in a legalised form. According to them, customary law would prescribe exactly what to do in particular situations and they would all act according to the rule. But what does the social practice of the rules look like? "If a researcher stays longer, he will discover that quite frequently people do not behave according to the – idealized – rules which have been stated in interviews or which have been pronounced in decisions of local authorities" (Benda-Beckmann 1989: 140).

Numerous ideal types of rules in relation to honour, theft, family relations or property relations are known and enumerated in interviews. But as mentioned, these recited rules and norms of customary law only rarely find repercussion in social practice. One might suppose that the *kanun* is only a cultural survival, but in interviews or even in the work of northern Albanian scholars (cf. Gjuraj 2000) the *kanun* is considered to have a vital and prominent role. Is this wishful thinking or

---

[2] On Gjeçov cf. Fox 1989a: XVI-XIX; Godin 1953/1954/1956: 7 FN 4 (1953); Pupovci 1971: 81-88; Zojzi 1981.

[3] For translations of Gjeçov's kanun of cf. Fox 1989b (English) or Godin 1953/1954/1956 (German, new edition edited by Robert Elsie; Gjeçov 2001).

[4] Cf. Elezi 1983; 2002; Illia 1993; Meçi 1995; 2002.

does the *kanun* transcend the law as expressed in rules? Does the law *kanun* refer to broader cultural concepts that, despite 46 years of stone-age socialism and a difficult democratisation process, continue to persist?

Questions about the local knowledge of modern legal concepts and local references to a customary law – be they word for word or not – say little about the relative obsolescence of the *kanun*. The existence of legal regulations and their practice has to be considered separately. A certain legal prescription can, based on the specific situation, lead to different outcomes, i.e. law can also be interpreted arbitrarily. But this does not change the fact that the particular rule is still present. This means that even in the case that an accurate transcription of the *kanun* would exist, one could only make a statement about the application of *kanun* if the actual social practice of the listed articles are to be taken into consideration.

Law does not stand alone, i.e. the social practice of the *kanun* appears as an expression of wider cultural and social conditions. Clifford Geertz (1983: 173) states that law is not bound to norms, rules, principles or values "but [is] part of a distinctive manner of imagining the real." Lawrence Rosen (1989: 5) stresses that it might be fruitful to see law as part of a wider notion of culture, as one part of concepts that extend into many spheres of social life. A particular society and its practice of law stand in relation to one another similar to how economic practice is interwoven with all other spheres of social life. Thus, in the following I will show how the socio-economic structures as understood in relation to the *kanun* are still relevant today.

One of the most important factors in the social role of the *kanun* are the *fis*-relations in northern Albania. Already the leading socialist ideologists knew that it was imperative to prise open the traditional clan and tribal structures in order to install the socialist model of society (Logoreci 1977: 181). For this reason the regime tore down large family houses and built in their place smaller houses or apartments or relocated people out of their isolated hamlets into often completely new villages. With the collectivisation process in agriculture, the socialist state aimed to deprive the local population of its economic foundation (Champseix/Champseix 1990: 33, 1992: 80; Dojaka 1987: 95). But already during socialism, reports were published about the 'survival' of the *fis* in northern Albania (Zojzi 1977) or about the still predominant social role of extended families. The head of the house still oversaw family life, especially in those regions where the *kanun* had for centuries held a prominent position. He watched over the division of labour in the household, distributed the different tasks and administered alone the material wealth of the family (Alia 1989: 20; Dojaka 1987: 99; Gjergji 1973: 84). The socialist regime also had difficulties in implementing collectivisation in northern Albania, which often lead to the situation that extended families continued to manage their fields together (Schwanke 1969; Teich 1969). On a local political level, some extended families could even rely on a certain degree protection from the socialist regime, especially if the families had supported the partisans in the 'war of liberation' (Dumont 1983). Finally, the socialist government under Enver Hoxha itself reproduced clan structures on the political level (Logoreci 1977; Schwandner-Sievers 1996).

Despite certain continuities, it has to be stressed that the socialist regime no doubt managed to profoundly modify the northern Albanian social field. The far-reaching self-administration of Ottoman times, the supra-regional interconnectedness of the *fis* and the economic foundations of northern Albanian traditional society were partly dismantled or at least completely reorganised. But still, *fis* structures were preserved in socialism and beyond and provided a fertile ground for a postsocialist revalorisation of traditional family relations that are an important pillar of the customary law practised today.

THE *FIS* IN POSTSOCIALIST NORTHERN ALBANIA

Before describing the present-day situation, I will briefly describe northern Albanian patriarchal kinship structure as it is related to the *kanun* in an ideal-type form. An understanding of this structure is necessary to illustrate the ideal importance of the family. But the presentation of an exact model of the northern Albanian *fis*-relations is difficult - for two reasons. On the one hand, different terms denoting individual elements of kinship structure are or were in use in the different parts of the northern Albania (Baxhaku/Kaser 1996: 17-22; Kaser 1992: 181-191). On the other hand, there are important variations in the importance and even the existence of the individual parts. This is due to the changing political situation in Albanian history and especially because of the intervention of various reigning powers and governments in the socio-economic structure of the *fis* (cf. Ulqini 1991, 1995).

The denomination of the individual parts of the *fis* are either of an ancestral or of a territorial nature.[5] The basic unit of the ancestral dimension is the family (*familja*), both as a social and an economic unit. The head of the house (*i zoti i shtëpisë*) presides over the household and manages the division of labour among family members, administers material wealth, represents the family in the public sphere and is also personally liable for the misconduct of family members. The family is synonymous to the territorial category 'house' (*shtëpi*). If a family gets too complex or insurmountable problems arise within a family unit, it may split. One part of the family moves out of the parental house and constructs a new house, often simple right beside the first. Both houses together form a brotherhood (*vllazni or vëllazëri*), which is presided over by the head of the senior household. The Albanian term for clan is *fis*, which is a group of related families and brotherhoods. Membership in a *fis* is based on a most often mythical common male ancestor. The leader of the *fis* is called *i pari i fisit* (head of the clan). Marriage within the clan is not permitted. The kinship unit *fis* may correspond to a hamlet (*mëhallë or lagje*), to a group of hamlets, to a village or even to an entire region. The leader of the hamlet, which after 1944 was only an informal position, is called *i pari i mëhalles*. Today a *kryeplak* is formally elected as head of a quarter. Three or four hamlets or quarters form together a village (*fshat or katun*). The highest level of this territorial dimension was until the end of the Ottoman occupation the *bajrak* (banner). It was

[5] For a more detailed description of the ancestral and territorial axes of northern Albanian kinship structure cf. Voell 2004: 149-167.

introduced by the Ottomans towards the end of the 17th century in order to better integrate the highland regions of Albania into the Ottoman administration system. The borders of the *bajrak*, which are still common knowledge today, were conceived on the basis of topographic conditions but took *fis*-borders into consideration.

In the turbulent years after the fall of socialism in 1991, kinship relations in general formed a more or less stable frame of reference.[6] Today's importance of *fis* and brotherhood can be traced back to this period between 1991 and 1997, which was shaped by political unrest, mass emigration, general strikes and economic breakdown. Northern Albania was marked by material poverty and many people left their villages to the plains around Tirana or looked for work abroad. The infrastructure was only poorly developed in the north and the local population were often excluded socially by the rest of the population because of their so-called 'primitive customs'. Northern Albania was furthermore far from having a working administration. But still, as many elders never cease to stress in interviews, the general situation remained comparatively quiet in the north. Despite the lack of functioning state institutions, the *kanun* and the continued relevance of family relations made it possible, as the elders say, to survive the first stormy postsocialist years without falling into anarchy. If the *kanun* did in fact play such a role in this period is today only difficult to reconstruct. Population density dropped so low in the even in the socialist past sparsely populated north after the mass emigrations of 1991 and 1992 that massive unrest is alone for this reason hardly conceivable. But the *fis* without a doubt did acquire an important social position so that today the *fis* must be seen as a powerful social parameter.[7]

The members of the family continue to form a social and economic unit. They generally work on their own on their small plots. Larger fields are rare in the narrow valleys of the north. Furthermore the families own one or two cows, sometimes only goats that offer a little milk. Agriculture has long been the most important sector of the local economy and the economic base of the specific northern Albanian family structures. After the fall of socialism, agricultural production in the form of small-scale farming regained in importance across Albania; 65 percent of the northern Albanian population continues to live in rural regions and work in the agricultural sector.[8]

It became clear in my interviews and also in large scale studies on the topic of landed property at the University of Wisconsin in Madison[9] that basic aspects of the northern Albania *fis*-relations, like patriarchy and patrilinear inheritance continue to be an important part of society (Wheeler 1998: 1-2). A contemporary household

---

[6] This section is based on Voell 2004: 178-189.

[7] Ethnographic studies of the first postsocialist years in Albania include Eberhart/Kaser 1995; Santner-Schriebl 1999; Schwandner-Sievers 1996; 1998; 2001; 2004.

[8] Cungu/Swinnen 1999: 605; Hashi/Xhillari 1999: 101; Lawson et al. 2000: 1500; Saltmarshe 2001: 69. In all Albania incl. the urban population, 52.6 percent of the population live from agriculture (Basic facts & indicators 2001, Albania. In: http://www.eu-esis.org/esis2basic/ALbasic7.htm (7 November 2005).

[9] Cf. http://www.ies.wisc.edu/ltc (7 November 2005); for publication cf. http://www.ies.wisc.edu/ltc/pubeur.html#alb (7 November 2005).

includes, beside the as a rule male head of the house[10] and his wife, one of his sons with his wife and children, who all together work in agriculture and the domestic sphere. Often several sons and their wives live together in the parental home. If a married son manages to accumulate enough material resources to found his own household, he will in general leave his parental home with his family. It may happen that the head of the house leaves a part of the family's fields to a married son, where he may build his own house. Numerous other factors might lead to the departure of the son with his wife from the parental household as well, including migration to the city, the marriage of a younger brother, who has a stronger claim to residence in the parental household, or even the social security system, which offers support only on the basis of the household and not according the number of family members (Gruber/Pichler 2002: 361; Lastarria-Cornhiel/Wheeler 2000: 130-131; Wheeler 1998: 24).

The anecdote at the beginning of this article may have given the impression that the head of the house in northern Albania no longer has much authority in the family anymore. But research shows that the social position of the head of the house is still predominant, or, as Rachel Wheeler (1998: 11) puts it, "In general, every family has a patriarch." Especially after the fall of socialism, with the growth of the social relevance of traditional kinship relations, the power of the heads of the house has increased, as has their position as representatives of the family in the public sphere. The economic developments in the 1990s and the growing influence of Western European values through the media and return migrants who experienced first-hand alternative family models nevertheless undermine the new power of the head of the families (cf. Lawson/Saltmarshe 2002: 499). Generally, it can be said that the position of the head of the house is esteemed and his word has a certain weight, but familial respect towards him is no longer unconditional. As long as his sons still live in their parental home and the household forms an economic unit, the head of the house is respected and his word followed. But the influence of the head of the house declines rapidly when his sons move out of their parental home and become economically independent.

Some related families may form a brotherhood (*vllazni or vëllazëri*) and often a brotherhood lives together in one hamlet, thus forming a spatial unit as well. But close economic relationships between the families within a hamlet are rare today. The traditional function of a head of the hamlet (*i pari i mahallës*) is still important; for example, in cases of conflict within the local community he is still the first person to speak to. In contrast to the *fis*, which today can hardly be delimited accurately, the brotherhood appears to be a relatively clearly defined unit and is today possibly the most important kinship unit. The brotherhood is the social recourse of the individual families and may in case of emergency or financial trouble provide assistance. In interviews, the 'unity of blood' is especially stressed in relation to brotherhoods, but the increasing individualisation of economic

[10] For exceptions and few contemporary so-called 'Albanian virgins' cf. Rapper 2000; Young 2001. Only 7 percent of all households have a female head, and this mostly in situations where the man in this position has died (Lastarria-Cornhiel/Wheeler 2000: 133).

development seems to be undermining the role of brotherhoods as well (Lawson et al. 2000: 1502, Lawson/Saltmarshe 2002: 497).

The formal counterpart of the head of the hamlet is the head of the quarter (*kryeplak*). This office was introduced in 1992; its holder is elected by the people of the quarter (*lagje*). The function of the head of the quarter is to ensure public order, in co-operation with the police. The office was also intended to form a link between citizens and the state administration and ensure that public services were accorded equally to all the people of the quarter (Saltmarshe 2001: 70-71). But the actual functions of the head of the quarter transgress his official duties. More often than not the head of the quarter is the member of a fis without the support of which he probably would not have been elected to this position. Therefore, the head of the quarter is not only the last man of the state in the administration hierarchy but also the representative of the traditional structures in the village. The position of a head of the quarter was explained to me as "*kryeplak është gjys kanun e gjys shtet*" – he is 'half kanun' and 'half state'. He is a *pikë takimi* – a meeting point. Since the head of the quarter is responsible for the maintenance of order, he will try to solve a conflict if a conflict arises, for example a problem in relation to landed property. It is not considered important if he follows the procedures prescribed by the state or by customary law. What is important for him is to find a compromise that is acceptable to all conflict parties. The head of the quarter is, in an ideal form, a mediator between traditional and state processes and offices.

Several brotherhoods form together a *fis*. The contemporary significance of the *fis* is not easy to describe; it depends among other things on where the *fis* is located. In marginal regions, like around the city of Kukës in northeastern Albania, the members of the *fis* often still live together in their hamlets, surrounded by their fields. Here the *fis* continues to be a sizable economic and social factor (Lemel 2000: 52-53). In contrast, in the lowlands around Shkodra it is very difficult to delimit a concrete *fis*. There the members of the *fis* rarely live together because the original homogenous settlement quarters no longer exist or have been undermined by extensive migration. The *fis* here is more like a network in which its members may find mutual support and economic aid. Loans are granted preferably to relatives, because kinship is considered to be the highest form of security. Douglas Saltmarshe, for example, describes how for the granting of a loan a kinship relation is even 'artificially' created through a form of godparenthood in order to embed the transaction in kinship relations (Lawson et al. 2000: 145; Saltmarshe 2001: 95).[11]

Difficult economic conditions lead to the increasing social relevance of the family and the commitment to their *fis* appears to be stronger among poor families. The relationships within of the *fis* become weaker, in contrast, when individual parts of the *fis* become economically independent of the rest. In addition, migration, both within Albania and abroad results in growing social contacts outside of the *fis* and the brotherhood, which in turn lose more and more influence as leading social group of reference. But the *fis* continues as an important network of dependency. It is an information network, which as a result of the positioning of *fis* members in

---

[11] For godparenthood cf. Doja 1999: 233-238.

administration and free enterprise allows access to services to other *fis* members (Lawson et al. 2000: 1502; Lawson/Saltmarshe 2002: 101; Saltmarshe 2001: 499).

Just as the informal position of the head of the hamlet continues to exists, so does the head of the *fis* (*i pari i fisit*). But as a *fis* is today is so difficult to delimit and since its members live scattered across the country and abroad, the head of the *fis* only have very limited possibilities for enforcing their point of view. A very differentiated picture prevailed in my interviews. On the one hand it was said that the head of the *fis* has no importance today. In Ottoman governed Albania, the leader of the *fis* surely was the first person to talk to on issues affecting the *fis*. But today, as many people stated, nobody would respect them anymore and they often only appeared at weddings and funerals in their old function. On the other hand, interview partners stressed the important role of the head of the *fis* as mediators in resolving conflicts. But these persons seem to be exceptions and tend to be asked to mediate due more to their experience or charisma than to their office as head of a *fis* as such. Some heads of *fis* are also powerful because of the current or past economic position of their *fis*, or even because of relationships with influent people in politics or administration.

THE *FIS* IN A TIRANA SUBURB

North of Tirana, on the road to Shkodra, countless one-family houses stand on very fertile land, the former experimental fields of the agricultural university and the land of a co-operative state farm, laid dry in the socialist period and afterwards cultivated intensively. After the end of the socialist state, many people migrated to the capital from the rest of the country, driven by poverty and unemployment, to re-establish themselves on the fields around the city. Around 54,000 people lived in 2002 on an area of 23 km^2 (in 1990 they numbered only 6000).[12] The place has been named Kamza and is a fusion of shanty villages, among them the village of Bathore. In Bathore around 30,000 live on an area of only 400 ha. The migrants are formally squatters, the land having been transferred to employees of the former state farm. But even repeated police raids could not stop the continuing flow of migrants. The legal status of the migrants vis-à-vis the land they are living on is even today largely unclear. The people who live in Bathore in former stables or in simply constructed cement block houses that are often look half-finished came for the largest part from northern Albania. Few of these houses have their own well, much less running water. Water must be carried from the nearby agricultural university buildings. Many of the houses are – legally and not – connected to the electricity network. But the existence of power lines, especially in the winter

[12] http://www.ihs.nl/downloads/projects/2003%20Albania_Draft%20Kamza%20ProcessMapping.pdf (8 November 2005).

months, does not necessarily mean electricity. The ordinary electric power problems in Albania seem to prevail in Bathore in an exponential form.

At the time of my research in Bathore (November 2001), the administrative organisation was very complex.[13] The reason for this was on the one hand the unclear relationship of this residential area with the community of Kamza. One part of the shanty village had officially been annexed to Kamza, but the other part still had the status of an independent village. On the other hand, the lack of local state administration structures needs to be mentioned. The recent establishment of administrative structures in an illegal settlement, where the people are in theory only squatters, is opposed to well-rehearsed and organised set of kinship networks. The official administration has few resources and no power and can only provide help and services in Bathore with the support of the numerous non-governmental organisations (NGOs) working in the area in health, social and infrastructural sectors. The NGOs get the credit for the work; and many people in Bathore accuse the members of administration of only looking out for their own personal interests.

My research in Bathore intended examine whether the northern Albanian *fis*-relations of the primarily northern Albanian population were also present in this suburb of Tirana; is the *fis* in Bathore a relevant social factor? As expected, the answer was ambiguous, but it is possible to say that the *fis* in Bathore, where the state administration is weak, developed to become an important component of social life.

In the first stage of each interview with people from Bathore, the migrants nearly unanimously said without hesitation that the *fis* played a significant role. They said that the *fis* was a relationship based on the same blood and therefore the *fis* offers a naturally strong form of cohesion in an alien surrounding. But as the interviews went on they also stressed that in practice, the *fis* is not as strong as in theory and that the *fis* should instead be conceived as a network and not as a clearly defined kinship unit (cf. also Santner-Schriebl 1999: 196).

The families that migrated from the early 1990s onwards to Bathore came one by one. No complete *fis* or brotherhood ever moved as a unit. Still, the families tried to settle close to family or kin who already lived there. Later this was no longer possible because of the density of the settlement. Nevertheless, the members of one's *fis* remained the first contact in Bathore, even if the families only ever meet for festive events such as weddings or funerals. Some *fis* and brotherhoods migrated in large numbers to Bathore and the neighbouring communities while other families have only few kin here.

The importance of the *fis* as a social network is not necessarily a desired relation, as I was told, but the lack of administrative structures and their present-day weakness, the difficult economic conditions and the social exclusion that the northern Albanians had to face in the capital led to the situation that kinship relations became the prime or most important frame of reference for the population in Bathore. The quality of kinship relations seem to increase the longer the related families live in Bathore. Especially those people who were among the first to

[13] This section is based on Voell 2003; for Bathore cf. also Metaj/Dashi 1998; Santner-Schriebl 1996; 1999.

migrate to the area underlined the importance of the *fis*. A *fis* with a lot a families in Bathore is called, like in their home region, a strong *fis* (literally a *derë e fortë* - a strong door). Their elders and leaders are respected in the neighbourhood, also because there is a strong *fis* behind them. But the interconnection between the individual households in a brotherhood of a *fis* does not follow any observable order. This is on the one hand because of the distance between different family units and on the other hand because of the economic conditions. There is no agriculture where they could possibly work together and they have no common economic interests. Each household is responsible for itself. Only in times of crises and cases of conflict do kinship relations become important.

But unlike in northern Albania, the leaders of the *fis* (*i pari i fisit*) have little authority. The name of the head of the *fis* can often be cited, even if he lives far away in the north of the country. One group of people stressed that for them, the head of the *fis* continues to be an important figure and his word still had weight, even in Bathore. Certainly, nobody would go to him about the minor day-to-day problems just to hear his word on these issues. But for subjects like blood feud or larger family problems, the opinion of the head of the *fis* is still considered. But these cases appeared to me to be ideal-type descriptions, only rarely was I given concrete examples where the head of the *fis* had a word to say in Bathore. A second group of people said that they had a head of the *fis* but that his influence on social life in Bathore was non-existent. On the contrary, in Bathore individuals had emerged in the place the head of the *fis*. These people are not the same individuals as the leaders of the *fis* in the hamlets like they can be found in northern Albania, they do not occupy inherited positions nor are they officially elected and they do not have the power to enforce concrete decisions.

My questions concerning the heads of kinship groups or quarters elicited standard responses almost every time that at the moment the situation was one of disorder in Bathore but that soon a new leader would be found. But obviously there are no leaders whose authority could be based on kinship relations. Instead, elders had emerged, who are respected because of their charisma, experience in family business, authority and also because of their age. They are the strongmen in the loosely structured kinship relations and are the first contact persons in cases of conflict in the quarter. The words of these elders have a certain weight in the quarter and especially in their family. But among the younger generations, which are economically independent of their parents and their extended families and have little use for traditional hierarchies and the advice of family elders, their authority is weak. In cases of conflict, nevertheless, like theft, struggles around property or family disturbances, the first person to go to is the elder. Thus the elder must be conceived of as an adviser and not as a head or leader.

The prime frame of reference in day-to-day social life in Bathore is the quarter and the local families organised in a brotherhood or *fis*. In the quarter, where the first migrants from northern Albania settled, meetings of the elders of the different families take place. These are not regular meetings, but it appears that recurring consultations about conflicts in the quarter are taking place, although they are not very organised. The meetings may even take place spontaneously, on the street or in one of the numerous little bars. Issues discussed include thefts or conflicts about property borders established in the first years of settlement in Bathore. The projects of the diverse NGOs in the area are also discussed here. If, for example, the elders agree to an infrastructure project and occupied ground is needed for this project, the elder's talk to the family living there and try to convince them that the project, such as the construction of a canalisation system, is a useful project. If the owner cannot be convinced of the necessity of the infrastructure project despite the fact that the rest of the neighbourhood are for it, they cannot be forced to consent. It could happen, nevertheless, that the family is ostracised from social life in the quarter.

CONCLUSIONS

Elsewhere I have demonstrated that if traditional structures that stand in relation to the *kanun* (like the *fis*-relations discussed here) continue to be relevant, the *kanun* might also in the near future remain an important part of northern Albanian society (Voell 2004). My argument was based on the dialectic relationship between habitus and the social field in the sense Pierre Bourdieu applied it. Through socialisation, the individual internalises the socio-economic structures of his environment, i.e. the social field.[14] These structures are internalised as dispositions of action and form that what Bourdieu called habitus. It forms a frame for social action as structured by the individual social field and delimits the possibilities of individual social action. Through social action based on these internalised dispositions, the individual in turn validates the social field. There exists a close and mutual relationship between the social field and habitus (Bourdieu 1972: 301-302). In homogenously structured societies with little contact to the outside, habitus is perpetuated because of its alternating relationship with the social field, which only shows little movement, if any. If an individual always encounters those schemes of cognition in which it was socialised, they will have little chance to question their internalised dispositions.

But the situation in northern Albania is more complicated, society is not as closed as in the ideal situation. The family and the brotherhood still form a solid frame of reference, especially in rural regions, where they are the basis for a common economic relationship in which traditional hierarchies continue to be important. In the mediation of conflicts or in the provision of services, if one member of a *fis* is in the 'right' position in the administration, *fis*-relations remain a relevant structure in society. But the *fis* and the legal conceptions that stand for it exists in competition with other frames of reference. Bourdieu (1980: 93-94, 102) argues that the habitus does not disappear from one day to another; habitus has a certain degree of 'inertia'. Drastic social changes do not result in the immediate reconsideration of habitus and a new habitus does not evolve very quickly. Long-established strategies are increasingly challenged, but this does not immediately affect day-to-day social life.

[14] For a definition of social field cf. Bourdieu/Wacquant 1992: 97.

Fis-relations play an important part in the inertia of traditional structures in northern Albania and - in turn - the customary law. Socialisation within traditional family structures is crucial for the maintenance of the social field of the *kanun*. From early childhood on, as Bourdieu underlines (1994: 139-140), the individual internalises social practices, and this takes place primarily within the family. Here the individual experiences the schemes of cognition of the social field that integrates the family and ensures its continuity. Much of this process is the internalisation of symbolic constitutions of meanings relevant within the family. Stephanie Schwandner-Sievers (Schwandner-Sievers 1999: 134) defined these as an 'inherent symbolism' deduced from Albanian mythology as a dialectic value system. She writes that 'oppositional categories' that describe symbolic classifications between friend and foe, honour and shame or loyalty and betrayal form the thinking of the northern Albanian population (Schwandner-Sievers 1996: 96; 2001: 102).

I have deliberately avoided recounting specific rules from the *kanun* to either verify or refute its existence. It is not difficult to animate people in northern Albania to explain how one should behave in a particular situation according to the *kanun* or what the *kanun* says about the organisation of extended families. The answers to these kinds of questions generally come without hesitation and in a very precise form. After several interviews in Bathore, we asked ourselves if our interlocutors had been told but our coming long before we finally did come and had had time co-ordinate their responses to our questions with one another. But when we began to ask about concrete examples of specific conflicts, the answers came with less confidence. For example, numerous families were apparently in long unresolved conflicts about an inheritance in which one party based their argument on the *kanun* while the other on state law, depending on which was more favourable for their respective position. The *kanun* exists and one cannot say that because the people do not all act according to the word of the *kanun* that it does not exist anymore.

One way to study the practice of the *kanun* is to analyse the ideal-type procedures given in the *kanun* and its complex social practice as presented in case studies. Another possibility is to describe parts of the social field of the *kanun* and to discuss their continuing relevance. In this article I discussed how traditional *fis*-relations continue to remain a relevant part of social life, even if they are no longer the sole frame of reference. *Fis*-relations are challenged increasingly but it is difficult to escape the influence of *fis* and brotherhood – and with them the *kanun*. The daughters are smiling, but they are not laughing.

BIBLIOGRAPHY

Alia, Zana 1989 Die Familie und ihre Struktur in der SVR Albanien. Tiranë: 8 Nëntori.

Baxhaku, Fatos and Karl Kaser 1996 Einleitung. In: Fatos Baxhaku and Karl Kaser (eds.) Die Stammesgesellschaften Nordalbaniens. Berichte und Forschungen österreichischer Konsuln und Gelehrter (1861-1917). Vienna: Böhlau pp 7-26.

Benda-Beckmann, Franz von 1989. Scapegoat and Magic Charm: Law in development theory and practice. In: Journal of Legal Pluralism and Unofficial Law Vol. 28 pp 129-148.

Bourdieu, Pierre 1972 Esquisse d'une théorie de la pratique (Collection Points: Série essais, 405). Paris: Seuil.

Bourdieu, Pierre 1980 Le sens pratique (Le sens commun). Paris: Les Éditions de Minuit.

Bourdieu, Pierre 1994 Raisons pratiques: Sur la théorie de l'action (essais, 331).

Bourdieu, Pierre and Loïc J. D. Wacquant 1992 An Invitation to Reflexive Sociology. Chicago: University of Chicago Press.

Champseix, Élisabeth and Jean-Paul Champseix 1990 57, boulevard Staline. Chroniques albanaises (enquètes). Paris: La Découverte.

Champseix, Élisabeth and Jean-Paul Champseix 1992. L'Albanie ou la logique du désespoir (enquètes). Paris: La Découverte.

Cungu, Azeta and Johan F. M. Swinnen 1999 Albania's Radical Agrarian Reform. In: Economic Development and Cultural Change Vol. 47(3) pp 605-619.

Doja, Albert 1999. Amitié, alliance, parenté: idéologie et pratique dans la société traditionelle albanaise. In: Georges Ravis Giordani (ed.) Amitiés: Histoire er Anthropologie. Aix en Provence: Presses de l'Université de Provence pp 217-255.

Dojaka, Abaz 1987. Transformations des rapports à l'intérieur de la famille. In: Ethnographie Albanaise Vol. 15 pp 95-103.

Dumont, René 1983. Finis les Lendemains qui Chantent, Tome1. Albanie, Pologne, Nicaragua: Finis pour tous les mondes. Paris: Seuil.

Eberhart, Helmut and Karl Kaser (eds.) 1995. Albanien: Stammesleben zwischen Tradition und Moderne. Vienna: Böhlau.

Elezi, Ismet 1983 E drejta zakonore penale e shqiptarëve dhe lufta për zhdukjen e mbeturinave të saj në Shqipëri. Tiranë: 8 Nëntori.

Elezi, Ismet 2002 E drejta zakonore e Labërisë. Tiranë: Toena.

Fox, Leonard 1989a. Introduction. In: Leonard Fox (ed.) Kanuni i Lekë Dukagjinit = The Code of Lekë Dukagjini. New York: Gjonlekaj pp xvi-xix.

Fox, Leonard (ed.) 1989b. Kanuni i Lekë Dukagjinit = The Code of Lekë Dukagjini. New York: Gjonlekaj.

Geertz, Clifford 1983 Local Knowledge. Further Essays in Interpretative Anthropology. New York: Basic Books.

Gjeçov, Shtjefën 2001 Der Kanun: Das albanische Gewohnheitsrecht nach dem sogenannten Kanun des Lekë Dukagjini kodifiziert von Shtjefën Gjeçov. Pejë: Dukagjini Publishing House.

Gjergji, Andromaqi 1973 Disa probleme në lidhje me zhvillimin familjes së sotme fshatare. In: Studime Historike Vol, 27 pp 73-86.

Gjuraj, Tonin 2000 Gjakmarrja në rrethet Shkodër, Malësi e Madhe. Shkodër: Qendra "Dretësi dhe Paqe".

Godin, Marie Amelie 1953/1954/1956. Das albanische Gewohnheitsrecht. In: Zeitschrift für vergleichende Rechtswissenschaft Vols. 56, 57, 58 pp 1-46; 5-73; 121-198.

Gruber, Siegfried and Robert Pichler 2002 Household Structures in Albania in the Early 20th Century. In: History of the Family Vol. 7(3) pp 351-374.

Hashi, Iraj and Lindita Xhillari 1999 Privatisation and Transition in Albania. In: Post-Communist Economies Vol. 11(1) pp 99-125.

Illia, Frano 1993 Kanuni i Skanderbegut. Shkodër: Argjipëshkvi i Shkodrës.

Ivanova, Julia V. 1960 Kanuni i Lekë Dukagjinit (Shprovë e karakteristikave historike). In: Buletin i Universiteti Shetëror të Tiranës, Seria Shkencat Shoqërore (Tiranë) Vol. 14(2) pp 95-124.

Kaser, Karl 1992 Hirten, Kämpfe, Stammeshelden. Ursprünge und Gegenwart des balkanischen Patriarchats. Vienna: Böhlau.

Krastev, Péter 2000 The price of amnesia: Interpretations of vendetta in Albania. In: Antonina Zhelyazkova (ed.) Albanian and the Albanian Identities (The Fate of Muslim Communities in the Balkan, 5). Sofia: IMIR pp 194-217.

Lastarria-Cornhiel, Susana and Rachel Wheeler 2000. Family and property rights: implications for gender and farming. In: Harold Lemel (ed.) Rural Property and Economy in Post-Communist Albania. New York and Oxford: Berghahn pp 126-156.

Lawson, Colin, Allister McGregor and Douglas Saltmarshe 2000 Surviving and Thriving: Differentiation in a Peri-urban Community in Northern Albania. In: World Development Vol. 28(8) pp 1499-1514.

Lawson, Colin and Douglas Saltmarshe 2002 The psychology of economic transformation: the impact of the market on social institutions, status and values in a northern Albanian village. In: Journal of Economic Psychology Vol. 23 pp 487-500.

Lemel, Harold 2000 Tenure security, land use, and investment. In: Harold Lemel (ed.) Rural Property and Economy in Post-Communist Albania. New York and Oxford: Berghahn pp 50-74.

Logoreci, Anton 1977 The Albanians: Europe's Forgotten Survivors. London: Golllancz.

Meçi, Xhemal 1995 Kanuni i Lekë Dukagjinit: Varianti i Pukës. Tiranë: Çabej.

Meçi, Xhemal 2002 Kanuni i Lekë Dukagjinit: Në Variantin e Mirditës. Tiranë: Geer.

Metaj, Ilirian and Etleva Dashi 1998. Bathorja: mozaik subkulturash dhe mosmarrëveshjesh. In: Pajtimi Vol. 3(2) pp 49-54.

Pupovci, Syrja 1971 Burimet për studimet e kanunit të Lekë Dukagjinit. In: Studime Historike Vol. 25 pp 75-98.

Rapper, Gilles de 2000 Entre masculin et féminin. La vièrge jurée, l'héritière et le gendre à la maison. In: L'Homme Vol. 154/155 pp 457-466.

Rosen, Lawrence 1989 The Anthropology of Justice. Law as Culture in Islamic Society (The Lewis Henry Morgan Lectures, 1985). Cambridge: Cambridge University Press.

Saltmarshe, Douglas 2001 Identity in a Post-communist Balkan State: an Albanian Village Study. Aldershot: Ashgate.

Santner-Schriebl, Silvia 1996 Feldforschung in den nordalbanischen Bergen: Der Sieg der Moderne im Postkommunismus am Beispiel des schnellen Wandels brüchig gewordener Traditionen im Dukagjin [diploma thesis]. Graz.

Santner-Schriebl, Silvia 1999 Wertewandel in Stammesgesellschaften am Beispiel der nordalbanischen Hochgebirgsregion Dukagjin und der Ghettos in Tirana und Shkodër [PhD thesis]. Graz.

Schwandner-Sievers, Stephanie 1996 Zur Logik der Blutrache in Nordalbanien. Ehre, Symbolik und Gewaltlegitimation. In: Sociologus Vol. 46(2) pp 109-129.

Schwandner-Sievers, Stephanie 1998 Wer besitzt die "Lizenz zum Töten" in Albanien? oder: Fragen zu Gruppensolidarität und Gewaltlegitimierung in einer "anderen Modernisierung". In: Jan Koehler and Sonja Heyer (eds.) Anthropologie der Gewalt. Chancen und Grenzen der sozialwissenschaftlichen Forschung. Berlin: VWF pp 71-88.

Schwandner-Sievers, Stephanie 1999 Humiliation and Reconciliation in Northern Albania: the Logics of Feuding in Symbolic and Diachronic Perspectives. In: Georg Elwert (ed.) Dynamics of Violence. Processes and De-Escalation in Violent Group Conflicts (Sociologus Suppl. 1). Berlin: Duncker & Humblot pp 127-145.

Schwandner-Sievers, Stephanie 2001 The Enactment of "Tradition": Albanian Constructions of Identity, Violence and Power in Times of Crises. In: Bettina E. Schmidt and Ingo W. Schröder (eds.) Anthropology of Violence and Conflict (European Association of Social Anthropologists). London: Routledge pp 97-120.

Schwandner-Sievers, Stephanie 2004 Times past. References for the construction of local order in present-day Albania. In: Maria N. Todorova (ed.) Balkan identities: nation and memory. London: Hurst pp 103-28.

Schwanke, Robert 1969 Wirtschafts- und Sozialentwicklung Albaniens vor und nach dem Jahre 1912. In: Walter Althammer (ed.) Die wirtschaftliche und soziale Entwicklung Südosteuropas im 19. und 20. Jahrhundert (Südosteuropa-Jahrbuch, 9). Munich: Trofenik pp 192-210.

Teich, Gerhard 1969 Das albanische Dorf (Von der Agrar- zur Industriegesellschaft, 16). Darmstadt: Hoppenstedt.

Ulqini, Kahreman 1991 Bairaku në organizimin e vjetër shoqëror: Fundi i shek. XVII deri me 1912. Tiranë: Akademia e Shkencave.

Ulqini, Kahreman 1995 Organizimi i Vjetër Shoqëror tek Shqiptarët. New York: Eagle Press.

Voell, Stéphane 2003 The Kanun in the City: Albanian Customary Law as a Habitus and its Persistence in the Suburb of Tirana, Bathore. In: Anthropos Vol. 98 pp 85-101.

Voell, Stéphane 2004 Das nordalbanische Gewohnheitsrecht und seine mündliche Dimension (Reihe Curupira, 17). Marburg: Curupira.

Wheeler, Rachel 1998 Past and Present Land Tenure Systems in Albania: Patrilineal, Patriarchal, Family-Centered (Working Paper: Albanian Series, 13). Madison: University of Wisconsin Press.

Young, Antonia 2001 Women who become men. Albanian sworn virgins (Dress, Body, Culture). Oxford and New York: Berg.

Zojzi, Rrok 1977 Survivance de l'ordre du fis dans quelques micro-régions de l'Albanie. In: Aleks Buda (ed.) La Conference Nationale des Études Ethnographiques (28 - 30 juin 1976). Tiranë: Académie des Sciences pp 185-206.

Zojzi, Rrok 1981 Shtjefën Gjeçov – un patriote et homme d'études éminent de la culture populaiere. In: Culture Populaire Albanaise Vol. 1 pp 171-184.

10. De-centring Albanian Patriarchy? Sworn Virgins and the Re-negotiation of Gender Norms in the Post-Communist Era

Antonia Young and Jenna Rice

This article seeks to address some of the questions that have surfaced about the place of the *virgjinesha* (sworn virgin) within Albanian patriarchy. In traditional patriarchal society in the southern Balkans, there has long been an option for ensuring a male heir where none actually exists: a girl or woman herself, or her parents as early as at her birth, may declare that she has become a man. A woman thenceforth dresses as a man, performs men's work and mixes socially as a man. It has often been asked whether gender roles in northern Albania are rendered more malleable due to the ability of some women to become men through the simple change of appearance and social role. We would here like to examine the norms that underwrite Albanian patriarchy and question whether sworn virgins, by virtue of their gender-crossing, destabilise or reinforce these norms. In so doing, we will trace the tension between the prevalent return to tradition in the mountainous regions of northern Albania in the postsocialist era on the one hand, and the new spaces for the negotiation of gender and patriarchy which the tradition of the sworn virgin carves out on the other. This paper will challenge the conflation of virgins with lesbians and ask what it means to talk about changing gender when sexuality itself is not relevant to the interests that motivate the transformation. It will then turn to those virgins who inhabit the traditional role only partially or in new ways to attend to the concerns and desires that animate their decisions to become men, thus aiming to complexify the way in which the destabilisation of norms is conceived.

Paradoxes of Re-traditionalisation

The role of the sworn virgin in northern Albania today can be analysed within the context of the return to tradition in rural Albanian society in the post-communist period. The German anthropologist Stephanie Schwandner-Sievers (2004: 106) explains that in her fieldwork she encountered, "a reversion to pre-communist values, structures, symbols and rituals as a pool of information for a new contemporary local order."

Certain analysts have pointed to the paradoxes according to which traditional, pre-communist forms of knowledge were revived in 1991 at the end of the nearly fifty-year communist dictatorship (see, for example, de Waal 2005; Schwandner-Sievers 2004). Prior to the communist period, the source for local order and tribal organisation had been the legal code known as the *kanun*, a set of orally preserved laws. This legal code was first set to paper by Shtjefën Gjeçov a century ago. The 1262 articles of the *Kanun of Lekë Dukagjini* – one version of this code – cover all aspects of mountain life, from the regulation of economic and family organisation, hospitality, brotherhood, the clan and boundaries, to work, marriage and livestock. However, Enver Hoxha's regime placed a ban on the *kanun*. As Clarissa de Waal (2005: 17) explains it:

> Seen by the communist government as a symbol of subversion and resistance, the *Kanun* was outlawed and even reference to the *Kanun* by locals in those areas where it had been practiced could lead to imprisonment.

It came as a surprise to discover the widespread knowledge of *kanun* law amongst the younger generation shortly after the fall of communism and de Waal suggests that, "suppression of the *Kanun* probably contributed to its survival and clandestine transmission to the young (except in the case of prominently communist families)." And paradoxically, the very measures meant to control the population – the restrictions imposed on the internal movement of peoples and a total ban on immigration – facilitated the maintenance of traditional life, especially in the inaccessibly mountainous regions.

Notably, since the end of the Hoxha dictatorship in 1991, there has been a resuscitation of reference to the *kanun*. The mass migration of men and de-collectivisation of land that marked the end of the communist period had a particularly dramatic effect on rural Albania. De Waal (2005: 17) documents the way in which the de-collectivisation of land precipitated a revitalisation of the *kanun*, particularly those laws relating to conflict resolution and land rights "The implementation of those parts of the *kanun* which deal with dispute settlement, property division and rights of way, was an important practical means of dealing with the existing legal hiatus. Adherence to the *kanun* as a symbol of identity and guide to behaviour might, it was hoped, act as a cohesive force in a society whose official ideological basis and practice of half a century had been discredited almost overnight" (de Waal 2005: 84).

Schwandner-Sievers (2004: 112) underscores the fact that

> variations of *kanun* rules persisted through time, space and person, differing in details of interpretation as to how to behave properly in feuding, and in respect of the guidelines prescribing how to save, restore or prove 'honour,' social status and pride.

She later remarks that

> it appears that in many north Albanian mountain villages certain interest groups have asserted control over local order via reference to the powerful myth of *kanun* and, partly, through reference to memories of a pre-communist [past] of social order (ibid: 117).

The *kanun* is thus a set of laws that is plural in its interpretation and manifestations, and that has re-asserted its legitimacy in the postsocialist era.

The patriarchal norms in northern Albanian agrarian society that inform gender roles are mediated and reinforced through reference to the *kanun*. These laws, under which the people of northern Albania lived for many centuries prior to the communist era, give a detailed description of the rigidly gendered division of labour that informs gender roles today. The *kanun* meticulously outlines the nature of men's and women's work. Traditional men's work includes all heavy manual work (chopping wood, scything, harvesting, protecting animals and property), talking to visitors, drinking and smoking with visitors, making all family decisions, representing the family outside the home and avenging family honour. Women's tasks include conceiving, bearing and rearing children, cooking, maintenance and cleaning of the family house, serving the men and guests, carrying water and firewood, weaving wool and sewing clothing.

The *kanun* also outlines the conditions under which a girl or woman can become a *virgjinesha*. It specifies that women can become social men in certain cases where there is a structural need for a male household head. Since all decision-making is taken by household heads (who by definition are male), a woman who chooses to fulfil the role, where there is no suitable male capable of doing so, must become 'male'. A father of several daughters and no sons may also decide to bring up one of his daughters as a man from birth in preparation for the necessary future role of household head. A woman may additionally opt to become a sworn virgin if she wishes to refuse her pre-arranged marriage without incurring dishonour on the family of her betrothed. In these cases, the female thenceforth dresses as a boy/man, performs male tasks and mixes socially as a male. With the change she swears virginity and may never revert to her birth gender.

When speaking here of gender, we are referring to social conventions that inform the distinctions between femininity and masculinity. We do not posit some incontrovertible difference between a corporeal, biologically rooted 'sex' and a socially and historically constructed 'gender'. Rather, following Judith Butler, we maintain that sexual difference itself is a contingent and culturally inscribed perception. Butler asserts that sex is not, "a bodily given on which the construct of gender is artificially imposed, but... a cultural norm which governs the materialisation of bodies" (Butler 1993: 2). In line with Butler, then, we will only speak of a distinction – or in certain instances, disjuncture – between 'sex' and 'gender' in cases where our interlocutors assume one to exist.

By changing gender, *virgjineshë* assure the persistence of the family household and preserve the honour of their family or, when the move to become a *virgjinesha* is used as a strategic means to refuse an objectionable marriage partner, the family of their betrothed.

The notion of honour is central to this re-traditionalisation. The household head, a position that is invariably occupied by a male, is seen as responsible for the preservation of family honour. Lule, for example, became a *virgjinesha* when his family realised that his elder brother was unfit to act as household head and represent the family at village councils. He explains, "I promised each of my parents, when they were dying, that I would ensure that the family was not dishonoured." Likewise, choosing to become a sworn virgin is the only honourable alternative to marriage.

ASSUMED HOMOSEXUALITY

Western feminists have tended to interpret sworn virgins within the paradigm of homosexuality. Questions about the destabilisation of gender norms are often accompanied by an assumption that sworn virgins in fact are (repressed) lesbians. What does it mean to understand gender transformation in a context where the primary point of reference in their gender orientation is not sexuality at all? Not only are *virgjinesha* and lesbian not commensurate gender identities, but this presumption contradicts the way these wo/men articulate their worldviews.

Ian Whitaker asserts that such a consideration would be quite beyond the comprehension of societies in which sworn virgins live (Young 2001: 67n21 & 22). Homosexuality for men was illegal in Albania until 1995, when the law was repealed that punished even those with a 'tendency' toward homosexuality with a prison sentence of up to ten years. Homosexuality was not even considered to be an option for women. Lesbianism is hardly discussed or even understood, while male homosexuality is still treated with hostility, although in Tirana it is gaining some acknowledgement, though certainly not acceptance. Whitaker (1981: 149) reports that

> [t]he idea that womenfolk back in the valleys might wish to indulge in lesbian associations was viewed partly with abhorrence, and partly with a disbelief that any pleasure could be associated with such activities.

While we do not wish to imply that homosexuality does not exist, particularly among women, we would like to point to its marginal and censured place within Albanian society, and clearly differentiate between lesbianism and the socially sanctioned, legally codified role of the sworn virgin.

Rather, *virgjineshë* constitute a third sex, but one with ambiguous classificatory autonomy.[1] On the one hand, sworn virgins remain distinct from most men in that they are not sexually integrated; on the other, it seems that many *virgjineshë* may be so fully accepted in their role that they may not be viewed as women-who-have-become-men at all but simply as men. These thoughts were provoked by Young's friend, Agim's, sudden awakening to the fact that maybe he knew of three sworn virgins with whom he had regular contact. In 1996, Young's fieldwork led her to several villages in northern Albania in which *virgjineshë* lived. Before embarking for these more rural locations, Young enquired whether Agim knew of any other sworn virgins living in Shkodra. He did not. But upon Young's return, he explained that he realised that there were actually some living in Shkodra, and within half an hour had put Young in touch with three further sworn virgins.[2] It may seem surprising that all three live under female names. Yet it supports our suggestion that their role as men was so fully accepted that the retention of their birth names was insignificant to those around them. It thus seems possible that their status as sworn virgins might either be of such little significance that it barely registers in the minds

---

[1] See Littlewood and Young 2005; cf. Young (2001: 19) where they discuss Réné Grémaux's observation that some of the sworn virgins he had studied did not receive the full social rights of men (Grémaux 1989, 1994). For example, Grémaux cites an instance in which Tonë, a Catholic, was buried in men's attire, but refused the ritual lamentation customary among his tribe of origin. We were not able to observe any instances of social differentiation and imagine such occurrences to be rare. Of greater significance are the ways in which *virgjinesha* are perceived by people within their communities. Our interlocutors all stressed that they see the *virgjinesha* they know as men.

[2] Young refers to these three sworn virgins as Lindita, Gemma, and Angjelina (Young 2001).

of those around them, or on the contrary, that those who know might feel honour-bound not to divulge it. There is the possibility that a significant number of sworn virgins living in villages and towns are so fully integrated as men that they are no longer or not commonly remembered or recognised as *virgjineshë*.

Although *virgjineshë* become fully integrated men, there are moments where a tension emerges between their lives as men and their understood biological sex. For example, in Kincses and Michalski's film "Pashke und Sofia" (2003), Anila recalls an instance when he was thought to be a potential marriage partner: "Once I visited a family. When the girl came in she told her father that of the boys she liked [me] the most."

Anila tells his story in a tone that indicates that he was pleased at having been taken for a man, and further, fallen for by a young woman. Yet his story, which he interrupts with bursts of embarrassed laughter, also points to the gap between his sexual status and that of other men.

Likewise, when Pashka is asked about marriage, he laughingly explains that, "women cannot marry women; only men marry women." Here he refers to himself by his biological sex. But there is a tension between this and his later statement that he feels like a man on the outside and inside. It is important to note, however, that these tensions do not seem to surface frequently in Albanian communities in which sworn virgins live, and may have emerged as a reflexive result of the anthropologists' questions.

Thus the only way in which sworn virgins are not fully enfranchised as social men is sexually, being, by definition, forbidden from engaging in sexual relations. However it is important to note that there is no concept here of denial of sexuality, as this, itself, is of little importance. Indeed, if we attend to the concerns that animate some women's decision to become *virgjineshë*, it is evident just how inappropriate it is to presume that virgins are, in fact, lesbians, for what is at stake is honour. Such honourable gender change is not open to many, for the transformation is only welcome when it is seen to be useful: typically when there is no man to head a household. The carefully considered choice to become a man, or to raise a daughter as a son, is made as a great tribute, and the subject earns status and respect.

Based on the value placed upon honour, the notion of reverting to one's birth gender is unimaginable. A discussion recorded by Jan and Cora Gordon in the 1920s points to the bounds of the thinkable, which remain true for sworn virgins today:

> "Looking closer we began to doubt the sex of this person..."
>
> "That girl... has vowed never to marry, so she dresses like a man and does man's work."
>
> "But if she breaks her vow, we said, does her family pursue her to kill her?"
>
> "She doesn't ever break her vow... she would be ashamed to. And, anyway, no man would want her any more than he would want his sister..."
>
> "Yet we repeated our questions, 'If? If? If?' we insisted."
>
> "She would have to leave the clan then... she would be disgraced for ever."
>
> "But they would not kill her? we asked."
>
> "Oh, no. She can marry if she likes, but she would not want to. You understand... she has sworn she won't (Young 2001: 43)."

All of our interlocutors stressed the respect that they receive from their family and community, which also points to the fact that *virgjinesha* and lesbians are not commensurate gender identities and that, furthermore, such a presupposition does not attend to the concerns about family honour that animate the decision to become men.

Given the nature of peasant life, labour demands and spatial proximity, sexuality takes on a unique character. As Berit Backer has observed about conceptions of love in the village of Isniq in Kosova,

> [t] he Isniq ideal of a man is not the Don Juan and eternal seducer – on the contrary. A flirt is considered unreliable, whereas a man who keeps women at a distance and treats them with 'respect' is an honourable person to be trusted in public affairs. To fall in love and to be interested in the opposite sex is a phenomenon everyone remembers from their youth, and it is accepted as something to grow out of. But until that happens one cannot be taken seriously (Backer 2003: 199).

The same can be said about northern Albania. Honour is a central value, the dictates of which inform the ways in which love and courtship are viewed and experienced. Furthermore, the trope of romantic love does not occupy the imaginations and idealisations of relationships as it does in the West. If anything, 'falling in love' is an unwelcome inconvenience in a society in which all marriages are arranged per the dictates of the *kanun*.

DRAG QUEENS, SWORN VIRGINS AND THE SUBVERSION OF NORMS?

How, then, does the position of the sworn virgin relate to the patriarchal norms outlined by the *kanun*? It is important to highlight certain Western feminists' assumptions about the relationship of drag to norms. It is often assumed that the ability of women to dress as men and thereby gain greater freedom and respect undermines the rigid divide between males and females. Changing from woman to man is traditionally a ritualised process involving the taking of an oath. Historically the oath was made in front of twenty-four witnesses and bound the sworn virgin to live as a celibate man, though the custom of swearing is now rarely observed. In strict contrast to women, sworn virgins wear men's clothing, smoke, drink alcohol and sometimes carry knives and/or guns. They adapt their own speech and mannerisms to conform to a masculine self-presentation. Others relate to them as men, usually using male pronouns both in addressing them and in speaking of them. They may adopt male names. It might appear that this ritualised change of appearance by which women gain accession to the male social domain challenges or subverts Albanian patriarchal norms. We have previously evoked Judith Butler in defining what is intended by our use of 'gender'. In order to assess the relationship of *virgjineshë* to the norms, it is useful to compare the experience of the sworn virgin's change of attire as it stands in relationship to these norms with the cross-dresser's relationship as analysed by Butler.

"Gender is drag," asserts Butler (1993) in Bodies that Matter. By this she suggests that gender is performative and that no performance of gender is more fundamentally authentic or real than any other. Butler argues that norms mould all subjects into the symbolic order. These norms are deeply constitutive of the self, for in order to delineate one's viability within the hegemonic order, the subject must continuously cite the very norms that initiated its intelligibility. In Butler's view, norms both govern the subject's formation and demarcate the boundaries of an inhabitable sociality. In speaking of the force of certain norms, Butler introduces the Derridean notion of iterability into gender performativity to account for the way subjects are shaped by norms. In Derrida's view, speech acts must be formulated according to an "iterable" model, that is, they must be able to be repeated under different circumstances, which is made possible as a result of their conformity to a codified structure. Signification occurs, accordingly, through the performative reiteration of gender norms, in turn materialising a certain kind of body – one whose coherence is predicated upon its adherence to these norms. Yet at certain moments, in instances that do not seek to approximate the familiar terrain of hegemonic norms, or do, but in an unfamiliar way, the norm is destabilised and thrown into question. Drag queens expose the constructed nature of gender norms and, consequently, denaturalise them. Butler states that

> drag is subversive to the extent that it reflects on the imitative structure by which hegemonic gender is itself produced and disputes heterosexuality's claim on naturalness and originality (Butler 1993:125).

The belief that one's anatomical sex clearly corresponds to either 'man' or 'woman' and that this biological status is separate from one's gender is the culturally normative belief that initiates the transgressive power of a cross-dresser's clothing. It is thus the tension caused through the apparent mismatching of anatomical sex, gender identity and gender performance that reveals the contingency of the constructs upon which these performances are based.

However, unlike the performance of a drag queen, which denaturalises the imitative structure through which gender norms are produced, the wearing of men's clothing by the *virgjineshë* substantively enacts the transformation into a man. In this case, donning men's attire does not mark a parodic resignification of heterosexual gender constructs; instead it is a socially sanctioned entry of a virgin woman into the role of man. Pashke explains that, "to dress as a man earns the respect due to a man". And it does so because the change from female to male attire is inscribed within a context in which the tradition of the *kanun* provides the necessary condition to legitimate the choice.

It is important to note that unlike the drag queen, for whom clothing stands in a (hyperbolic) relationship of signification to the self, the change of dress of the sworn virgin is both a signifier of this transformation and materially enacts and inaugurates this change. Cutting hair is symbolically important and usually the first step in making the change. Pashke, who died in June 2006, took the decision to become a *virgjinesha* at the age of eighteen when his uncle, with whom he lived, was taken to the hospital in Shkodra, some 80 km away. Becoming a man enabled him to make the journey on foot two times a month for the duration of his uncle's illness. Although Pashke had never met another sworn virgin, he knew of his traditional rights according to the laws of the *kanun*. Thus a friend of Pashke's recalls that, "when the harvest began, when she came back she cut off her hair and decided [to become a man]. For me she is a man now" (Kincses and Michalski 2003). A neighbour of Pashke's comments that, "they are a very correct household, Pashke and her uncle; but I do not relate to Pashke as a woman. I think of her as a man."

It is interesting to note the centrality of the concept of 'correctness' in the neighbour's remark. By becoming a man, Pashke was able to preserve the family honour. The change of dress and self-presentation thus both indexes this transformation and materially affects the change. Indeed, Pashke was buried in formal male attire. The symbolic character of dress and comportment in indexing the change from woman to man is illustrated by the example of the cigarette Pashke wore behind his ear even though he actually did not smoke.

It is important to recall that, as Butler herself reminds us,

> the political and geographical context in which I work is, of course, in the United States, and it is connected to some of the political questions that have emerged within the United States and within England (Butler 2001: 9).

One must be cautious when assuming that examples external to Butler's theory can be easily accommodated within her language, a fact that Saba Mahmood (2005: 163) has also pointed out in her discussion of Butler's notion of performativity in relation to members of the Egyptian 'mosque movement': "Butler herself cautions against such a 'technological approach' to theory wherein the theory is articulated on its self-sufficiency, and then shifts register only for the pedagogical purpose of illustrating an already accomplished truth" (Butler at al. 2000: 26). Such a perfunctory approach to theory is inadequate, she argues, because theoretical formulations often ensue from particular examples and are therefore constitutively stained by that particularity. In order to allow a particular theoretical formulation to travel across cultural and historical specificities, one needs to rethink the structure of assumptions that underlie a theoretical formulation and perform the difficult task of translation and reformulation."

Indeed, Butler would not have prescribed the application of her theorisation of drag to the assessment of gender dynamics in northern Albania. By evoking Butler, we strive for the opposite: namely to reveal the gap rather than the similarity between the phenomenon in Albania and the example of cross-dressing in the United States. We seek to demonstrate that the dress of sworn virgins is a very different experience of dress that relates to Albanian patriarchal norms in a way altogether removed from the example of drag queens.

We would like to suggest that it is not drag or cross-dressing, itself, that works to destabilise gender norms. Indeed, the very role of the sworn virgin sustains patriarchy by assuring the continuity of a patrilineal order even when men are scarce. Butler also calls into the question the extent to which heteronormativity is, in fact, subverted by drag queens' performances and suggests that this denaturalisation can serve to reconsolidate these norms. Yet for *virgjineshë*, the change of dress does not, itself, stand in a relationship of subversion or reinforcement of patriarchal norms. Rather, it is those wo/men who inhabit the role of 'sworn virgin' in partial and new ways who unsettle the structures of Albanian patriarchy.

SWORN VIRGINS ON THE MARGINS

> "I did it [changed gender role] after my father died ten years ago. I wanted to be free; now I can walk for hours in the mountains and nobody can touch me; I am free now; I can do what I want and nobody can tell me anything; I can even have my money and buy what I want (G./D. cited by Andrea Pieroni 2010: 44)."

If there is a destabilisation taking place, it is thus rooted elsewhere. Those sworn virgins who do not occupy the role in traditional ways mark an example of a relation to the norm that is neither that of simple reinforcement nor destabilisation. We would like to attend to the ways in which certain wo/men live the category 'virgin' in ways circumscribed neither by the dictates of *kanun* nor by conventional practice.

In his discussion of the relationship of people to the natural environment, Andrea Pieroni describes his encounter with a *virgjinesha* he refers to as G./D.:

> I was greatly surprised when the head of the household in which I was staying suggested that I visit the summer settlements in the alpine pastures, which were many hours walk from the village, with his sister for a guide. His sister, G., is 40 years old, she cuts her hair short like a man, she dresses like a man, and in the village she is known by the male name of D. or djalë (*lad*).

He continues:

> I was amazed to observe how G./D.'s knowledge of the environment encompassed both the home gardens close to the houses, which is generally the domain of the women, and the alpine pastures located very far from the village, which is generally a male domain. G./D. learnt about the home gardens during her/his childhood and especially when she/he was a teenager, but now she/he has taken on a male role in gathering plants. Hence she/he would never gather nettles or Good King Henry leaves, although she/he knows how to recognize and process them (ibid).

G./D. explains his reasons for only performing men's tasks, saying, "I do not like to cook and do not like any of the things women do at home: washing clothes, ironing, and sewing" (ibid.). It is interesting to note the emphasis on personal choice in the two above citations. This espoused individualism markedly contrasts with the concerns of family honour expressed by the more traditional sworn virgins but is nevertheless a common theme when sworn virgins are asked to comment on their decision.

The somewhat older Xhemma lived most of his life under strict Communist leadership and also claimed to have taken on the role of sworn virgin by his own choice to gain access to more freedom, and to mix socially in the male world (though not as a woman). He died of lung cancer in 2004. He justified his position as a sworn virgin when his brother-in-law died and his role as uncle became very important to his sister's children.

Anila, in his twenties, lives a very outgoing life in his native village and clearly feels very much in control. He experienced late childhood and adolescence in a time of tremendous change in Albania. These changes have filtered down to the village mostly in disruptive ways; the telephone no longer worked, mail was no longer delivered and the public health care system collapsed; most of the young men left in search of work elsewhere and many families left, too. Where there were once 149 families, there now live only 18 permanent resident families (although plenty return for the summer months to tend their land and enjoy country living). Anila, who prefers to be called Rrok (a male name) feels complete freedom to walk long distances in the area and to pay social visits to other households, something which normally only men do. He displays a significant number of the attributes of the more traditional sworn virgins: male attire, short hair, assertive male gestures and a self-confident stride, but his reason for assuming the role is not traditional. There is no social need for Anila to act as a sworn virgin. He explains that it not only gives him freedom to wander around the village; it more importantly affords him protection against the dangers of kidnapping. Anila explains these fears: "These days you can't trust anyone. Even the most respected woman might be taken as a prostitute. They take you away from your family. You don't know anyone there" (Kincses and Michalski 2003). Even though he might be recognised as a biological woman, as a sworn virgin he is not perceived as attractive by men.

Thus, G/D, Xhema and Anila do not assume the role of sworn virgin in the traditional way or for the traditional reasons. All three assert reasons for becoming *virgjineshë* that are fully removed from the *kanun*, although Xhema retroactively justified his decision by citing a more traditional motivation. Further, the position of G/D and Anila is on the margin of society in as much as they use both female and male names and express a resolute individualism. And this liminal position is enabled by the tradition of the sworn virgin, it provides a model, a vocabulary, and a history that make it an intelligible, if altered, social position.

Whereas in the past, women became men either for reasons of inheritance or in order to find an honourable solution to an objectionable marriage, here women use the model of the sworn virgin, adhering to it to varying extents, for protection or in order to expand their social options. As sworn virgins they are entitled to greater freedom as they can leave their homes whenever they wish, socialise with the men of the village, travel freely and take up a trade. This allows them to assume certain responsibilities and pursue certain ends – careers typically reserved for men. And yet, by not committing to either one or the other, they are opening up room for the subversion of these rigid roles.

TOWARDS A TRANSCENDENCE OF THE PATRIARCHAL ORDER?

On the one hand we are witnessing in Albania a return to tradition; on the other, paradoxically, it is the place the traditional sworn virgin carves out in society that is opening up new spaces for the negotiation of gender and of patriarchal norms. Yet it is also important to note that although these wo/men do not live the role of *virgjinesha* to the letter of the *kanun* and thus undermine the rigidity of Albanian patriarchy to access new freedoms, they nonetheless are bound to remain virgins.

We are nevertheless not suggesting that a radical change to the patriarchal order might take the shape of the mass subscription of Albanian women to ambiguous *virgjinesha* roles. Indeed, it is difficult to predict what place sworn virgins will occupy in the future in Albania's rapidly changing society, or for how long the tradition will persist. Rather, we have aimed to provide one example of how traditional roles are being occupied in new or modified ways, making space for the negotiation of gender roles and tradition. If there is, then, something endemic to sworn virgins that de-centres Albanian patriarchy as mediated by the *kanun*, it does not reside in the simple flexibility of some women to become social men through change of dress and comportment. And whereas traditionally the 'sworn virgin' helps assure the continuity of a patrilineal social structure, here the patriarchal order is transcended by new, diverse and individualistic modes of experiencing and inhabiting gender roles and functions.

BIBLIOGRAPHY

Backer, Berit 2003 Behind Stone Walls: changing household organization among the Albanians of Kosova, edited by Robert Elsie and Antonia Young. Pejë: Dukagjini Publishing House.

Butler, Judith 1993 Bodies that Matter: On the Discursive Limits of Sex. New York: Routledge.

Butler, Judith 2001 Agencies of Style for a Liminal Subject. Conversations with Judith Butler: Proceedings from the seminar "Crisis of the Subject", held in Ohrid-Republic of Macedonia 11-14 May 2000, Katerina Kolozova and Zarko Trajanoski (eds.) "Euro-Balkan" Institute.

de Waal, Clarissa. 2005. Albania Today: A Portrait of Post-Communist Turbulence. London: I.B.Tauris.

Gjeçov, Shtjefen 1989 Kanuni i Lekë Dukagjinit = The Code of Lek Dukagjini. New York: Gjonlekaj.

Gordon, J. and C. J., 1927. Two Vagabonds in Albania. New York: Dodd Mead.

Grémaux, Réné 1989 Mannish women of the Balkan mountains. In J. Bremmer (ed.) From Sappho to de Sade: moments in the history of sexuality. London: Routledge.

Grémaux, Réné 1994 Woman becomes man in the Balkans' in Gilbert Herdt, (ed.) Third Sex, Third Gender. New York: Zone Books.

Kincses, Réka and Karin Michalski 2003 Pashke und Sofia (film) 30 min.

Littlewood, Roland and Young, Antonia 2005 The Third Sex in Albania: An Ethnographic Note In: Alison Shaw and Shirley Ardner (eds.) Changing Sex and Bending Gender New York and Oxford: Berghahn pp 74-84.

Mahmood, Saba 2005 Politics of Piety: The Islamic Revival and the Feminist Subject. Princeton: Princeton University Press.

Pieroni, Andrea 2010 People and plants in Lëpushë. Traditional medicine, local foods, and post communism in a north Albanian village. In: Manuel Pardo de Santayana, Andrea Pieroni and Rajindra K. Puri (eds.) Ethnobotany in the New Europe. People, health and wild plant resources pools. Oxford: Berghahn pp 16-50.

Schwandner-Sievers, Stephanie 2004 Times Past. References for the Construction of Local Order in Present-day Albania. In: Maria Todorova (ed.) Balkan Identities. Nation and MemoryLondon: Hurst pp 103-128.

Whitaker, Ian 1981 A sack for carrying things: the traditional role of women in northern Albanian society In: Anthropological Quarterly Vol. 54 pp 146-56.

Whitaker, Ian 1989 Familial roles in the extended patrilineal kingroup in Northern Albania. In J. G. Peristiany (ed). Mediterranean Family Structures. Cambridge and London: Cambridge University Press pp 195-203.

Young, Antonia 2001 Women Who Become Men: Albanian Sworn Virgins, Oxford, New York: Berg.

11. Alternative Publics: Reflections on Marginal Collective Practices in Communist Albania

Smoki Musaraj

The peculiar relationship between the founding of imagined communities and the emergence of a novel sense of simultaneity – of shared time that connects individuals across space – is a distinctive feature of both nation-building and modernity more generally (Anderson 1991). Yet, as Kathleen Stewart (1996) has pointed out, the extent to which this concept of simultaneity and national homogeneity accounts for 'other' collective desires for alternative cultural spaces within the nation-state remain an open question. Focusing on the experience of the communist regime in Albania, this article pursues this tension between the official narrative of the modern nation-state and 'other' temporal and cultural spaces contemporaneous with it.

Recent studies of the Albanian communist history take different methodological approaches to 'whose story' to tell and 'how.' In his survey of the 20th century history of the Albanian nation-state in the Albanian journal Përpjekja, Bernd J. Fischer (2004) underlines the nationalist impulse of the Albanian communist state.[1] Fischer focuses mainly on the tactics of leadership of the notorious leader of *Partia e Punës* (Party of Labour), Enver Hoxha, to account for major political decisions that defined the communist nation-state in Albania after World War II. Albeit one of the most accurate and thoughtful ones of its kinds, Fischer's history is one of big events and big heroes. It approaches national politics from a realist perspective where key actors pursue particular interests.

On the other hand, a later contribution to the same journal by Enis Sulstarova (2005) suggests that a deeper understanding of the communist historicity requires also a micro-approach. We need to turn our attention, Sulstarova argues, to the study of everyday practices of survival as an unexplored site in the study of the communist period in Albania (Sulstarova 2005: 94). She rightly states that there is a need to understand the experience of living under the communist regime not simply as a passive reaction to the structures of domination, but as a constant struggle with attention to creative practices of subversion (ibid 2005: 94).

In this article I wish to address the question of the Albanian national community under communism by looking at two sets of daily practices that were marginal to the official discourse of historical progress: the monotonous temporality of the food queues and the illicit watching of foreign – especially Italian – TV programmes. I base my discussion on a series of individual and group interviews with Albanian

[1] Fischer writes: "The Yugoslavs were right to consider [Enver] Hoxha as a nationalist, and he would not cease to be such even he wanted to. When Hoxha came to power he faced the task of rebuilding Albania from the foundations, or at least from whatever had remained from [King] Zog's time (Fischer 2004: 114)."

immigrants in New York who came to the United States after the regime change of the 1990s. These interviews were taken during summer 2005. At the time of the interviews, most of the interviewees were taking English as Second Language courses in New York.

Unlike the official rhetoric of the 'New Man' and the new nation, the two sets of practices I consider here embodied a systemic tension of the communist regime. Queues for food rations engendered the idea of a public of necessity, maintained and performed daily through the ritual waiting for unpredictable outcomes. Watching foreign TV, on the other hand, became a secret space of collective enjoyment of the forbidden 'foreign' (*i/e jashtme*). Through these reflections on marginal – yet, ubiquitous – practices in communist Albania, I want to explore alternative modes of sociality in tension with the official narrative of historical progress and perpetual revolution. Instead, this article suggests that queues and television consumption were themselves sites of confrontation between different notions of national community. Secondly, I want to emphasise the tension that arose between these forms of collectivity engendered through these two practices, a tension that perhaps anticipated the hollowness and short life of the system.

NATIONALISM AND TEMPORALITY IN THE ALBANIAN COMMUNIST STATE

As observed by recent historical accounts of the Albanian communist regime, the official rhetoric of the nation post-World War II rested on the premise of historical progress, of constant revolution and the construction of the 'New Man' (see i.e. Blumi 1999, Lubonja 2002, Fuga 2004: 51). In this sense, this regime embarked on a modernist temporality, which, in Reinhart Koselleck's words is determined by "specifically historical determinants of progress and regress, acceleration and delay (Koselleck 2004: 103)." Thus, in the official historical most events before the end of World War II was filed in the category of 'regress' and 'delay' while the communist future offered 'progress' and 'acceleration.' Yet, in its mundane activities, while severing the ties to the past, the new (communist) nationalist project in post-World War II Albania was very much concerned with creating a distinct temporality of the present, a temporality that would instil a community with a collective morality. In all Eastern European countries more generally, the present was articulated as faithfulness to the only legitimate political Party – in the Albanian case, *Partia e Punës* (Party of Labour). As Katherine Verdery (1996) points out, across Eastern Europe the (communist) national community required a reformulation of the basic social units towards cultural homogeneity:

> Throughout the region, Communist Parties pursued policies designed to narrow both the gaps between and the sources of antagonism among social groups and to create social homogeneity. [...] [These policies] aimed to minimize the differentiation of social interests and to make everyone equally dependent on state handouts. The regimes presented this as a moral imperative, making morality (rather than political interests) the basis of political community. By homogenizing the social field, the Party

> could justifiably claim to represent and serve the interests of society as a whole, a collective subject from which it had ostensibly effaced meaningful differences (Verdery 1996: 93).

The centralisation of private property was the most widespread transformation that aimed at such homogenisation. In this aspect, the nationalising strategies of the communist state in Albania resembled those of many countries of the Eastern Bloc.[2]

In its efforts to establish a distinct moral community with an internal temporality, the Albanian communist state introduced a distinct relationship to space and time. Activities such as mandatory volunteer service, forced distribution of university graduates in rural areas necessitated movement of people away from traditional family and clan-entrenched residences and workplace. People's locations became extremely politicised. Traditional forms of sociality were largely dismantled. Yet, through these dislocations and relocations, new kinds of public synchronicity emerged. In cities, regional differences, family relations were placed at the secondary level. Instead, the Party-state mediated collective identity through the systematic control of daily life activity including the food distribution system and the spaces of cultural production.

Having already instituted homogenising activities such as the collectivisation of agriculture and mandatory volunteer service, the state mediated much of social time. Writing about similar practices in Romania, Verdery (1996: 40) has described this phenomenon as a "seizure of time" from private enterprise, household consumption and sociability. Meanwhile, leisure time, private time gave way increasingly to time sacrificed to a myriad of state obligations. Ardian Vehbiu's recollection of the history of transformation in Tirana's urban landscape offers an interesting insight into a new notion of social time during communism:

> The regime tried very seriously to eradicate from the cultural consciousness the idea of a public square as a socialising place. It was the time when, still following the footprints of the Chinese Cultural Revolution, free time [*koha e lirë*] was looked at suspiciously, as a survivor of the bourgeois notion of work-as-burden; hence the urban residents were required to socialise in schools, factories, in the workplace, in neighbourhood meetings, in military training [*zbore*], in public trials, in amateur theatre competitions and in forced volunteer work [*aksione*], where it was easy for the officers, secretaries of the party and other authorities to manipulate the self-consciousness of the group (Ardian Vehbiu 2003: 46, my translation).

To Ardian Vehbiu's list of the new spaces of socialisation during the communist regime in Albania, one could also add *rradhën e qumshtit* (the milk queue), a term that stands for the long lines of waiting for rationed food (not only milk) or fuel. While sharing the pathos of sacrifice for the greater (national) good, unlike the 'schools, factories, the workplace, neighbourhood meetings, military training, public trials, amateur theatre competitions, in forced volunteer work' *rradha e qumshtit* developed spontaneously as an unintended consequence of the existing system of food distribution exacerbated by the scarcity of the 1970s and 1980s.

---

[2] For a thorough discussion of the history and consequences of the agrarian reforms and property ownership reforms in post-war Albania see Artan Fuga (2004)

RRADHA E QUMSHTIT OR 'WAITING FOR GODOT'

In the last decades of the communist period, as Albania severed ties with the other members of the Eastern Bloc, food scarcity became a growing concern. Everything was rationed, including milk, eggs, meat, and butter. Food rations were assigned by the nuclear – as opposed to the extended – family and distributed through designated local stores. The milk ration was two litres per family. Combined with increasing scarcity, the food distribution system created a constant state of anxiety that motivated the population to start the queues at much earlier hours than the hours of operation of the stores. Paradoxically, this constant standing in line, the routine of plugging oneself into the food distribution system synchronised urban dwellers with the nation as a body.

Yet, it was not only scarcity that necessitated such social and psychological dependency on the state. It was, again, the system of distribution itself that reinforced the image of the state as a mediator of consumption. Rations were determined according to family size and handed out by location. Ration lists were thus another form of grounding families to their residencies. One could not seek milk or other rationed products in another neighbourhood, let alone another city. *Rradha e qumshtit* arose as an inevitable form of coping with consumption needs vis-à-vis state organisation and distribution of supplies.

As such, the system of food distribution displayed some of the mechanisms through which the Party-state functioned as a modern nation-state, concerned with the monitoring and disciplining of its subjects' life functions (cf. Foucault 1995). Writing about the Romanian experience of communism, Verdery suggests that queues enabled the "immobilisation [of] bodies in food lines to the enhancement of central power (Verdery citing Campenau 1996: 46, cf. Humphrey 2002)." What had once been a more private activity – food consumption – was now the domain of the state.

The *rradha e qumshtit* in particular has become a legend in people's memory of communism. During summer 2005, I interviewed a group of Albanian immigrant women, between the ages of late thirties to late forties, who had lived in Albania for most of their lives and had immigrated to New York after 2000. At the time of the interview, some of these women were working in cleaning jobs, mostly temporary, but many were still unemployed and struggling with learning the language and adjusting their skills and experience to their new residence. All of them had worked in Albania in skilled professions such as teaching, administration or civil engineering.

Our conversation was triggered by a passing comment one of the women had made regarding an afternoon of socialising among other friends. Expressing content about spending time aimlessly, she said: "It quenched my nostalgia for the milk queue! (*Na hoqi mallin e rradhës së qumshtit!*)." Intrigued by this expression of 'nostalgia' (*malli*) I then started to ask them about their memory of the milk queue. I soon realized that the nostalgia was not an emotion directed to a lost past but rather a form of critique that these women directed towards their current living conditions. Yet, at the same time, the comment brought back instantaneously the memory of the communist experience as a specific sense of temporality: a senseless waiting.

In contrast with the idyllic tone of the first comment, when questioned in more detail about *rradha e qumshtit*, Miranda[3] replied:

> I get a headache when I think about the milk queue. We used to put our stones on the line and then other people would throw them away and then we would start fighting. One night here in New York I had a dream about my [passed away] mother who was telling me to go and buy *gjizë*[4] at the milk queue. Just think about it, poor woman, all her life she spent it in queues [conversation with author, summer 2005].

To those who waited in the lines of the communist rations, *rradha e qumshtit* represents a "structure of feeling", that is, a historically specific epistemology lived and remembered as embodied sensibility, a "thought as felt and [a] feeling as though (Williams 1977: 132)." In these recollections, *rradha e qumshtit* and its physical 'symptoms' are an expression of how communist history has marked the individual body and memory. Miranda associates *rradha e qumshtit* with physical discomfort – a headache – and with a haunting memory – her anxious dream.

Rradha e qumshtit represented all other queues precisely because of its daily waiting for a receding horizon. Most importantly, the expression "*te rradha e qumshtit*" (at the milk queue) is used today – at times despondently but often nostalgically – to indicate a waiting without a clear horizon, a suspension of time, a temporal unknown, the Albanian equivalent of 'waiting for Godot.'[5] Hence the expression itself designates a particular experience of time as valueless and frozen. Like Samuel Becket's 'Godot', the queues assumed a real and pervasive presence of a perpetual absence. Waiting for the 6 o'clock milk was such a regular activity that it constituted an important daily ritual. This effected most dramatically women's negotiation of their family expectations and their new role in the gender-equal communist economy:

> *Rradha e qumshtit* was very stressful especially for women who had to think about how to procure milk for their children. The stress extended throughout the whole day and children were also affected. Women, who were working during the day, had to think ahead about how to plan for spending the night at the queue [conversation with author, summer 2005].

As this comment indicates, queues introduced a temporal rhythm that penetrated family life and individual life. One's whole day was organised around the queue. Hence, as much as they performed a state-mediated structure of social distribution, the queues engendered a daily tune of frustration that challenged the communist notion of solidarity with the Party. The queues were a striking visual representation of a systemic failure of the planned economy. Hence, they became sites of constant surveillance. Political conversations were taboo, as everywhere in public spaces. In fact, many of the women I talked to stated that they were certain there were spies among the people queuing next to them, spies

---

[3] All names of the informants in this article have been fictionalised.

[4] A local dairy product.

[5] In reference to Samuel Becket's "Waiting for Godot." It is no coincidence that the Albanian dramatization of 'Waiting for Godot' received much attention from the Albanian public. The expression '*në pritje të Godosë*' (waiting for Godot) is also used in informal conversation to indicate the waiting for something that will most probably not come.

that sought incriminating information. Explicit political conversations were banned from these spaces, however, one's behaviour, one's attitude towards the activity of queuing itself was highly political. Lumja told the following story:

> An old man had been waiting in line since 3AM and when he reached the counter, the supplies had run out. After being in line for so long and being exasperated he exclaimed: 'may this meat never be eaten' [*mos u hëngërt kurrë ky mish*]. He was sent to prison for cursing the authorities [conversation with author, summer 2005].

This incident illustrates how a mundane activity such as queuing constituted a performative element of the communist nation. Challenging this ritual waiting was read as challenging the very system of power. Although the old man had not mentioned any higher authorities in his curse, Lumja associates the arrest with his rejection of the temporality of the queue; hence, as a defiance of the state authorities. Yet, at the same time, this incident indicates the weakness of this system, the threat that these daily frustrations posed to the system.

Staying in line was not simply an act of pure survival. Similar to the annual parades or the volunteer projects, adhering to the system of distribution and to queuing represented a rite of passage for national belonging. Yet, unlike the parades, the queues were not part of the official set of rituals but they represented a kind of collectively shared secret bound by an unspoken shame[6] – the shame of the state in the face of a growing gap between reports of overproduction and the reality of scarcity.

Through these daily rituals, a different sense of time as repetition of the same coexisted with the official modern notion of time as progress. The queues thus constituted a different experience of the present from the official 'myths' of progress in Albanian historiography.[7] In queues, time was experienced as a 'Waiting for Godot', with an increasingly receding future rather than a perpetual revolution in the present. That said, studying the ways queues operated in communist Albania, in Michel de Certeau's words, only "privileges the productive apparatus (which produces 'the discipline') (de Certeau 1984: xv)." Understanding the social historicity of the communist experience in Albania requires also a study of the 'ways of operating' or 'tactics' that "constitute the innumerable practices by means of which users reappropriate the space organized by techniques of sociocultural production (Ibid)." While sacrificing private time to the public queues, I suggest in the following, especially after the 1970s, Albanians reappropriated what was officially intended as a rigidly monitored public space – Television – turning it into an alternative space of enjoyment in the privacy of one's home, through the secret watching of foreign TV programmes. The pervasiveness of these televised places both as a practice but also as a topic of daily informal conversation,

---

[6] See Andrew Shryock's discussion of the notions of cultural intimacy and public secrets Shryock 2004) Shryock combines Michael Herzfeld's notion of 'cultural intimacy' and Michael Taussig's notion of 'public secret' to describe cultural practices that, in representing something shameful about the collectivity of the nation, produce a peculiar intimacy that continues to bond the said community.

[7] A number of articles in Schwandner-Sievers and Fischer's Albanian Identities (2002) for instance take a critical stance towards the notion of history as progress reflected in official discourse in history books and literature.

constitute a crucial area for studying the "clandestine forms taken by the dispersed, tactical, and make-shift creativity of groups or individuals already caught in the nets of 'discipline' (ibid)."

CHRONOTOPES OF A TELEVISED ELSEWHERE: ALBANIAN WATCHING OF FOREIGN TV

Albania's 'imitation' of the Chinese Cultural Revolution in the late 1960s and early 1970s politicised much more dramatically culture and daily self-fashioning.[8] Purging of anything 'foreign', including styles of dressing, walking, and comportment, took the centre stage of national politics. Ironically, the cult of the foreign is as much of a marker of memories of communism in Albania as *rradha e qumshtit*. This (publicly) secret fascination with the foreign during communist Albania created a sharp contrast with the official suspicion of anything foreign, a suspicion that permeated all levels of society, including that of arts and literature.[9]

A judge during the communist regime currently living in Ridgewood (Queens), New York, Agron described this shift in Albania:

> Until 1967, 'cause I am one of those old officials [*kuadro*] and at the time I was in high-school, so until 1967 [the political system] used to be more open. In 1967 there was the 'open letter' [*letra e hapur*],[10] where [the political authorities] attacked religion and many other things. The Cultural Revolution took place during that time. On the basis of this revolution they started to write letters of public accusation [*fletë-rrufetë*] as in China. These practices came here and they started to attack the white dress for instance. They categorised it as bourgeois things.
>
> There were different directives. Sometimes the authorities became more strict and conservative, sometime more liberal. From the 1970s there was a wave of liberalisation. In 1971 there was Italian music, they broadcasted the European Festival [Eurovision]. Even Enver [Hoxha] spoke on behalf of the youth. 1967 was a black year, then they started to soften up. In the end of 1971 they started again to attack everything, the 11th Festival [of Albanian light music] [*Festivali i 11-të*], and many other things, fashion, dress. It was the time of public accusations. The 'voice of the mass' [*zëri i masës*] started, any random person would come out in public and say something negative about you and then you would find yourself in political trouble. During my time as a student, around 1963, we used to have long hair. In 1969-1970 the rules against men with long hair became very strict. When I was a student we used to stay out very late,

[8] Isa Blumi (1999: 303) emphasises the cultural dimension of the so-called 'class wars' of the late 1960s-1970s

[9] See for instance Fatos Lubonja's (2002) analysis of the Albanian communist literature during the late 1960s and especially its use of ancient myths – such as Ismail Kadare's use of the myth of the Trojan Horse in *Përbindshi* (The Monster, 1965) – to reinforce the myth of Albania's "isolation and bunkerisation" p.98

[10] Refering to a letter written by Enver Hozha to the public announcing the turn of Albania away from the Soviet Union and a new series of purges against intellectuals and urban dwellers infected by bourgeois or revisionist culture. See Blumi (1999)

> dancing and so on. Come 1969, the Chinese came and so did the *fletë-rrufetë* and so… [group interview with author 3/6/2005].

Agron's account is typical not only of his classmates but more generally of his generation, a generation that experienced a period of cultural openness followed by an abrupt and radical isolation that was to last for the next two decades. Agron's account is also typical in its attention to historically specific details such as the annual European music festival Eurovision, the Italian music festival San Remo, the importance of dress and general look (such as the length of haircut), all of which mark the embodied memory of another kind of public intimacy: the fetishisation and enjoyment of anything foreign. While in official discourse defined as signs of the immoral and corrupt outside – be that the bourgeois West or the revisionist East, in informal conversation foreign things and TV programmes were markers of an increasing secret jouissance, a fascination with anything foreign.

While seizure of time and redistribution of resources localised membership to the nation in the neighbourhood publics, the single TV Channel, Albanian Radio-Television (*Radio Televizioni Shqiptar – RTSH*), aimed at creating a homogenous national culture in the space of imagination. This other medium of the national project was disjointed from the reality of the publics of necessity. RTSH represented the state of affairs in Albania bluntly ignoring the reality of scarcity and sacrifice. In addition to this deliberate fictional image of the nation, TV technologies also enabled another suspension of national time, an escape into an 'other' world of imagination. As the Albanian Cultural Revolution targeted anything 'foreign' – be it a commodity or a visual representation – the status of the 'foreign' became a cult. A former primary school teacher currently living in Ridgewood with her son's family, Hanife reiterates some of the same icons of Italian TV as Agron. When asked why she would watch foreign TV, Hanife focused on the curiosity for something different:

> We would watch foreign channels during those periods of time when the class war [*lufta e klasave*] would soften a bit. We were curious to see what was happening outside [*jashtë shtetit*] since we had never been outside ourselves. We wanted to see a movie, listen to music. Just human curiosity. To see San Remos [annual Italian music festival], Eurovision [annual European music festival], a soccer match. Some families were under surveillance. They would be surveyed more than others. Specific families would be targets and they would tell them 'put down their antennas otherwise we will send you to internment' [conversation with author, summer 2005].

In her brief summary of the reasons for watching Italian TV, Hanife combined 'human curiosity' for anything foreign with the fear of persecution. Her last comments suggest that, while it was public knowledge that everyone who owned a TV would try to access foreign programmes, this knowledge could potentially be used against someone whose political status was already being questioned. In fact, as Hanife points out, access to viewing the one and only TV channel was extremely selective and reflected the hierarchy of social status within Albanian society and vis-à-vis the state. Obtaining a permission (*autorizim*) to own a TV was a highly bureaucratic and political process incumbent upon one's 'biography,' i.e., whether anyone in the close family had any political stain. Like the distribution of food but perhaps more dramatically, TV set distribution reflected and reinforced social differences across the space of imagination.

TV also provided the possibility for privately accessing foreign TV signals. To prevent people from watching Italian TV the Albanian state dedicated much effort on placing zhurmuesa (signal scramblers) and into measuring the sizes of antennas. Despite and perhaps because of all these obstacles, most urban residents were regular viewers of foreign TV channels including Italian ones (RaiUno, Raidue, RaiTree, and private stations, Italia Uno, Canale 5, Rete Quatro, and Telenorba) and Yugoslav ones (such as Titograd and Crne Gora TV).

A counter-public developed behind the closed curtains, the muted volumes, the bigger antennas, the late nights of the Italian music festival, San Remos, of the European music festival, Eurovision as well as occasional American TV series such as Dallas or Fame. Indirectly, TV offered the possibility of accessing other 'scapes' of imagination. Paradoxically, despite the notorious isolation from the outside world, through these new technologies Albania was part of what Arjun Appadurai describes as "a shift in recent decades, building on technological changes over the past century or so, in which the imagination has become a collective, social fact. This development, in turn, is the basis of the plurality of imagined worlds (Appadurai 1996: 5)." I want to suggest, with Appadurai, that this other space-time of illicit foreign TV watching was a social fact of communist Albania. It suffices to mention that the majority of Albanians are fluent in Italian even though by and large they have never sat on an Italian language class nor did they have any access to Italian books at the time. It was only due to hours of watching Italian TV programmes that Albanians acquired Italian as a second mother tongue. For a period of time and especially in the northern regions, a similar phenomenon took place with Serbo-Crotian which, in addition to representing the language of the 'enemy', has a Cyrillic alphabet while Albanian has a Latin one. Finally, so entrenched was foreign TV, and in particular Italian TV, that Albanian familiarity with pop-culture icons such as Popeye or Fame is filtered by the Italian-dubbed versions – *Braccio di Ferro* and *Sarano Famosi* – that they watched during the 1980s.

This 'structure of feeling' associated with watching foreign TV manifested its social force especially in the aftermath of the 1990s fall of the communist regime. As Nicola Mai suggests, the flux of Albanian refugees towards Italy in the early 1990s was very much motivated by the cult of Italy as a land of beauty and pleasure, an image that had been cultivated through the daily watching of Italian TV programmes. There was a sense among the boat-refugees that they were quite confident about where they were going simply from years of watching Italian TV as an alternative cultural space to the dominant national one. These chronotopes – alternative space-times – of illicit TV watching in late night hours are as much of a landmark of the lived experienced of the late communist regime as the queues. Unlike the queues however, watching foreign TV reclaimed the private space of the home as a secret space but also as an alternative (public) space of enjoyment.

Paradoxically, this form of enjoyment experienced in secrecy behind closed curtains, was a collective experience, also a form of public intimacy formed around enjoyment rather than shame (as the was the case with the queues). Landmark events such as San Remo, Eurovision or the World Cup were topics of public conversation the day after their secret viewing. In other words, watching foreign TV was a well-known and well-kept secret.

In contrast, watching foreign TV in Albania today does not carry the same meaning, nor the same passion and desire. Nicola Mai is right to describe the pervasive watching of foreign TV during communism as a place of suppressed desire. In his account of the influence of Italian TV on Albanian youth before and after the fall of the iron curtain, Mai stresses the elements of entertainment and pleasure of Italian channels as the main allure for the Albanian audience:

> What Albanian viewers found in Italian television was a cultural landscape of beauty and pleasure that contrasted with the cultural monotone offered by both Albanian television and society. [...] The appeal of Italian programs must be understood in terms of their radical difference from cultural products available in Albania and of their potential function to make tangible an aspect of life that the local culture was lacking and had not been able to provide. What Albanians appreciated most in Italian television, I would contend, was a cultural landscape of pleasure and beauty which both responded to and surpassed their most audacious fantasy (Mai 2001: 100-101).

Mai is right to describe desire as a driving force behind the fascination with foreign TV programming. Yet, I want to add that the practices of watching in themselves constituted those "clandestine forms of tactical and make-shift creativity (de Certeau 1984: xv)" that groups engendered at the heart and in spite of state disciplinary mechanism. Slavoj Zizek (1993) introduced the term 'enjoy your nation as themselves' to describe a national experience of collective unity through mocking and purging the familiar foreign, in his case, the other ethnic group in former Yugoslavia after the collapse of the federation. I am suggesting that the longing for foreignness in communist Albania became a form of enjoying the nation through its own negation. This longing was, in fact, one of the alternative spaces of collective enjoyment that co-existed tacitly with quite different social imaginaries of the nation.

Finally, the accounts discussed here are recollections of past experience and hence illuminate the embodied memory of given historical experience. Like Miranda's headache and dream of the queues, watching of foreign TV has had a profound cultural and social effect on the post-1990 developments among the Albanian community both in Albania and abroad. Thus, currently I have observed a phenomenon among the Albanian immigrants in New York that, I think, draws our attention to the ongoing social impact that the fascination with the foreign TV during communism still have on people's everyday lives. Most of the Albanian students that I taught came to the ESL classes with almost no knowledge of English. When these students have an English speaker as a teacher who has no knowledge of Albanian and they desperately want to communicate in a common language they revert not to Albanian or English but to Italian, a language in which they communicate with ease. Italian is still associated with whatever is 'foreign' (*i/e jashtme*) hence it is used in circumstances when a speaker encounters a situation foreign to his/her background. Yet, at the same time, the fluency in Italian is proof of it being a special kind of foreign, much closer than the New York boroughs; a familiar stranger that has been domesticated and reappropriated.

CONCLUSION

In this article I have tried to challenge the traditional methodological separation between meta-historical accounts versus micro-ethnographic accounts of the communist experience in Albania. Inspired especially by Michel de Certeau's writing on the practices of everyday life, I suggested looking of the history of communist Albania from an anthropological angle that analyses what are considered as 'marginal' practices of both subjection and escape from dominant political discourses of the time. Thus, I suggested that much more than the narrative of historical progress and perpetual revolution and its critique, the memory of *rradha e qumshtit* and the illicit watching of foreign TV media embodied the lived experience of communist regime in Albania during the 1970s and 1980s. Existing as unintended 'structures of feeling' of the official regimes, both practices caused an ongoing tension with the official discourse of the nation, a tension that underlies especially the last gasps of the regime.

Yet, the two activities could not be more opposed in terms of the kind of historical imagination that they enabled. Queues represented a distinct temporality – a 'waiting for Godot' – made possible by the state-mediated system of food distribution and the grounding of food rations by location of residences. People experienced queues as a physical burden, a painful memory of planned economies. Within the more general literature of East Europe, queues confirm the communist negation of individual privacy and agency and the submission to the system of food distribution (i.e. Verdery 1996, Glaeser 2004). Yet, this view of communist period does not fully encompass all forms of sociality and lived reality.

In contrast to the queues, watching foreign TV, a practice perhaps more specific to Albania than other Eastern European countries, represents an alternative use of time and space of imagination. This practice created another form of sociality and public intimacy that capitalised on enjoyment rather than deprivation. These practices, I have argued, reclaimed that sense of the private, which is in symbiotic relationship with another national public that would come alive in informal conversations and exhilarations over the fetishised foreign.

Finally, both sets of practices exceed the historical boundaries of the communist regime in Albania and manifest themselves today as embodied sensibilities of a particular temporality – like the 'waiting for Godot' – or of a specific cultural language – like the familiar-strange disposition towards Italian cultural products. The study of these practices is hence useful not only to mount a critical approach to the historiography of the Albanian communist period but also to understand better the continuities, tensions and discontinuities of imagined national publics, of forms of sociality and of informal modes of social imaginaries.

BIBLIOGRAPHY

Anderson, Benedict 1991 Imagined Communities: Reflections on the Origin and Spread of Nationalism, New York: Verso.

Appadurai, Arjun 1996 Modernity at Large: Cultural Dimensions of Globalization. Minneapolis: University of Minnesota Press.

Blumi, Isa 1999 Hoxha's Class War: The Cultural Revolution and Its State Formation, 1961-1971. East European Quarterly, Vol. 33(3) pp 303-326.

de Certeau, Michel 1984 The Practice of Everyday Life. Trans. Steven Randall. Berkley: University of California Press.

Foucault, Michel 1995 Discipline and Punish: The Birth of the Prison, London: Vintage.

Fischer, Bernd J. 2004 Shqipëria si laborator politik – zhvillimi i shtetit shqiptar gjatë shekullit të njëzetë (Albania as a Political Laboratory – The Development of the Albanian State in the 20th Century). Përpjekja Vol. 10 pp 101-116.

Fuga Artan 2004 Shoqëria Periferike: Sociologji e Ndryshimit në Shqipëri. (Peripheral Society: Sociology of Change in Albania) Tiranë: Botimet Ora.

Humphrey, Caroline 2002 The Unmaking of Soviet Life: Everyday Economics After Socialism, Ithaca: Cornell University Press.

Glaeser, Andreas 2004 Monolithic Intentionality, Belonging, and the Production of State Paranoia: A View Through the Stasi onto the Late GDR. In: Andrew Shryock (ed.) Off Stage/On Display: Intimacy and Ethnography in the Ages of Public Culture, Stanford: Stanford University Press pp 244-278.

Reinhart Koselleck 2004 Futures Past: On the Semantics of Historical Time, Trans. Keith Tribe, New York: Columbia University Press.

Lubonja, Fatos 2002 Between a Virtual World and a Real World. In: Stephanie Schwandner-Sievers and Bernd J. Fischer (eds.) Albanian Identities: Myth and History, London: Hurst and Company pp 91-103.

Mai, Nicola 2001 Italy is Beautiful: The Role of Italian Television in Albanian Migration to Italy. In: Russell King and Nancy Wood (eds.) Media and Migration: Constructions of Mobility and Difference, London: Routledge pp 95-109.

Schwandner-Sievers, Stephanie and Bernd J. Fischer, (eds.) 2002 Albanian Identities: Myth and History, London: Hurst and Company.

Stewart, Kathleen 1996, Space on the Side of the Road: Cultural Poetics in an 'Other' America. New Jersey: Princeton University Press.

Shryock, Andrew 2004, "Introduction" In: Andrew Shryock (ed.) Off Stage/On Display: Intimacy and Ethnography in the Age of Public Culture, Stanford: Stanford University Press pp 3-30.

Sulstarova, Enis 2005 "Mbijetesa e perditshme nen komunizm" (Everyday Survival under Communism), Perpjekja Vol. 9.

Vehbiu, Ardian 2003 Kulla e Sahatit (The Clock Tower), Tirane: K&B.

Verdery, Katherine 1996, What Was Socialism and What Comes Next. Princeton: Princeton University Press.

Williams, Raymond 1977 Marxism and Literature. Oxford: Oxford University Press

Zizek, Slavoj 1993 Tarrying with the Negative: Kant, Hegel and the Critique of Ideology, Durham: Duke University Press.

12. A Fading Musical Memory? National Identity Construction in Lab Epic Songs

Eckehard Pistrick

The epic historic songs of the Balkans have a significant value for the cultural self-definition of constructed national, regional, religious or ethnic groups. They form the core of a form of oral history transmitted and highlighted by traditional musical forms such as ballads or multipart singing. This insight has remained uncontested since the ground-breaking studies of Milman Parry and Albert B. Lord in interwar Yugoslavia 1933-1935 (Lord 1960). Recently this tradition has witnessed a wide-ranging process of transformation, which began already in the communist period (1946-1991) and was intensified with musical globalisation, which has had a significant impact on the musical traditions of the whole of Southeastern Europe. This process of musical change since 1991 is footed in a context of migration, demographic change, urbanisation, the collapse of the state-directed economy and a deeply-rooted identity crisis that lead not only to dramatic social and economic changes but also to remarkable cultural shifts, which in turn lead to a redefinition of what was understood as 'traditional', 'rural' and 'authentic' in Albanian musical practice. Ethnomusicological fieldwork has confirmed that this process has resulted on a local level in a thorough reconfiguration of vocal and instrumental, unamplified and amplified soundscapes (cf. Sugarman 1997: 336-340, Pistrick and Dalipaj 2008).

In this paper[1] a particular musical repertoire, that of the *këngë epike historike* (epic historic song), defined by population group (the Lab people) and location (the Saranda region in southern Albania) will be analysed. In comparing texts and music recorded by ethnomusicologists such as Erich Stockmann, Qemal Haxhihasani or Benjamin Kruta over the course of fifty years, one can observe not only the transformability of songs in an oral music tradition, but also the 'musical impoverishment' that has taken place over half a century. 'Musical impoverishment' should be understood in this context as "a substantial loss of or reduction in musical expressions (Kartomi 1981: 239)." Applied to the case of Albania, this term seems appropriate to describe the shrinking knowledge of texts and the decreasing variety of regional singing styles. The first extensive collection of transcribed Albanian folk music, material from the so-called Stockmann expedition of 1957[2] does not yet bear the imprint of the communist aesthetic

---

[1] The research for this article was done in 2004 before 'Albanian iso-polyphony' was added to the UNESCO immaterial word heritage list in 2005. The place of vocal musical practice in society has changed to a certain degree since that time.

[2] Berlin Phonogramm Archive. A selection of the Stockmann recordings has been the subject of a non-profit CD publication: Ahmedaja 2012.

doctrine of *folklori i ri* (new folklore)[3] and the "and a state-directed cultural objectification and politicization of culture (Handler 1988: 11-15; 154-155)" as exemplified in the National Folk Festival of Gjirokastra established in 1968.[4] The Gjirokastra Festival, whose aim was among others to preserve, revive and reconstruct vocal traditions, shaped the image of Albanian music abroad and the aesthetic ideals of folk music within the country until today. The drifting between authenticity and folklorism became a distinctive feature of the festival. After the collapse of the communist regime and the "age of migration," as Castles and Miller (1993) put it, vitally important questions arose, menacing the continuity in performing traditional songs as a form of social communication. The following material was collected during fieldwork in the region of Saranda in southern Albania in April and September 2004. This region bordering Greece includes parts of two larger territorial units: the Labëria and the Çamëria. It is characterised by its rural character,[5] its good agricultural conditions but also for one of the highest migration rates in the whole of Albania. While the relatively prosperous administrative centre of Saranda has become a point of concentration for multipart singers and is home to three multipart choirs, smaller towns such as Delvina, the villages of Borsh on the Ionian coast and Xarra and Mursia in the transition area between the Labëria and the Çamëria are marked by the traumatic impact of migration and demographic change.[6] Each village can be characterised according to its specific musical tradition. While Borsh lies close to Himara and is influenced by the Himara four-part style, the neighbouring villages of Xarra (Muslim) and Mursia (Orthodox) are characterised by their intermediate position between the Lab and Çam singing styles, subdivisions of the Tosk singing style. During fieldwork it became obvious that singing, once a participatory activity, strengthening and reaffirming social bonds and shared moral values, has acquired especially in urban contexts the character of a performative genre, executed by a few semi-professionals forming *shoqata kulturore* (cultural associations). These 'cultural associations' are the legacy of the *shtëpi të kulturës* (houses of culture) established as urban centres for cultural development parallel to the establishment of the co-operatives in the 1960s and 1970s.[7]

---

[3] The term originally defined the aesthetic agenda of adapting the traditional music repertoire to communist realist principles. It is applied in a wider sense to multipart compositions in the 1990s.

[4] Although Stockmann recorded a few newly texted partisan songs, songs in praise of the communist party and Enver Hoxha, the major part of the recordings nevertheless reflected traditional musical textures and practices.

[5] According to the Statistical Office of the Municipality of Saranda, in 2004 62 percent of the population live in the 99 villages in the region.

[6] Cf. Kaser 2002: 182. In the case of the villages of Fterra and Çorraj he remarked that the main part of the village population consists of the grandparent and children's generation, 28 percent of the population being over 60 years of age.

[7] The houses of cultural in urban centres were established earlier than those in rural contexts.

EPIC SONGS AS A REFLECTION OF NATIONAL IDENTITY

Orally transmitted songs, especially epic and heroic songs, are of outstanding importance for Albanian self-perception, especially because they cannot be traced back through a long written tradition (Reuer 1993: 715). Ismail Kadare put the historical significance of epic songs in the following words: "No outstanding personality of the Albanian world has passed through this world without a song (Kadare 1987: 34)." The songs presented here belong to the genre of epic songs, more specifically epic historic songs, which have to be clearly differentiated in performance practice and content from *këngë epike legjendare* (epic legendary songs). While the latter group is mostly performed by a vocal soloist with an accompanying instrument and draws on material from the time before and during the Ottoman occupation, often based on orally transmitted legends, the former is executed predominantly in a choral style and with reference to actual historical events. These songs are also called *këngë trimash* (heroic songs) in Albanian. They can be subdivided further according to their content. Arshi Pipa, for example, distinguishes between a) songs of national liberation (praising national heroes), b) songs of social revolt (praising popular leaders who fought against feudal lords and governments), c) vendetta songs (connected with blood feud activities), d) songs of *kaçaks* or *hajduks* (praising outlaws or rebels) (Pipa 1978: 17).

In order to understand the context of epic songs, one has to shift attention to the historical ties of such products of artistic folk creativity. The Ottoman times are in many cases points of reference for epic singers. This period serves as background for a verbal and musical representation of the historical identity of the singers' own nationality. This discourse may take place in context with nationalist claims based, according to Hering, on a "backward-looking utopia", the desire to restore a fictive status quo ante as it may have existed before the Ottoman period (Hering 1989: 360). The stereotyped image of illegitimate Ottoman rule serves as a justification for conflicts motivated by nationalist claims or desires for self-determination and freedom. In addition to this justification of political opinion, in a large number of cases the moral code is the motivating force behind this folk tradition; honour and shame, suffering and revenge, betrayal and the ensuing punishment are in this case the themes that are sung about. The characteristics of the heroes remain the same in either case: their endurance in fighting the invaders, their continuing readiness to resist and their anarchic will for freedom. The praise of the heroes is expressed in formulas that are shared across national borders: they produce a uniformity in historic songs and hide what is distinctive in them (Scaldaferri 2003).

The historical reliability of epic songs is limited, as Skendi demonstrated with the songs of the *klephts* and the *hayduks*; these songs "do not give but glances of isolated facts and events (Skendi 1956: 669)." This includes the fact that names and dates may be changed and that facts may be altered and confused. Idealisation, standardisation and nationalist falsification can be found in epic folk songs as it is not the "nature of the oral heroic poetry to reproduce with exactness the facts, events and personages (Skendi 1956: 672)." Therefore it is not surprising that a folksong in some respect loses its aesthetic abstract and poetic value the more it becomes real, verifiable history.

The epic song belongs to the sphere of what has been called 'mythistory', myth serving in Schöpflin's structural-functionalist interpretation as a "way of organizing history, so as to make sense of it for a particular community (Schöpflin 2002: 26)." Central myths relevant to the epic singing tradition in southern Albania are the a) myths of territory, b) myths of redemption and suffering (including the ante mural myths, which argue a national sacrifice to save Europe from the invasions of barbarians and Orientals) c) the myth of unjust treatment d) the myth of divine or profane election (in terms of moral superiority) and e) the myth of military valour (cf. Schwandner-Sievers 2002: 10-11).

Most of the epic historic texts refer to solitary men and their relation to a specific historical situation. Women rarely appear in these texts and are portrayed not as individuals but as character types, "who serve to heighten the tragedy of the male hero's death (Sugarman 1997: 256)." The events are mostly described within a frame of subjectified geographic description or a frame of precise historical dates. The tragic events find their echo in sensitive descriptions and personifications of nature, in "weeping mountains and trees" (in the song for Gani Butka) or "mountains poured black" (in the song Malet e Borshit).

Two kinds of main characters can be distinguished, the trans-regional, institutionalised hero and the regional hero. To the first category belong such figures as Skanderbeg, Abdyl Frashëri, Çerçiz Topulli and Ismail Qemali. These heroes represent a proud national history reflected and personified in their lives and deeds. All of them are in one way or another connected with the concept of nation, independence and self-determination. And all of them are associated with a constructed perception of history as a line of continuity along which threats and challenges to Albania, as well as Albania's reactions to these pressures, remained consistent. The genre of epic songs is characterised by historical continuity; its texts reach without interruption from the medieval heroes to the central figures of the *Rilindja Kombëtare* (National Renaissance) and Enver Hoxha.

Regional heroes on the other hand represent the values, history and characteristics of a specific region and its inhabitants. They do not belong to the national pantheon, but they are constitutive for the collective memory of a certain region. These regional heroes, such as the *kapedani* (local chieftains or captains), are used for distinguishing a specific regional group (whether defined by religion or ethnicity) within the constructed nation, what Benedict Anderson has called the 'community of anonymity' (Anderson 1983).

In singing, the singer makes history audible, present; Erich Stockmann (1987) spoke of the singers as being convinced of the mission of their singing, namely to remember events from the past of the Albanian people and to keep them present in their consciousness. In his statement the musicologist distinguishes three levels of interpretation that play a role in every performance of any epic (historic) song: 'singing the past', 'singing the present' and 'singing the future.'

THE INTERRELATION OF CONTENT AND PERFORMANCE IN EPIC SONGS

Musical performance is linked to social occasions; social gatherings in most cases require some form of music. Prominent gathering places for multipart singing today are bars or cafes, which function, as Castelo-Branco (2005) put it in reference to the Alentejo region in Portugal, as 'informal training grounds.' The singers taking part in these informal events change from occasion to occasion and the division line between performers and audience, so common for musical performances in Western Europe, is in rural Albania still a flowing one. Singers constitute in the act of singing their own audience and are often their own fiercest critics.

The basis for musical execution and tonal point of reference in southern Albanian polyphony is the *iso* or drone, a continuous or repeated rhythmic tone. This drone is executed in many cases by all persons present, binding together performers and audience in a collective experience. Every performer is in this case at the same time attentive listener and conscious interpreter. All occasions in which members of a village community come together to make music serve in some respects as "practical socialization (Sugarman 1997: 224)." Young and old come together in these events, stabilising and reaffirming their social order. An important sociological feature of singing is in this respect the division of singers according to age and gender. The singing process itself is intended to create a blending of sound so as to create a "sonic community" as Lortat-Jacob (2005) has called it, mirroring a presumed harmonious interaction in village life. Social order is reflected occasionally even in the composition of multipart groups. In a performance in Borsh the mayor of the village sung the *marrës* (first voice) despite his limited abilities as singer. He thereby intended to present and make audible his superior social role both to the foreign visitor and to members of his own community. This view of the social functionality of song was already expressed by Lomax (1959) and Sugarman (1997). It is based on the concept of "ethnoscientific structuralism", a concept that summarises the idea that a community produces music because "something in that music's structure is consistent with central patterns of thinking and of behaving within the culture (Sugarman 1997: 24)." Sugarman suggests, based on the case of *muhabet*-singing,[8] that singing fulfils the function of social exchange within a wider range of symbolic concepts, which include the concepts of *nder* (respect), *radhë* (order) and *muhabet* (intimacy or appreciation) (Sugarman 1997: 138, 182ff). Albanian authors also have written about the influence multipart songs could have on social bonds. Kadare described multipart songs both as expressions of individuality and community: "In multipart songs the blending, communication, the outpouring of the individual to the collective, and, vice versa the surge of the collective to the individual reach their highest peak (Kadare 1987: 35)." This double character, combining collective and individual historical experience is one of the characteristics of the epic songs being discussed here. Thus,

[8] The term *muhabet* in this context refers to communication through conversation, storytelling, singing, dancing and/or playing musical instruments; cf. Sugarman 1997: 58.

considering these multiple meanings and functions of singing as a different level of communication, without observing the performance circumstances, the true value of a song within a cultural framework cannot be deciphered.

First, the style and the vocal technique chosen for performance is of special significance. The song *O Kurvelleshi me famë, shumë herë re në zë* (O famed Kurvellesh, many times we have heard of you) for example, which recalls the German massacres in the Kurvelesh mountains during World War II is performed with the vocal technique *kthen me grykë* (turning with the throat) (Kruta 1987: 57). This vocal technique and the use of the emblematic interval of the minor seventh., is closely related to the lament repertoire and is used, for example, at the arrival of the *krushq* (the men sent to pick up the bride) in the house of the bride.[9] In choosing this particular vocal technique for this epic song, one associates the song with a mood of mourning and the singer is showing personal involvement in the described historic events.

Secondly, the performance situation of epic historic songs is highly significant. The relationship between musicians and audience, the physical behaviour of the musicians, their stance, gestures and facial expressions are as relevant in interpreting epic songs as are the musical and textual analysis. Sitting or standing in a circle is considered essential for producing a good vocal sound with aesthetic qualities. Usually, a semi-circle is formed around the *marrës* (first voice; 'he who takes the song') with the *kthyes* (second voice; 'he who turns the song') on his right and the *hedhës* (fourth voice; 'he who throws') on his immediate left, so that these voices can be in continuous acoustic and eye contact. The singers in the second row, who form a semicircle behind the soloists, are all *iso* (drone) singers. These parts in Albanian multipart singing are generally indivisible from one another because of the interwoven relationships between them that form the inner logic of Lab singing. The singers in Lab multipart singing play unchangeable, irreplaceable roles.

Epic songs require a special quality of sound adapted to its heroic textual world. In Lab multipart singing men and women generally sing with force and full voice in chest register.

> While singing, the soloists not infrequently fall into a state of complete rapture. Completely immersed in singing, they forget their surroundings. In some cases they get so worked up about a certain issue that they are unable to perform a complete melodic line so that they can only produce sole tones in a suggestive manner (Stockmann and Stockmann 1958: 104, my translation).

Because epic historic songs belong almost exclusively to the sphere of men's singing, they are also connected with the vocal ideals of men's singing, such as the *zë të trashë* (thick voice), the wide range of ornamentation techniques, frequent interjections of exclamation and energetic rhythmic accents. The singing style represents the aural counterpart of the visual representations of gender. The men usually sing in an extroverted emotional manner, "to induce a transcendent experience (Sugarman 1997: 278)", although this is not the primary intention. Singing can therefore be understood as "aural representation of

---

[9] Here it fulfils the function of a *vajtim i vërtetë* (a real lament); cf. Kruta 1989: 136.

their own emotional state with the intention of inducing a similarly heightened state in the others (Sugarman 1997: 276)."

A CASE STUDY: ABDYL FRASHËRI

In the region of Labëria several songs have been created, dedicated to the historical figure Abdyl Frashëri (1839-1892), the two most popular among these are *Kurvellesh e Gegëri* (Kurvellesh and Gegeria) and *Avdul shitë pasurinë* (Abdyl sold his fortune). The latter example will be presented in the following in four different interpretations and text versions to demonstrate recent changes in Lab epic songs. The material stems from interviews and recordings made in Albania during fieldwork in 2004 and from archival sources kept in the Institute for Cultural Anthropology and Art Studies, Tirana. First evidence of the song comes from a text notated in 1936 in Delvina and a text kept in the Institute for Cultural Anthropology and Art Studies notated by Luçi, which dates from 1947 and comes from Kuç, a Kurvelesh village situated just 12 kilometres northwest of Borsh. All other sources indicate that this song is well known in the whole of the Labëria, Kurvelesh and Toskëria, in a region stretching from Saranda to Berat (Haxhihasani and Dule 1981: 262). A version of the song was also recorded by Erich Stockmann in 1957.

Together with his two younger brothers, Naim (1846-1900) and Sami (1850-1904), Abdyl Frashëri laid the foundations for the awakening of Albanian national identity in the *Rilindja Kombëtare* a movement that emerged in 1878 in the wake of the signing of the Treaty of San Stefano. On 10 June 1878, three days before the Congress of Berlin, the League of Prizren was founded to articulate the Albanian position on the territorial revisions in the Balkans. Abdyl Frashëri was a leader in this League; he sent two protest telegrams to Istanbul and to the ambassadors in Berlin to prevent a partitioning of Albanian-inhabited territory. Of special interest is the Memorandum for Albanian self-determination of 13 July 1878, which was sent to Lord Beaconsfield, the head of the British delegation at the Congress of Berlin (Vickers 1995: 39). In this memorandum, Frashëri appealed in the name of all Albanians to the European sense of responsibility and especially to Great Britain as *mësuesja e lirisë së popujvet* (teacher of the free peoples), demanding the right to self-determination following the Greek example (Qorri 1944: 52).

But all efforts to prevent a partition proved to be in vain and remained unheard. During the Congress of Berlin the existence of an Albanian people was denied by the Great Powers. Bismarck, one of the fiercer supporters of a partitioning of Albania claimed that "an Albanian nation does not exist. Albania is nothing but a geographical term (Stavrou 1993: 17, my translation)." The Treaty of Berlin was seen later not only in Albanian nationalist circles as 'Tomb-treaty for Albania'. Despite this failure, Frashëri continued his political mission.

On 30 March 1879, Abdyl Frashëri and Mehmet Ali Vrioni left Preveza (South Albania) to visit the principal European capitals of Rome, Vienna and Berlin, where they tried to present the wishes of the Albanian people to European statesmen. This mission was stylised in the texts of songs such as *Kurvellesh e Gegëri*, where it is stated that *Avdul bej nga Frashëri dhjetë her' vate Frëngji* (Abdyl Bey from Frashëri went ten times to Europe). The efforts of Abdyl Frashëri, who came from the village of Frashëri in southern Albania, were considered to be an example of national consciousness and made him a hero, even though he fought his battles on the field of diplomacy.

Textual Analysis

The textual structure of *Avdul shitë pasurinë* (Abdyl sold his fortune) is reminiscent of a popular song dedicated to another Albanian politician: Ismail Qemali. Here again the story is one of a lonely hero who travels selflessly to save his nation (primarily from territorial partition) to the court of an unknown country, where he talks to the highest political representatives. The text culminates in the self-representation of the hero with name, nation and national aspirations.

The song in the version from Xarra has seven stanzas, each consisting of three verses which derive from one original verse, augmented through partial or complete repetition (a+b+a'+b'+b''). Important textual features remain the same in the example from Borsh. The five stanzas show the same verse structure (a+b+a'+b'+b'').

Another version was sung by the multipart ensemble 'Jonianët', one of three such ensembles at home in Saranda. This group was the first of these to be formed after the dissolution of the system of culture houses and the establishment of *shoqata kulturore* (cultural associations) in 1993. The group is an example of the continuity of multipart singing within urban contexts and the successful transmission of repertoire and style from one generation to the next. The current leader of the group was trained by Kiço Kapedani, one of the most famous *rapsods* (rhapsodic singers) of the region who even sung for the Stockmann expedition in 1957. The 'Jonianët' version shares many textual features with the version from Borsh. The five-line structure as described above is maintained. Interesting is the last stanza, which was performed occasionally in concerts by the group. It is a typical sort of contemporary commentary on an orally transmitted text containing a generalised message, in our case bravery and the quest for freedom for the Albanian people. This version is musically more elaborated than the text might intimate.

The example from Mursia with five stanzas also resembles the version from Borsh. The descriptive second stanza is omitted although the singer remembered the last stanza of the 1951 version. Both text versions from Borsh and Mursia omit specific historic details and do not describe Frashëri's political intentions or his territorial demands such as in the historiographically descriptive 1936 example. These impoverished text-versions evoke an abstract, indefinite hero open to different interpretations. The text is used mainly to describe the events and the dialogue, depriving the historical figure of Abdyl Frashëri of its specific political intentions and achievements. The shared textual content of all three versions are the three or more introductory stanzas culminating in the two stanza dialogue between Bismarck and Frashëri. Within this frame, descriptive details may change, also due to dialectal differences, 'dividing into pieces' can be *copa copa* (Kuç), or *çikë çikë* or *copë e çikë* (both Saranda). 'Textual impoverishment' becomes more visible after these first five stanzas. The musically highly elaborated version from Borsh is textually the poorest, with five stanzas showing only a third of the textual content presented in the fourteen stanzas from Delvina as recorded in 1936. This oldest recorded example shows that the dialogue between Frashëri and Bismarck was originally developed as a monologue by the Albanian hero, whose political message made up more than the half of the Delvina-text, namely eight stanzas. This monologue had been reduced to a six-stanza-scheme by 1951 and to three stanzas in Xarra 2004 to vanish completely in the Borsh-version. The opposite trend may be seen in the version from Saranda, which refers to the version from Delvina with its four monologue stanzas and the reintroduction of a lost verse praising the constructed character of the Albanian nation.

Metric Analysis

The general metrical structure of this song can be best observed in the example from Xarra. The basis of a stanza is a thirteen-foot verse (8+5) combined with a five-foot verse (2+3), which can be repeated. The metric structure is complicated by the introduction of filling syllables (*-je,-jo,-ja*), which transform the metric structure significantly.

The example from Borsh shares with the Xarra-example the thirteen-foot first verse and the repeated five-foot verse at the end of every stanza. The iambic character is here more explicit because supported by a $^3/_8$ measure. We find the same features already mentioned in the Xarra-example, such as augmentation of the verse-foot by the introduction of syllables such as *-je*, *-ja*, and *-jo* and exclamations such as '*more*' and very typical at the end of every b'-part "*oja mana mana*."

The Saranda-version is deprived of all syllable additions found in the village tradition. Only the exclamation '*more*' is used as a connection between the two parts of the first thirteen-foot verse.

In the Mursia-version each stanza is made up of the thirteen-foot verse (8+5) and is performed in iambic metre. It is significant that the soloist also uses the 'syllable calculation technique' in adding the same syllables as the Borshiots during the repetition of the first line: "*ska-ja-mi*" and "*Fra-ja-shë-ri.*" With this technique the metric structure is transformed again.

Musical Analysis

All four versions of the song are examples of the elaborated three- or four-part singing style of the Lab multipart tradition. The Lab singing style is in general a text-bound recitative form, which shows an extraordinary interdependence between verbal and musical parameters. The result of this interdependence is that most songs are based on a melodic-metric line, which can be altered during the course of the piece.

The examples from Saranda and Xarra were performed in three-part style, the example from Borsh in four-part style and the example of Mursia solo. While typical harmonies created between the voices remain constant, the elaboration and ornamentation of the respective voices can differ considerably.

The tonal range of the *marrës* can, for example, be restricted to a major third and consist only of three tones, as in the Xarra-example or stretch up to the expressive interval of a minor seventh in the Saranda-example.

The rhythmic and tonal appearance of the *kthyes* is also subject to change. In the example from Borsh the second voice loses its melodic importance while the *hedhës* assumes a dominant role, not only as provider of sonic timbre but as imitator of the rhythmical figures of the *kthyes*.

A typical feature of all discussed examples, with exception of that from Saranda, appears to be the gradual microtonal rise of the pitch-centre. This phenomenon is caused by the growing tension of the singers' voice and the growing emotional identification with the text during the act of singing. The microtonal rise, together with the insertion of exclamations, indicates the personal involvement of the singer with the epic textual world.

Every performance is characterised by a distinctive aesthetic quality of singing. While in the case of Xarra the style especially of the leading voice can be described as introvert, the Borsh performance is distinguished by an expressive style, rich in overtones. The voice part of the marrës was here clearly used to show the singers virtuosity with rhythmic differentiations and different tone colours. These different aesthetic approaches stem partly from the age of the singers. While the group of aged peasants from Xarra performed in the style of the *këngë pleqërishte* (songs of the old men) with a restrained dynamic, slow performance and rich melismatic cantilenas, the young men of Borsh formulated their aesthetic view according to the concept of the *këngë djelmurishte* (songs of the young men) in a fast tempo with harsh rhythmic contrasts. In addition, the regional differences between Borsh, situated close to Himara, a distinguished centre of a popular four-part-singing style and the Greek-border village of Xarra, without a functioning musical life, cannot be underestimated.

The Mursia-example is sung by a soloist, who tries to combine typical features of the *marrës* and the *kthyes* in one voice. This way of singing is singular because normally the multipart structure is considered indivisible. The single voice even shows the typical features of Lab multipart singing such as the gliding tone at the end of the piece, the transitional passages between *marrës* and chorus with o-/-u vocals and the above mentioned typical syllable additions.

Abdyl Frashëri (Goseck /Germany, 26.6.2005)	
Abdyl prishe pasurinë një barrë flori (2x) një barrë flori.	Abdyl you spent your fortune Which was a sack of gold, (2x) Which was a sack of gold.
Hipe vaporrit e shkove more për në Gjermani, (2x) për në Gjermani.	He boarded on a steamship and Went to Germany, (2x) Went to Germany.
Oh vajte te Bismarku brënda more ndënje në skamni (2x) ndënje në skamni.	He went to Bismarck inside, In front of the throne, (2x) In front of the throne.
Të pyetën dhe të thanë more: "Djalë nga je ti?" (2x) "Djalë nga je ti?"	He asked him and said: "Boy where are you from?" (2x) "Boy where are you from?"
"Unë jam nga Shqipëria, mor' Abdyl Frashëri, Abdyl Frashëri."	"Unë jam nga Shqipëria, mor' Abdyl Frashëri, Abdyl Frashëri."
"Ju lutem mendoni mirë ju për Shqipëri ju për Shqipëri."	"Please think thoroughly About Albania, About Albania."
"Mos e bëni copë e çikë mor' sikur s'ka njeri sikur s'ka njeri."	"Do not split it into pieces As if there were no humans, As if there were no humans."
("Se Shqipëtarët janë trima mor' vdesin për liri, vdesin për liri.")	("Because the Albanians have courage And will die for their freedom, Will die for their freedom.")

Avdul Frashëri (Borsh/Albania 12.9.2004)	
Avdul shite pasurinë, një barrë flo-jo-ri, (2x) oja mana një barrë flo-jo-ri.	Abdyl you sold your fortune Which was a sack of gold, (2x) Which was a sack of gold.
Hipe vaporrit e shkove, vajte në Gjermani (2x) o iso more vajte në Gjermani.	He boarded on a steamship and went, Went to Germany, (2x) Went to Germany.
Vajte te Bismarku brënda, ndënje ne ska-ja-mi, (2x) oja mana mana ndënje ne ska-ja-mi.	He came inside to Bismarck, Where he sat on the throne, (2x) Where he sat on the throne.
Në Bismarku kur është shtëpi e ti: „Djalë nga je ti?" (2x) „Djalë nga je ti ?"	It was in Bismarck's house: "Boy where are you from?" (2x) "Boy where are you from?"
Unë vij nga Shqipëria, Avdul Fra-ja-shëri, (2x) oja mana Avdul Fra-ja-shëri."	"I come from Albania, Abdyl Frashëri, (2x) Abdyl Frashëri."

Avdul Frashëri (Xarra/Albania, 8.4.2004)	
Avdul shite pasurinë një barrë flo-jo-ri, (2x) një barrë-je flo-jo-ri.	Abdyl you sold your fortune Which was a sack of gold, (2x) Which was a sack of gold.
Hipe vaporrit e shkove vajte në Berli, hajde (2x) Vajte në Berli.	He boarded on a steamship and went to Berlin, (2x) went to Berlin.
Vajte te Bismarku brënda ndënje në-je skami,(2x) Brënda në-je skami.	He went to Bismarck Inside in front of the throne, (2x) Inside in front of the throne.
"E i djalë në shtëpi-jo nga je ti?" hajd- (2x) "Djalë nga je ti?"	"And boy in the house, Where are you from?" (2x) "Boy where are you from?"
"Un' jam nga Shqipëria, Avdul Fra-ja-shëri, (2x) Avdul Fra-ja-shë-je-ri."	"I am from Albania, Abdyl Frashëri,(2x) Abdyl Frashëri." „
"Kam ardhur të bën me fjalë për Shqipë-je-ri, (2x) ju për Shqipëri."	I came to intercede with the word For Albania, (2x) For Albania."
"Ju lutem mos e bëni pjesë-pjesë sikur s'ka-ja njëri, hajd-o (2x) sikur s'ka njëri."	"Please do not split it into pieces As if there were no humans, (2x) As if there were no humans."

Avdul shite pasurinë (K. Danga, Mursia/Albania 15.9.2004)	
Avdul shite pasurinë ç'e barë flori Avdul shite pasur' i ç'e barë-je flori, ç'e barë flori.	Abdyl you sold your fortune Which was a sack of gold, Abdyl you sold your fortune Which was a sack of gold, Which was a sack of gold.
Vajte në Bismarku vetu ndenje në-je ska-ja-mi ndenje në-je ska-ja-mi.	He went alone to Bismarck, here he sat on the throne Where he sat on the throne.
Dhe Bismarku s'është j'shtëpi: "Djalë nga je-je ti?" Dhe Bismarku s'është j'shtëpi "Djalë nga je-je?" "Djal-o nga je-je?"	And Bismarck in his house: "Boy where are you from?" And Bismarck in his house: "Boy where are you from?" "Boy where are you from?"
"Unë jam nga Shqipëri-u-a, Avdul Frashëri, Unë jam nga Shqipëri-u-a, Avdul Fra-ja-shëri, Avdul Fra-ja-shëri."	"I am from Albania, Abdyl Frashëri, I am from Albania, Abdyl Frashëri, Abdyl Frashëri, "
"Të rritur-e n'ato male, me libra në gji." "Të rritur n'ato male, me libra-ja në gji, me libra-ja në gji."	"I was brought up in these mountains, with a book on the breast." "I was brought up in these mountains, With a book on the breast, With a book on the breast,"

Avdul shite pasurinë (Kuç-Kurvellesh/Albania, 1951; cited in Haxhihasani and Sako 1956: 213-214)	
Avdul shite pasurinë, një barrë flori. Hipe vaporrit e shkove, vajte në Berli.	Abdyl you sold your fortune, Which was a sack of gold. He boarded a steamship and went, Went to Berlin.
Vajte te Bismarku brënda, ndënje në skami.	He came to Bismarck inside, Where he sat on the throne.
Ç'të pijen edhe të thanë: "Djalë, nga je ti?"	They drank something and he also said: "Boy, where are you from?"
"Unë jam nga Shqipëria, Avdul Frashëri."	"I am from Albania, Abdyl Frashëri."
"Ju lutem, shikoni mirë, ju për Shqipëri."	"Please, look carefully, For Albania."
"Mos e bëni copa-copa, sikur s'ka njëri."	"You cannot split it into pieces, As if there were no humans."
"S'jemi Grekër as Bullgarë, as prej Malit Zi;"	"We are neither Greeks nor Bulgarians, Nor from Montenegro;"
"Jemi vetëm Shqipëtarë dhe duam liri;"	"We are just Albanians And desire freedom;"
"Të rritur n'ata male, me libra në gji."	"I was brought up in these mountains, With a book on the breast."

Abdyl pasurin' e shite (Delvina/Albania, 1936; cited in Haxhihasani and Dule 1981: 164)	
Abdyl, pasurin' e shite, një barë flori.	Abdyl you sold your fortune, Which was a sack of gold.
Hipe vaporit e shkove, vajte në Berlin.	He boarded on a steamship and went, Went to Berlin.
Bismarkun ta pjekie doje, për një bisedim;	He wanted to meet Bismarck, For a discussion;
T'i hije brënda kërkoje, po s'keshe fuqi;	He went inside and searched, But his strength was failing;
Më në fund i hire brënda, ndenje në skamni.	Finally he went in, Where he sat on the throne.
"Burrë, ç'më ke për të thënë dhe cili je ti?"	"Boy, what do you have to say to me And who are you?"
"Nuk jam grek e as bullgar, as nga Mal' i Zi;"	"I am neither Greek nor Bulgarian, Nor from Montenegro;"
"Po nga kombi shqipëtar, Abdyl Frashëri."	"But from the Albanian state, Abdyl Frashëri."
"Ju, Bismark, s'punoni mirë dhe për Shqipëri,"	"You, Bismarck are not working for the good Of Albania,"
"Kërkoni ta copëtoni, sikur s'ka njeri."	"You intend to split it up, As if there were no humans."
"Gra e burra do luftojmë neve për liri;"	"Women and men will fight For their freedom;"
"Të drejtën do ta kërkojmë gjer të shuhemi."	"We claim our rights, Until we die."
"Gjirokastra edhe Korça nuk janë Gërqi,"	"Gjirokastra and Korça Are not Greece,"
"Ashtu Dibra edhe Shkodra S'janë Mal' i Zi."	"Even Dibra and Shkodra Are not Montenegro."

A STORY OF SURVIVAL? REPERTORY CHANGE AND CONSISTENCY WITHIN AN ORAL TRADITION

At the end of this case study, one might sum up the recent trends as a combination of three phenomena, namely 'generation reversal', the shifting conception of singing from a participatory activity to a performative activity[10] and 'musical impoverishment.' Villages are in the process of being 'muted', *pa këngë* (without song), as Stavro Zisos, the last singer from the village of Vrion, explained to me in an embarrassed tone. All the above-mentioned trends are connected in one way or another to the collapse of the communist regime, the collapse of organised cultural activity in rural areas, the end of the political and cultural isolation of the Albanian people and the curse of migration.

Considering that Albania is one of the youngest countries of Europe, with 42 percent of the total population being under 19 years-of-age (UNICEF 1998: 14-15), the reaction of the young generation to the experience of migration will be crucial for the persistence and survival of traditional music. Recent years have seen the advance of popular music into village households. This trend is supported by three main factors: 1) returning labour migrants from Greece and Italy, 2) the so called 'summer children', who bring the latest pop music from the larger cities into rural communities (provoking passive musical reception instead of active performance activities) and 3) Greek and Albanian television programming (cf. Tower 2002: 227). Television does not only carry the wave of popular music, it has in general replaced information exchange via song, it has substituted the 'oral tradition' with a pseudo-objective information stream. This means that the concept of *muhabet*, of communicating through storytelling, singing, dancing and/or playing musical instruments, has come to be considered inadequate in relation to emerging modern communication technologies. Songs on the other hand are expressions of traditional Albanian culture. They "refer to the individual, conceived exclusively as part of a family (or network of families) and in relation to its attendant needs and priorities (Mai 2001: 98)."

Sugarman comes to the conclusion that the repertoire of Prespa singing will reconsolidate itself between the contrasting poles of the old style songs and the newer media songs (cf. Sugarman 1997: 340). This challenge is also posed to the Lab repertoire. The orally transmitted form of multipart singing, learning to sing by listening and by practising in events and regular meetings of multipart groups seems to be far away from the age of mass media consumption.

What threatens the musical practice profoundly is the fact that music is losing its functionality. Contexts for singing are disappearing and singers die without having had the possibility to transfer their knowledge to others. Singing as intergenerational practice, practised on any communal occasion is no longer the general case. The shift of singing from a participatory to a performative activity seems to be redetermined (cf. Sugarman 1997: 342).

---

[10] This development began with the *folklori i ri* movement.

On the other hand, traditional music has assumed a new integrating role after the collapse of the communist regime. This revival is the result of the preceding stigmatisation of the aesthetic dimension during the communist dictatorship. Singing epic historic songs today, recalling and reinterpreting national or regional history also means repositioning and reaffirming Lab identity within new contexts such as globalisation. Stuart Hall argues that globalisation, "rather than undermining nationalisms, can activate and underwrite them (Hall 1992: 302)." But is this the case in Albania? We cannot answer this question yet but it is important to stress that the musical tradition itself is not bound exclusively to the concept of nation. It is bound as well to regionalism (relating music to the *krahina*) and above all to the convictions of individuals, to their beliefs and values. Music can be seen in this context as interacting element, as mediator between person, region and nation, the different levels of collective identity.

One of the most astonishing features of Lab singing is its ability to renew itself over the course of time. This ability, rooted in an amazing virtuosity to adapt musical versatility and textual knowledge to changed conditions is expressed in improvisations such as the *përshëndetje* (songs of well-being), in new emigration songs built on formulas of the ancient *këngë kurbeti* or in political satirical songs. These examples show that this style of singing is not only rooted in the past but also able to comment on contemporary aspects of day-to-day life. As long as Lab multipart singing does not lose this decisive quality, this unique tradition can be considered a living multipart tradition.

BIBLIOGRAPHY

Ahmedaja, Ardian (comp.) 2012 Discovering Albania – Recordings from the collections Traeger Albanien 1903 and Stockmann Albanien 1957 of the Berlin Phonogramm-Archive. Audio-CD, Tirana: Ulysses-Foundation.

Anderson, Benedict 1983 Imagined Communities. Reflections on the Origins and Spread of Nationalism. London and New York: Verso.

Castelo-Branco and Salwa El-Shawan 2005 Vocal Polyphony in Portugal: The Case of Alentejo. Paper given at the conference Multipart Singing on the Balkans and in the Mediterranean, Vienna 11-13 March 2005.

Castles, Stephen and Mark J. Miller (eds.) 1993 The Age of Migration: International Population Movements in the Modern World. London: Macmillian.

Hall, Stuart 1992 The Question of Cultural Identity. In: Stuart Hall, David Held and Tony McGrew (eds.) Modernity and its Futures Cambridge: pp 273-326.

Handler, Richard 1988 Nationalism and the Politics of Culture in Quebec, Madison: University of Wisconsin Press.

Haxhihasani, Qemal and Zihni Sako (eds.) 1956 Këngë Popullore Historike. Tirana: ASHSH.

Haxhihasani, Qemal and Miranda Dule (eds.) 1981 Epika Historike, Vëll. 2. Tirana: ASHSH.

Hering, Gunnar 1989 Die Osmanenzeit im Selbstverständnis der Völker Südosteuropas. In: H.G. Majer (ed.) Die Staaten Südosteuropas und die Osmanen (Südosteuropa Jahrbuch 19). Munich: Südosteuropa-Gesellschaft pp 355-380.

Kadare, Ismail 1987 The Autobiography of the People in Verse, Tirana: Shtëpia Botuese "8 Nëntori".

Kartomi, Margaret 1981 The Process and Results of Musical Culture Contact: A Discussion of Terminology and Concepts. In: Ethnomusicology, Vol. 25(2) pp. 227-249.

Kaser, Karl 2002 Dörfer in der Krise. In: Karl Kaser, Robert Pichler and Stephanie Schwander-Sievers (eds.) Die weite Welt und das Dorf, Vienna: Böhlau pp 162-187.

Kruta, Benjamin 1987 Regard Typologique de la polyphonie Labe (La polyphonie de trois voix près du bourdon et du bourdon). In: Culture Populaire Albanaise, Vol. 7 pp 23-57.

Kruta, Benjamin 1989 Polifonia dyzërëshe e Shqipërisë jugore. Tirana: ASHSH.

Lomax, Alan 1959 Folk Song Style- Musical Style and Social Context. In: American Anthropologist, Vol. 61 pp 972-954.

Lord, Albert B. 1960 The Singer of Tales. Cambridge (Mass.): Harvard University Press.

Lortat-Jacob, Bernard 2005 Chord and Dischord in Polyphony. Paper given at the Conference Multipart-Singing on the Balkans and in the Mediterranean, Vienna 11-13 March 2005.

Mai, Nicola 2001 Italy is beautiful. The Role of Italian Television in Albanian Migration to Italy. In: Russell King and Nancy Wood (eds.) Media and Migration. Construction of Mobility and Difference, London: Routledge pp 95-109.

Pipa, Arshi 1978 Albanian Folk Verse: Structure and Genre. Munich: Dr. Rudolf Trofenik.

Pistrick, Eckehard and Dalipaj, Gerda 2008 Celebrating the imagined village – Organising and Commeting Local Soundscapes and Social Patterns in South Albanian Feasts. In: International Journal for Euro-Mediterranean Studies; Issue: Arts and heritage in the Mediterranean, Vol. 1, 2 pp 163-191.

Qorri, Besim 1944 Shqipnija e Vërtetë. Studim Historik dhe Ethnografik. Tirana.

Reuer, Bruno B. 1993 Musik. In: Klaus-Detlev Grothusen (ed.): Albanien, Südosteuropa-Handbuch Vol. 7 Göttingen: Vandenhoeck and Ruprecht pp 714-727.

Scaldaferri, Nicola 2003 Itinerari di frontiera: I canti epici albanesi nel contesto dell'epica balcanica. In: Maurizio Agamennone and Gino L. di Mitri (eds.) Atti del convegno internazionale di studi l'eredità di Diego Carpitella. Etnomusicologia, antropologia e ricerca storica nel Salento e nell'area mediterranea, Nardò pp 93-111.

Schöpflin, George 2002 The Nature of Myth. Some Theoretical Aspects. In: Stephanie Schwandner-Sievers and Bernd J. Fischer (eds.) Albanian Identities. Myth and History, Bloomington: University of Indiana Press pp 26-30

Schwandner-Sievers, Stephanie 2002 Narratives of Power. Capacities of Myth in Albania. In: Stephanie Schwandner-Sievers and Bernd J. Fischer (eds.) Albanian Identities. Myth and History, Bloomington: University of Indiana Press pp 3-25.

Skendi, Stavro 1956 The Songs of the Klephts and the Hayduks- History or Oral Literature? In: Südost-Forschungen Vol. 15 pp 666-673.

Stavrou, Christodoulos 1993 Die griechische Minderheit in Albanien. Frankfurt a.M.

Stockmann, Erich and Doris Stockmann 1958 Die vokale Bordun-Mehrstimmigkeit in Südalbanien. In: Les Colloques de Wégimont pp 85-135.

Stockmann, Erich 1987 Eine musikethnologische Sammelreise nach Albanien 1957 aus Anlass des 50. Jahrestages der Expedition, Klangwelt-Weltklang Feature. Berlin: Rundfunk der DDR.

Sugarman, Jane 1997 Engendering Song. Singing and Subjectivity at Prespa Albanian Weddings. Chicago: University of Chicago Press.

Tower, Caroline 2002 Jugend und Geschlechterrollen im Wandel. In: Karl Kaser, Robert Pichler and Stephanie Schwandner-Sievers (eds.) Die weite Welt und das Dorf, Vienna: Böhlau pp 219-238.

UNICEF 1998 Situation Analysis 1998 Children's and Women's Rights in Albania. Tirana: UNICEF.

Vickers, Miranda 1995 The Albanians. A Modern History. London: Tauris.

13. The History, Form and Function of the Old Bazaar in Tirana

Armanda Hysa

Tirana's old bazaar has never been studied in detail, neither by Albanian historians nor by ethnologists. The old bazaar nevertheless deserves to be examined, not only because it is the first urban core of the city. It also for centuries represented the economic, trade and financial centre of the community, a meeting place for people coming from surrounding villages, towns and cities, a place of recreation and amusement, a place to exchange experiences and a place where people could discuss politics and arrange marriages.

The effort to understand what the bazaar was and what it meant for the city is also an effort to understand the relationships between people, their ideas and mentalities, the basis of the city's economic development and the various customs and traditions that are not to be found recorded in any written documents.

The Bazaar and the City

One of the characteristics of the medieval Ottoman city was the way the market and exchange were organised. Handicraft production and trade were organised in corporations and guilds. After coming under Ottoman rule, Albanian cities grew in accordance to this model. The Ottoman city model clearly separated residential and economic spheres, as opposed to Western models where these spheres were mixed (Shkodra 1973: 67, Miho 1987: 70). Tirana was founded in the 17th century, at a time when the largest part of central Albania had already been islamised. Zija Shkodra (1973, 1981) has stressed the role the development of the market had in the development of urban life and the general growth of Albanian cities in the first two centuries of Ottoman rule. There were several reasons for this (Shkodra 1981: 167): The political situation in Albania was more or less calm in that time; no major conflicts were taking place on Albanian territory as was the case in the 15th century. The consequence was an increase in population and the demand for goods. Communication and trade between various parts of the Empire grew and as a result so did the number of urban centres. The ethnologist Rrok Zojzi argues in an unpublished manuscript that several of these new Albanian cities – among them Tirana – is closely related to the emergence of their markets.[1]

The legend goes that Tirana was founded by Sulejman Pasha Bargjin Mulleti, who initiated the building the complex (*imaret*) made up of a mosque, a public bath (*hamam*), an inn (*han*) and a bakery at the junction of an east-westerly and a north-southerly road. It is said that these were the first buildings established on an untouched plain; the residences of the pasha and other houses appeared later. The data, if not completely missing, is very difficult to interpret. Kristo Frashëri (2004) and Koço Miho (1987: 17) are of the opinion that a small village or hamlet served as a nucleus for what was to become the city.

Zojzi on the other hand argues that on the plain of Tirana a regular agricultural and animal fair known as the *Panairi i Shën Lleshit* (the fair of Saint Alexander) was held regularly. He argues that this fair began much earlier than its first documentation in 1781. His argument is based on the discovery of traces of a monastery and a fountain near today's central bus station (*parku i autobuzave*). Zojzi claims these are the remains of the monastery and fountain of *Shën Gjin* (Saint John) and dates it to the 14th century. The monastery is known to have been built on the plain bearing the same name. According to Zojzi, in the medieval era, fairs were always organised around monasteries. For him, these two facts support the idea of a fair existing before the wars of the 15th century. Zojzi argues that the old bazaar was situated to the east of the old fairground. This, as well as the fact that the old quarters of Tirana were located in a horseshoe around this fairground constitutes two more arguments affirming that the *Panairi i Shën Lleshit* was a continuation of an older fair and pivotal for the creation of the urban centre.

Both these hypotheses have their own logic, but at the same time they each have their weaknesses. It is true that Sulejman Pasha established the *imaret* in 1614. The commemorative slate on the Old Mosque (*Xhamia e Vjetër*) and the central role this family had in the city until the beginning of the 19th century are the evidence to this. While this does not say anything about the actual course of events they confirm that the social memory of these events was still alive up to the beginning of the 20th century, four centuries later. In any case, an *imaret* requires an existing infrastructure and people in need of its services if it is to be successful.

The 'fair' hypothesis has a certain logic as well. While it is true that traces of a monastery belonging to the pre-Ottoman period have been discovered, and that monasteries often served as centres for fairs in the middle ages, must this necessarily be the case for Tirana as well? The quarters of old Tirana are in fact situated in a horseshoe around a large open area. But in typical medieval Ottoman cities, the markets were traditionally on the outskirts of the communities. Thus, the political context would have stipulated that the bazaar and the fair would – at least initially – not have been in the centre of the town as was the case. The increasing of number of inhabitants and the natural growth of the city would have led to the

[1] Zojzi, Rrok. Tirana nëpër gojëdhëna dhe tradita etnografike (Dorëshkrim), AE pranë IKP 300/29 D 38; Zojzi, Rrok. Materiale të papërpunuara nga ekspedita e vitit 1955 në rrethin e Tiranës, AE pranë IKP, 35/1, dosja 37.

creation of new quarters around the fair and bazaar but this would have been a more recent phenomenon.

Having reviewed the facts, my own conclusion is that Tirana took shape as a town and then became an interregional market centre. In a *firman* of 10 December 1781 on the status of the fair we read among other things that

> To feed the poor, travellers and the faithful of the *zawiyah* of the *qadiri*, it was decided to finance this charitable service from revenues of the fair created near the *çarşı* [bazaaar] of the city of Tirana belonging to the jurisdiction of the *kaza* of *Akçehisar* [Kruja] (Frashëri 2004: 91, my translation).

Fair and bazaar existed parallel to one another by 1781.

I would agree with Shkodra (most recently in Shkodra 1994) that the creation of the city came as a natural regional development. The fertile land of this plain may well have attracted the attention of the beys and villagers of the surrounding area. The trade caravans that increasingly frequented the area as well as the growth of trade relations among the villages in the area benefited from the fact that they could meet at a central point, namely at the crossroads of Tirana. Sulejman Pasha then built the *imaret* in 1614 to serve this early bazaar. There was need of a han for the accommodation of merchants and a public bath. These would have been established to serve non-local merchants; would the merchants and travellers have had ties to the local population, it would have been an affront to take lodging in the inn - they would have stayed as guests in the houses of their friends and relatives. The construction of the bakery and then the mosque indicate that the bazaar had grown from a weekly to a daily institution that attracted not only peasants but craftsmen as well, who needed to be fed and given the opportunity to perform their regular prayers. Their construction also indicates that payment was made not in kind but in cash. Thus the bazaar of Tirana began to acquire the form it took in the late 19th and early 20th centuries. The construction of the *imaret* can be seen as the institutionalisation of a loose scattering of houses into a town. Thus the beginnings of the bazaar are intimately related with the emergence of Tirana as a town.

THE GROWTH AND ORGANISATION OF THE BAZAAR

The beginnings of Tirana's bazaar were agricultural – it was an open air market for the sale of agricultural goods. This can be seen at the denominations of bazaar's nine main markets: *leshna* (wool market), *orizna* (rice market), *krypna* (salt market), *hasra* (mat market), *dithna* (grain market), *djathna* (cheese market), *gjelna* (poultry market), *pema* (fruit market) and *qerret* (cart market).[2] The survival of these different markets into the 20th century is evidence to the fact that these activities never lost their importance in the local region. As the importance of the market grew, it also attracted local craftsmen who began to

[2] Zojzi, Rrok. Materiale të papërpunuara nga ekspedita e vitit 1955 në rrethin e Tiranës, AE pranë IKP, 35/1, dosja 37.

bring their products there. Later, craftsmen from farther away, from Kruja, Elbasan, Kavaja and so on began to bring their products there as well, which in turn stimulated the development of these trades in the town of Tirana itself. Craftsmen who in the past came weekly from their village began to build permanent warehouses where they left their material and merchandise. In the course of time some of these settled definitively in Tirana, produced their goods there and sold them on a daily basis, acquiring their raw materials from their family members who had remained in their hometowns. The cobblers are a distinctive example: every Thursday, which was initially the market day, they came from Kruja to sell their products where the National History Museum is located today. In the course of time some of these men settled in Tirana and began to produce their goods there. The potters, a trade associated with the village of Farka, are a similar example. With the turn of the 18th century Tirana counted about 500 families and 150-200 shops (Myderrizi 1937: 15).

The trades developed thanks to a great part to the immigration of a large number of people from Voskopoja at the end of the 17th century. They settled at the edge of the town near what is today *parku i madh* (Grand Park). A clear sign of their first settlement is the Church of Saint Prokopi, built around the turn of the 19th century (Hobdari 2001: 10). Their main occupations were stockbreeding and smithing, especially in copper and silver. When the forces of Kurt Pasha of Berat, who wanted to control the emerging market centre of Tirana threatened the town, they took an active part in defending the city. Thus they gained the sympathy of the city notables and a large space was left to them in the old bazaar to construct their shops and develop their trades. The incorporation of the Voskopojans in the bazaar played a significant role in the growth and increased diversity of the latter. A large number of shops and new handicrafts enriched the market. But the effects were not only economic in nature; it was also very important from a social perspective because it helped to integrate the Orthodox Vlach community into the town.

Thus a slow shift in the structure of the market can be observed. The central compositional unit giving the bazaar its quality and physiognomy became the shop of the craftsman, where both the production and sale of goods took place. This double nature of the shops as needing to exhibit the products as well as providing room to work the goods and store the raw materials defined their organisation and their construction. The shops were usually around five metres deep, had a single floor and were built in regular blocks. A normal block had about 15 shops facing another block of the same size along streets known as *sokaks*.[3] The goods were often displayed directly on the street under a large awning.

The growth of the bazaar in Tirana, like medieval urban planning as such, was spontaneous, although this medieval spontaneity was not free of any guiding principles. The existence of a medieval organisation of 'urban planners', the 'Agas of construction' clearly show that a certain degree of organisation and planning based on guiding principles did take place in this field (Riza 1988: 5).

---

[3] Zojzi, Rrok. Materiale të papërpunuara nga ekspedita e vitit 1955 në rrethin e Tiranës, AE pranë IKP, 35/1, dosja 37.

The blocks of houses were built along virtually parallel streets, the craftsmen practicing a single trade clustered together in these streets. The streets were quite wide ranging between distances of seven to ten metres and were paved with cobblestones. In the middle of the street there was a drainage channel. Streets built later and those that were renovated with time had this channel on either side of it. The streets in the bazaar were named after the crafts and trades they housed and included the butcher's and the barber's streets, both running parallel to Rruga 28 Nëntori, the blacksmith's street running diagonally between the Rruga e Barrikadeve and the Rruga e Dibrës, the coppersmith's street parallel to it and the silversmith's street, which extended parallel to the Rruga e Barrikadeve. These latter craftsmen were also known as *myhyrxhinj* or ring makers. The felt and *fez* maker's street was in the western part of the bazaar behind the *Hani i Elbasanllinjve* (Elbasani Inn). The street of the *terzi* (tailors specialised in the production of traditional costumes) was also known by the people of Tirana as *sokaku i cohaxhinjve* (street of cloth). It is not clear exactly where this street was but it may have been in the place known today as *rruga e rrobaqepësve* (the street of the tailors). By the 1950s the national dress had been largely abandoned and the old *terzi* had probably gone over to sewing modern clothing.

The *dyfekçinjtë* (rifle makers) had their street in the bazaar as well, but they disappeared quickly with the introduction of Western factory-made weaponry in the early 20th century. In the 1950s only two or three remained scattered in the bazaar. The same can be said for the pipe-makers. This craft flourished in the 19th century with over 40 shops in the bazaar. In the interwar period only ten remained and these were absorbed in the 1950s in the 'Migjeni' Artisanal Enterprise.[4]

A women's market emerged as well. There the women sold their stitched and crocheted handicrafts made of cotton and silk and handwoven cloth and clothing. Central Albania and the region around Tirana in particularly was known for these products. There was not a house in Tirana without at least one mulberry tree in the garden where silkworms were cultivated. At the end of the 19th century 100,000 metres wool and cotton cloth and 160,000 metres of silk was produced annually in Tirana (Shkodra 1994: 142) in household production. It was a very profitable activity for the families. Considering that most of the families thus produced their own handloom products, this production must have been exported to other regions of Albanian or even abroad. These merchants specialised in the exporting and importing of goods also had their streets, one of them running parallel to the Rruga 28 Nëntori and the other on the road beside the former City Hall (where the National History Museum is today).

Other merchants walked the streets selling their goods. These included the *kazazes*, sellers of silk *gajtan* or belts, as well as the sellers of pastries and *boza*, a refreshing drink made of cornflour. These walking salesmen had their shops spread throughout the bazaar. Similar institutions focusing on providing services instead of goods such as the coffeehouses, the taverns and several *han* were also distributed throughout the bazaar. Especially the numerous coffeehouses were important for

[4] Selimi, Yllka, Material i përpunuar nga ekspedita në qytetin e Tiranës. Zeja e punimit të pipave, AE IKP, 1096/1, 1978.

the craftsmen and merchants as they represented a gathering and meeting place for the people. As Friedrich Wallisch described it,

> [i]n front of the larger coffeehouses, where the middle-class discusses politics, the chairs and tables are set up row upon row on the street. In the very small coffeehouses, which are nothing more then narrow hovels, the men crouch on low wooden benches. Or one takes his place with drawn up legs on the windowsill. In his hands the reins of his horse standing outside the cafe[...] In the gloom of shop can be seen the red glowing charcoal under the small copper kettle; a guest is probably telling one of the bittersweet but pointed stories that have been passed on in ancient tradition from generation to generation (Wallisch 1931: 24, my translation).

But important negotiations took place in the coffeehouses as well, such as between peasants deciding on the marriages of their sons and daughters. They drank coffee there on such occasions in a betrothal ceremony known as *pirja e kafeve të vogla* (drinking of little coffees) that is still observed in large parts of the country today. The coffeehouse and tavern keepers also delivered the workshops, delivering up to 50 coffees a day.[5]

The available data related to the *hans* are very scarce. Besides the *han* built by Sulejman Pasha, there existed also the above-mentioned *Hani i Elbasanllinjve*, a very large single storey construction with an elaborate arched facade, and another han of two storeys beside the Clock Tower, which was destroyed soon after World War I. Living conditions in these *hans* were very simple, the rooms being furnished with no more than a place to sleep and a chair (Asais 1930). The wells were another vital public institution in the bazaar about which no data is available, not even about their number.

Finally, the clock tower or *kulla e sahatit* must be mentioned as a central element in the modernisation of the bazaar and of life in the city as a whole, it providing a means by which to organise day-to-day activities more effectively. Clock towers spread throughout the Balkans in the 16th century; in Tirana it was only built in the 1830s by Ethem Bey. The choice to build the clock tower so close to the Ethem Bey Mosque was visionary, this corner of the bazaar developing to become the centre of the city. Every main street in Tirana merges on the complex mosque-clock tower, which eventually became the symbol of the city (Miho 1987:90, cf. the description in Wallisch 1931: 21-22).

THE GUILDS AS AN ORGANISING STRUCTURE

With the increasing number of craftsmen establishing their workshops in the bazaar, its nature changed. What had once been a market for agricultural goods became increasingly a centre of production. This also effected the organisation of the bazaar and of life in the city. The Tirana craftsmen, like the craftsmen of other cities of the Ottoman Empire, were organised in guilds or *esnaf*. The *esnaf*

[5] According to Seit Abdullancës, former owner of such a café in the old bazaar.

organised and monitored the prices, the distribution of work among the individual craftsmen, the qualification of its members and oversaw the competition between villages and towns (Shkodra 1973: 221). The leaders of the *esnaf* were called *llonxha*, one of whom was elected chairman (*qehaja*). The role of the *esnaf* was not only of an economic nature. While they had strict rules that determined only the distribution of materials, labour and goods, they also provided a forum for organising the social relationships of their members and their members with the members of other *esnaf* and people who were not organised in guilds. Their moral codes of behaviour were as strictly respect as religious and other moral codes (Shkodra 1973: 253). The *esnaf* provided a form of social security for its weakest members, helping them after accidents or with celebrations and provided their members low interest credits. When one of its members died, the esnaf would manage that member's debts, credits or other accounts. In co-operation with other local institutions it compiled an inventory of the deceased's property and then distribute it among his heirs. The *esnaf* would also care for his children if they were still minors (Shkodra 1973: 255, 256). Finally, the *esnaf* organised the military service of its members should the Sultan call upon them to do so and they were responsible for maintaining public order. If their members broke any of its rules, the *esnafs* had the right to judge and taking legal measures against them (Shkodra, 1973:259). They also organised security in the bazaar. Initially, young unmarried apprentices and journeymen ensured the security of their own guild streets, but these were replaced by paid guards or *pasvan* at the beginning of the 20th century, the guilds paying their wages. Seventeen guilds were eventually active in Tirana, five of them of Orthodox Vlach origin, the remaining twelve being Muslim. These dominated the organisation of the bazaar until its demolition in 1959, even if the system of guilds had lost much of its influence towards the end of the 19th century. The economically and numerically most powerful guild in Tirana, as was the case in Shkodra and many other cities, was that of the curriers (*esnafi i tabakëve*). They had their own special quarter and even today the term tabakëve is associated with the mosque and bridge of the Ali Demi quarter. This guild was highly organised, both from an economic as well as form a social perspective. The rule of their chairman and the head of the volunteer police in the quarter was unquestioned. The construction of the bridge in the quarter, the *Ura e Tabakëve*, was completed using guild means.[6]

DEVELOPMENT OF THE BAZAAR IN THE 19TH AND 20TH CENTURIES

The Austrian diplomat Müller, who toured Albania in the 1830s, estimated that Tirana had around 1000 houses and 727 shops at the turn of the century (cited in

[6] Llagami, Ferit. Krijimi i shoqatës së tabakëve (lëkurëpunuesve) në Tiranë, Dorëshkrim, AE pranë IKP, 795/79

Shkodra 1981: 191). However accurate these figures are – and they may well be an exaggeration – it is clear that the town and the bazaar had grown significantly. This growth – twice the number of houses and more than three times the number of shops than a century previous – cannot be attributed to the natural growth of the population. This growth demonstrates simply the fact that Tirana had become a significant urban centre that had become a very attractive magnet for villagers of the surrounding area as well as from other more distant towns. But Müller visited the town after 30 years of violent feuding between the notable families of the city, which clearly harmed the local economy. Müller explains that many shops in the bazaar had been abandoned; around 480 were still occupied. Eighty years later their number would again reach 700 (Shkodra 1981: 200).

The potters' market in the early 20th century (courtesy of Jochen Blanken)

By the 19th century the old bazaar in Tirana was delimited at its corners by four mosques, the Old Mosque in the southeastern corner, the Ethem Bey Mosque in the southwest, the Karapici Mosque in the northwest and Stërmasi Mosque in the northeast. The oldest of these was the Old Mosque. Later, in the early 18th century, the Karapici and Stërmasit Mosques were built within a short time of one another. These mosques were named after the families that financed their construction. The Ethem Bey Mosque was built last in what was to become the centre of the city. Mulla Bey, a prominent member of the Mulleti family, which claimed a leading position in the city, financed its construction. The work to carry out this project started in the year 1789, but Mulla Bey died before it was completed and his son Ethem Bey reaped the benefits.

Four mosques in such a limited space of two to three hectares may seem to have been superfluous at first glance. But beyond their function as monuments to important families in the city, their existence is also a sign that religion played an important role in trade, not only for the merchants and craftsmen local to the area but also for visiting merchants and patrons of the bazaar and the fair. The people coming here were attentive not to neglect their prayers. This can also be said of the Christian Orthodox community, which built a large Christian Orthodox Church in 1863 where the Hotel Tirana International stands today (Shkodra 1994: 139).

The end of the 19th century saw a major change in the economic structure of many Albanian cities, Tirana included. The region was flooded with large quantities of low priced goods from abroad. Many local trade sectors – such as the rifle makers and the local cloth industry (cf. Busch-Zantner 1939: 70, Wallisch 1931: 23) – began to fail. The monopoly position of the local *esnafs* collapsed; they could no longer protect their members from competition and the whole structure began to disintegrate. The traditional function of the bazaar as a centre of production and of exchange shifted in favour of the latter. Even though production continued in many workshops until the demolition of the bazaar in 1959, the majority of shops shifted their focus to the sale of imported goods. By the beginning of the 20th century, the city was getting ever larger and a number of shops had opened in the other quarters as well. The old bazaar lost continually in importance despite a thorough renovation in 1905. The city's new status as capital and the demands of a modern capital city began to eat away at heart of the bazaar. The Karapici Mosque was demolished in 1930 and the Sulejman Pasha's *imaret* and *hamam* were demolished for aesthetic reasons, the latter in 1939. Although it was intended to replace the *hamam* with a more modern and larger public bath, this project was never realised.

The plowmakers' market in the early 20th century (courtesy of Jochen Blanken)

A large number of descriptions of the bazaar by Western European travellers exist from this period. Friedrich Wallisch was typical in his description of the bazaar between past and present:

> Here on the western edges of the city emerge the alleys of the bazaar, a maze of one-storey houses, store upon store, often with a low terrace, workshop and store most often in one. This is the teeming and tranquil, squanderous yet squallerous, confined and

> at the same time in its magnitude labyrinthian quarter of work and trade (Wallsich 1931: 22, my translation).

Like others before and after him, he felt here the presence of the ancient history of the city. But while the city planners foresaw a very functional organisation for the new capital, they shied away from infringing on the originality of the bazaar. One of them would write: "...the old bazaar – that in my opinion must remain as it is to give to the city a characteristic feature – is becoming richer with more and more goods. The shops are growing more beautiful everyday... (Asais 1930: 222)." Even the communist travel writer Ilja Ehrenburg could not help but be fascinated by the atmosphere of the Albanian bazaars

> with [their] colourful carpets, silk cloth, filigree products of silver made by skilled artisans where fatty patisseries and aromatic incenses are sold, where donkeys hung with strings of blue pearls meander slowly through the dust and where gramophones interrupt the call of the muezzin; coffeehouses with ever sleepy guests in white *fez*, old mosques and slogans in rough letters that resemble verses. And then the old parts of Tirana, just as labyrinthian, just as fanciful (Ehrenburg 1947: 92, my translation).

In the first half of the 20th century the bazaar proved too small to house all the merchants and tradesmen in the city and workshops and stores opened in the streets bordering on the bazaar. The tendency remained nevertheless for these new shop owners to gravitate towards the old bazaar because it was the symbol of the marketplace.[7] And the gap left by the weakened esnafs allowed for a new form of entrepreneurship, a further shift from the traditional oriental way of doing business towards an emerging free market.

In the process of enlarging and modernising the city, a municipal decision was thus taken in 1928 to shift the meat, fish and vegetable markets from the old bazaar to the old *varrezat e pashës* (cemetery of the pashas). This new market still exists today and is known as the *pazari i ri* (new bazaar). The decision led to the opening of about 60 new shops: "Elsewhere there were no shops for the above-mentioned goods, except for the shops of the fruits sellers."[8] After the creation of the *pazari i ri* many markets and streets lost their function or acquired new functions. Based on oral testimonies, some peasants nevertheless continued selling their products in the old bazaar, even though the municipality forbade it and the new market was not far away. They did this, for example, in the market of grains and straw-mats. This may have had two reasons, the first being a natural inertia after many centuries of trade in the old bazaar and the fact that the old bazaar continued to be more frequented than the new one.

This measure taken by City of Tirana could be considered a sign that the old bazaar had become too small to meet the needs of the rapidly increasing population. On the other hand, it may be interpreted as a necessary hygienic measure, the result of an increasingly modern self-perception. It was no longer felt acceptable to sell meat, fish and vegetables in the middle of the dust and disorder of the old bazaar

---

[7] Interview with Shyqyri Rreli and Gani Hajdari, who had their businesses in the old bazaar.

[8] Gazeta e Re, Sunday, 11.11.1928, No. 10, "Zbukurimi dhe pastërtia e kryeqytetit. Hali (merkato)" p 1 (my translation).

between the noise of the coffeehouses and the exhaust of cars – even if still few in number.

CONCLUSION

While the Old Mosque and many other older buildings were destroyed in the Battle for Tirana in November 1944 that de facto ended World War II in Albania, the old bazaar was hardly damaged. But the bazaar was increasingly neglected and by the end of the 1950s the situation had become critical. The radical changes of modernity on the one hand and the new communist regime on the other were too much for many of the trades practised in the bazaar and many of these were much in decay if not completely lost. The artisanal trades were merged into the 'Migjeni' Artisanal Enterprise and moved elsewhere in Tirana and the decision was made to tear down the old bazaar completely in the name of "building a new socialist life". After the demolition of the bath and the bakery and after the destruction of the Old Mosque, the oldest historic elements in the city, the old bazaar, ceased to exist in 1960. In its place was built the *Pallati i Kulturës* (Palace of Culture). In interviews, no old citizen of Tirana who remembered the old bazaar did not recall that moment with pain. They felt their soul and memory to have been violated. The younger generation is often not even aware that when go in search of the history and culture of their city in the National Library, they are standing on the ground where the Albanian capital has buried its own history.

BIBLIOGRAPHY

Asais, Francesco, 1930 Nella capitale d'un giovane regno. In: Emporium, Vol. 8. pp 221-232.
Busch-Zantner, Richard 1939 Albanien. Neues Land im Imperium. Leipzig: Wilhelm Goldmann Verlag.
Ehrenburg, Ilja 1947 Auf den Strassen Europas. Reportagen. Berlin: Verlag Volk und Welt
Frashëri, Kristo 2004 Historia e Tiranës. Tirana: Toena.
Hobdari, Mihal 2001 Banorët e parë vlleh të Tiranës. In: Arumunët e Shqipërisë, Tirana: Shoq. Arumunët e Shqipërisë.
Myderrizi, Osman 1937 Tirana në 1937. Tirana: Bashkia Tiranë.
Miho, Koço 1987 Trajta të profilit urbanistik të qytetit të Tiranës, Tirana: 8 Nëntori.
Riza, Emin 1991 Qyteti dhe banesa shqiptare e mesjetës së vonë. Tirana: ASHSH.
Shkodra, Zija 1973 Esnafet shqiptare, Tirana: ASHSH.
Shkodra, Zija 1981 Qyteti shqiptar gjatë Rilindjes Kombëtare. Tirana: ASHSH.
Shkodra, Zija 1994 Tirana - Capital City of Albania. In Harald Heppner (ed.) Hauptstädte in Südosteuropa: Geschichte, Funktion, Nationale Symbolkraft, Vienna: Böhlau pp 133-147.
Wallisch, Friedrich 1931 Neuland Albanien. Stuttgart: Franchkische Verlagsbuchhandlung.

CONTRIBUTERS

Nebi Bardhoshi is a legal anthropologist and researcher at Institute of Cultural Anthropology and Studies of Art in Tirana. He is also the founder of the Research Centre "Law, Norms, Tradition" at the Faculty of Law, European University of Tirana an lecturer of anthropology and law at the New York University of Tirana. Dr. Bardhoshi is author of several scientific works in field of social and legal anthropology on, among others, issues of legal plurality, legitimacy, collective identity, customary law and post-socialism. His interests also include the history of Albanian ethnographic thought, especially in the field of legal anthropology. He is author of the book Gurtë e kufinit: Kanuni, Pronkesia, Struturimi (Tirana: UET Press 2011).

Nathalie Clayer is a Professor at the EHESS (Paris) and a senior fellow researcher at the CNRS (Paris). She is the director of the CETOBAC (Centre d'études turques, ottomanes, balkaniques et centrasiatiques, CNRS-EHESS). Her research focuses on religion and state building in the Balkans, especially among the Albanians. Her most recent book is entitled Aux origines du nationalisme albanais (Paris: Karthala 2007).

Gerda Dalipaj studied psychology and anthropology at the University of Tirana before beginning her PhD at the University of Aix-Marseille 1. She worked as a researcher at the Institute of Folk Culture in Tirana from 2004-2009. Her master's research was on reciprocal aid in villages in the region of Shpati in Central Albania and has published on this and other issues in Albania and abroad. Today she is a member of BALKABAS at IDEMEC, where she is working on issues of family and spatial belonging in postsocialist Albania.

Siegfried Gruber is a postdoc at the Max Planck Institute for Demographic Research in Rostock/Germany. His main research topics are household structures and historical demography in the 19th and 20th centuries. His research interests include Albania and Serbia in Southeastern Europe and the city of Rostock.

Andreas Hemming is a freelance anthropologist, translator and research project consultant. From 2007 to 2010 he was co-researcher in the research project "Visual and Aural Representations of Identity in Albania" funded by the Fritz Thyssen Foundation, which included a nine month period of stationary fieldwork in the Mirdita district of northern Albania.

Armanda Hysa started working as a researcher at the Institute of Folk Culture, now Institute of Cultural Anthropology and Art Studies, in Tirana in 2001. Her main area of research is on material culture, focusing on the old bazaars, the *charshiyas* from a regional perspective, comparing the phenomenon in Albania, Macedonia, Bosnia and Hercegovina and Kosovo, and how such sites can become important objects in ethnic and historical identity process. She has published on the history of ethnography in Albania during communism and the transformation period.

Gentiana Kera is currently a lecturer at the Department of History at the University of Tirana. She is a PhD candidate at the Centre for Southeast European History at the University of Graz, where she was in the past researcher in several projects on the Albanian family and historical demography.

Smoki Musaraj is a postdoc at the Institute for Money, Technology, and Financial Inclusion at the University of California, Irvine. She received a PhD in Anthropology from The New School. Her dissertation, *Tales from Albarado: Pyramid Schemes and Ponzi Logics of Accumulation in Postsocialist Albania* explores how the Albanian pyramid schemes of 1992-1997 were made possible and legitimate through specific political and business practices, how they mediated the transformations of value and wealth across different temporal and spatial scales, and how their Ponzi logics of accumulation continue to operate in other area of economic life in contemporary Albania.

Enriketa Papa-Pandelejmoni is a lecturer at the Departament of History at the Faculty of History and Philology, Univerisity of Tirana. She is a PhD candidate at the Centre for Southeast European History and Anthropology at the University of Graz, where she was researcher in several projects on the Albanian household and family. Her research focuses on the interwar period in Albania.

Eckehard Pistrick is an ethnomusicologist and staff member of the institute for Music, Martin-Luther-University Halle-Wittenberg as well as associate at the CREM (Centre de Recherche en Ethnomusicologie) in Paris. His research focus lies on the links between music, memory and emotions and the practices of staging, folklorisation and appropriation of cultural heritage in the Mediterranean area. He has completed fieldwork in Albania, Greece, Macedonia, Bulgaria and Cambodia (2004-2010). After obtaining his M.A. in 2005 he organised an award winning concert tour with traditional Albanian musicians. Between 2007 and 2010 he held a position as co-researcher in a research project on "Visual and Aural Representations of Identity in Albania" funded by the Fritz Thyssen Foundation. He is PhD candidate at the Universities of Halle-Wittenberg and Paris Ouest-Nanterre.

Jenna Rice is a PhD student at Stanford University in the Department of Anthropology. Her dissertation research focuses on informal networks of charitable giving in Damascus, Syria.

Gilles de Rapper is a social anthropologist at the Institute for Mediterranean, European and Comparative Ethnology (IDEMEC, Aix-en-Provence). His research focuses on the transformations of post-communist Balkan societies. He is interested in border dynamics (migration, ethnic and national minorities, border conflicts and representations of national space), religious interrelations and transformations of kinship. He is specialised on Albania and Albanian communities in the Balkans.

Stéphane Voell is research fellow at the department of Cultural and Social Anthropology at the University of Marburg. From 2001 to 2003 he conducted a total of nine months of research in Albania, completing his PhD in 2004 on traditional law in northern Albania. He is currently working in the Caucasus on traditional law and religion in the Republic of Georgia.

Antonia Young is an anthropologist at the University of California, Berkeley and has been doing research in Southeastern European since the late 1950s. She is active as a expert witness in asylum cases and as an elections observer (in Albania, Kosovo, Macedonia and Bosnia-Herzegovina). The best known of her many publications on Albania is her groundbreaking work on Women who become Men: Albanian Sworn Virgins (London: Berg 2000).